D0810482

# LOVE LETTERS *from* GOD

## MY LOVE FOR YOU NEVER ENDS

## Lee Richards

**DUNAMIS**

LOVE LETTERS FROM GOD:
MY LOVE FOR YOU NEVER ENDS*

**Dunamis Word Publishing**
www.dunamiswordpublishing.com

ISBN: 978-1-68489-421-5 (Hardcover)
ISBN: 978-1-6848-9420-8 (ebooks)

# CONTENTS

# LOVE LETTERS FROM GOD

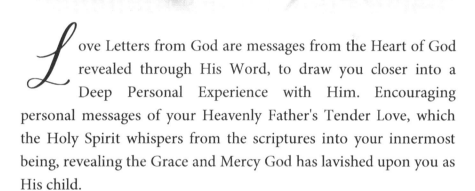

*L*ove Letters from God are messages from the Heart of God revealed through His Word, to draw you closer into a Deep Personal Experience with Him. Encouraging personal messages of your Heavenly Father's Tender Love, which the Holy Spirit whispers from the scriptures into your innermost being, revealing the Grace and Mercy God has lavished upon you as His child.

Each message offers encouragement in your daily life and provides inspiration and Strength as you cope with life's challenges. Let the Holy Spirit guide you through the letter, giving you rich and enlightened thoughts so you can experience for yourself the astonishing Love of Christ in all its infinite and innumerable dimensions.

God wants you to enjoy your New Life in Christ, to have Fullness of Joy, His Life to the fullest measure. When you are worried, anxious, feeling overwhelmed, run down, weak and distressed, these Messages from the Word of God can lift your spirits and give you a fresh God-Centered Perspective, Hope, and Victory!

The Holy Spirit makes the Word of God and God's Love alive to you in the Love Letters from God.

- He reveals to you How God sees you as His child, your new identity in Christ Jesus.
- The Endless Love of God poured out into your Heart through the Holy Spirit.
- How tightly you are sealed and kept secure in God's Love by His indwelling Presence.
- The Beautiful Fruit of Divine Love produced by the Holy Spirit within you.
- Every spiritual blessing lavished upon you as a Love Gift from the Father.
- The blessing of your new life hidden with Christ in God.
- How God is so rich in mercy to satisfy His Great Love for you.
- The Gift of Grace that is always more than enough.

The Holy Spirit reveals the Father's Divine Love in its infinite expressions given to Him and discloses it to you in the Love Letters from God. Your faith will explode as you hear the Word of God, the Holy Spirit will Stir your Heart and mind to apply His Spiritual healing to yourself and your friends as Christ Strengthens you to make an impact on someone else's life!

When you are worried, anxious, feeling overwhelmed, run down, weak and distressed, these Messages from the Word of God can lift your spirits and give you a fresh, God Centered Perspective, Hope, and Victory!

The messages found in the Love Letters from God evolved from being drawn morning-by-morning into God's Presence to listen as He opened my ears to hear His Word, I needed to hear. He led me to take a pen and paper and write down each message given through the scriptures; in the same way, He spoke them to me in the first person. I did and still do.

May you be comforted and encouraged in the Love Letters from God you have found. When you let the Spirit of God birth them in your heart, may God's Word be a joy to you and rejoice your Heart with His Passionate Love and Faithfulness, as you call up His Holy Name.

## SCRIPTURES FOR FURTHER READING:

Romans 8:16, 1 Corinthians 2:12, Ephesians 3:19, Romans 5:5, 2 Corinthians 1:22, Ephesians 1:13, Galatians 5:22-23, Ephesians 1:3, Colossians 3:3, Ephesians 2:4, Ephesians 2:8, 2 Corinthians 12:9-10, John 16:13, Jeremiah 15:16

## Get Ready to Experience a Life-Changing Relationship Hearing God's Heart

Each letter offers an encouraging message of God's Tender Love and Truth; the Holy Spirit whispers to your heart.

These love letters reveal God's heart, written as if God Himself is speaking His Word directly to you – words of unconditional love, comfort, encouragement, peace, and joy.

Let the Holy Spirit guide you through each letter, giving you rich and enlightened thoughts; so you can experience for yourself the astonishing Love of God in all its infinite and innumerable dimensions.

God invites you in each letter to embrace His Heart, to lift your spirits, and give you a fresh God Centered Perspective reassuring you His Love for you Never Ends!

# MY LOVE FOR YOU NEVER ENDS

*od's Love for you Never Ends, because He is Eternal and His Love for you is Eternal! His Love for you is all-encompassing, ordained before the foundation of the world, for you to be seen and known as holy and blameless in His Sight.*

*God has loved you from eternity past to the present, and He will love you for all eternity because nothing in all creation can separate you from His Love for you in Christ Jesus. His Love for you is higher than the highest heavens.*

*God loves you with the same passionate Love that He loves His Beloved Son Jesus. He being His greatest treasure reveals the great value God has for you in calling you His child.*

*Hear how Eternal God's Love is for you today.*

# Letter From God

Good Morning,

I Love you My Dear, Precious, Beloved, Blessed, Special, Beautiful child of My GREAT Love. And that is what you are!

My Love for you Never Ends! Because I AM Eternal, My Love for you is Eternal—It will Never Pass Away!

My Love for you is all-encompassing. I Loved you and Chose you before I laid the foundation of the world. Because of My Great Love, I ordained you to be holy and blameless in My Eyes, Even above Reproach, before ME in Love, My child. And that is what you are!

I have always loved you from All Eternity, and I will Always Love you through All Eternity. My Faithful Tender Love for you Continues forever! Let My All-Encompassing Love gives you Great Comfort and Confidence. There has Never Been a time when I have not Loved you, and Never a time when My Love will end.

My Eternal Love for you is rooted and grounded in My Love for My Beloved Son, Jesus. He purchased your freedom and redeemed you to be adopted and recognized as My child.

See the wonderful depth of My Marvelous Love I have lavished upon you, that I have adopted you into my family and call and count you as My child.

Additionally, I Love you with the same Passionate Love I have for Jesus. And I proved it by giving you the Gift of My Son, My Greatest Treasure, in for the forgiveness of your sins, Who I raised back to life to prove you have been made Right with ME for All

Eternity. Now, nothing can ever separate you from My Endless Love.

Nothing in All Creation will ever Separate you from My Love I have revealed in Christ Jesus. He Totally set you free from every trace of sin by the power of His Blood Shed on the Cross, and Permanently Canceled sins effect on you for All Eternity.

My Unfailing Love for you is Higher than the highest heavens and my Tender Mercy extends infinitely beyond the Grandeur of Heaven, who Loves ME. My Faithful Love towers over you as far as the east is from the west removing your guilt and shame forever. I am your Loving Father Who carried you in My Spiritual Womb until My Spirit birthed you and keep you in My Nurturing Love for All Eternity.

When I birthed you in My Endless Love with Eternal Life, this is the Eternal Life is found in My Son. Thus, you experience My Faithful Love that Never Ends, and My Tender Mercies and Compassion that Never Fails. Every Morning they are fresh and new, for Great and Abundant is My Faithfulness toward you.

You will never find an end to My Tender Compassion Extended to you, which is undeserved and cannot be earned; but is desperately needed to give you mercy for your failures, and Grace to help in time of need.

My Love flows through My Presence within you which is the source and root of your life. So, you are able to experience for yourself My Endless Love, Beyond Measure, in All its Intimate infinite dimensions that I continuously pour into you, filling you and flooding to overflowing with My Endless Love, My child.

I love you,

Daddy God. Amen.

*Give thanks to the Lord, for he is good.*
*His Love endures forever.*

PSALM 136:1, NKJV

## SCRIPTURES FOR FURTHER READING:

1 John 4:8, Ephesians 1:4, Colossians 1:22, Psalm 136:1, 1 John 3:1, John 17:23, Romans 5:8, Romans 4:25, Romans 8:38-39, Colossians 2:14-15, Psalm 103:11-13, John 3:5-7, 1 John 5:11, Lamentations 3:22-23, Hebrews for: 16, Colossians 3:12, Ephesians 3:17-19

## Prayer

Heavenly Father,

You are the source of Endless Love that will Never Pass away! Empower me to experience the great magnitude of Your Astonishing Love In all its dimensions. Your Endless Love for me transcends all understanding.

In Jesus' name. Amen.

# FILL YOUR THOUGHTS WITH MY THOUGHTS

*W*hat God says about you is more important than what man speculates about you. He speaks Truth into your Heart by filling your mouth with His Word. So, say what God says about you. It is already True!

Embrace the Truth of what He says about you, who He calls you, where He has seated you, and your Full Identity as His child. Because that is what you are! It will change what you say about yourself, and even accept from others that is not in-line with Who God says you are.

Fill your Thoughts with His Thoughts because He knows who you are and the price He paid to make you His Own child.

You are who God says you are! Let His Love pour into Heart today.

# Letter From God

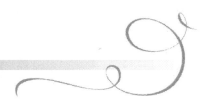

Good Morning,

I Love you My Dear, Precious, Beloved, Blessed, Special, Beautiful child of My GREAT Love. And that is what you are!

I Speak into your Heart My Truth, say what I say about you, fill your mouth with My Words which birth My Divine Persuasion in you as you respond to My Anointed Utterances.

I certify that My Word you utter into your Heart will Come to Pass. For in your utterance of My Word you are declaring what I had in advanced preplanned for you from the beginning, knowing all the work you would do, and the needs you would have in life to fulfill your destiny.

So, Speak My Word to your Heart that I speak to you; it does not return to ME unfulfilled. My Word Spoken through your lips will Always Perform My Purposes and fulfill the Divine Mission I Sent It out to do in your Life.

I AM Who sends My Word to you for your guidance, comfort, encouragement, provision, healing, counseling, help, Strength, wisdom and deliverance. I Living in you confidently confirm My Word I stirred your minds most holy emotions to embrace with your Heart. My Spirit Whispers into Innermost Being, "This Word is My Promise which I guarantee to you, My child. Believe It!" Speak My Word Boldly!

Thus, I persuade you to Believe the Promise of My Word, and to Cling to the Message of My Word I have birthed within you based on My Infinite Faithfulness, which Most Assuredly Guarantees It Will Come to Pass, in My Timing and My Way.

Embrace the Truth of Who My Words says you are, what I have already lavishly bestowed upon, and your rights and privileges as My Dearly Loved Child – your True Identity before ME. It reveals My Heart toward you, and Changes your expectations about what I am doing for you and how I see you holy and blameless before ME, in Love.

Your life is not your own, but Mine. Your Life is Hidden with Christ in ME. I now live within you, and empower your life through My Spirit Working Mightily in you to accomplish all I have Promised you in My Word, because you are Truly Loved and Fully Accepted by ME.

Fill your thoughts with My Thoughts, My Love, My Acceptance, My Forgiveness, My Mercy, My Comfort My Wisdom and My Presence, Knowing you are vitally united together with Me. And My Peace that Surpasses All Understanding will guard your Heart and mind by My Presence within you, flowing My Love through you. Then your Heart is always guided by My Peace, acting as umpire continually in your Heart, to settle all questions that come into your mind by My Divinely Persuading what I would have you to do, My child.

I love you,

Daddy God. Amen.

> *My word, I send it out, and it always produces fruit. It will accomplish all I want it to, and it will prosper everywhere I send it.*
>
> Isaiah 55:11, NLT

Romans 10:17, Isaiah 55:11, Isaiah 46:10, Matthew 6:8, Ephesians 2:10, John 1:1, John 10:30, Psalms 107:20, Jeremiah 1:12, Jeremiah 30:17, John 14:16-17, 26; Ephesians 6:19, John 1:12, 1 John 3:1, Ephesians 1:4-7, Colossians 3:3, Ephesians 3:20, Philippians 2:13

## Prayer

Heavenly Father,

Your Word you speak into My Heart through the Holy Spirit will accomplish what You sent it to do. You certify that the Promise of your Word in-birthed in me by the Holy Spirit will come to pass. So, I cling to Your Infinite Faithfulness.

In Jesus' Name. Amen.

# MY LOVE IS A DIVINE MAGNET

*G*od nurtures you in His Love that connects you in a mutual beneficial deep loving relationship with Him. He wants you to commune with Him daily to experience life-changing intimacy with Him. Come to Him with an open heart, knowing there is nothing in your past, present, or future that can ever diminish His Love for you.

*God draws you into His Presence, satisfying the deepest passions of your heart. He gives you a deep, longing desire to live in union with Him. In His Love, you find a safe place of shelter because He always gives you His best and thinks the best of you. He calls you His delightful child and covers you with tender mercies, wrapping you in the riches of His superabundant grace.*

*Come drink deeply from the living waters of His Spirit. Your Divine Helper Who has woven you into the very fabric of God's heart, supernaturally infusing you with divine strength to triumph over every situation. He pushes back intruding darkness and comforts you with His cascading Passionate Love.*

*Let His whispers transform your thoughts see yourself as does.*

# Letter From God

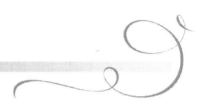

Good Morning,

I Love you My dear, precious, beloved, blessed, special, beautiful child of My GREAT Love. And that is what you are!

You must nurture Love to experience the mutually beneficial connection of a deep loving personal relationship. So, you need to commune with Me daily. I stir you to embrace My heart, which gives you the confidence to come boldly into My Presence to experience intimacy with Me.

Come, approach Me with an open heart, fully convinced that nothing could keep us apart. There is nothing in your past or present or future circumstances that can weaken My Love for you. Nothing will ever distance you from My Passionate Love. When you move your heart closer and closer to Me, you find I have always been close to you.

My Love is a Divine Magnet that draws you into My Presence to satisfy the deep passion of your heart. Now you are in union with Me, and My Passionate Love cascading in your heart births love for others. For Love is the attractive force of all True relationships. Love is your safe place of shelter that never focuses on what is wrong with you but always believes the best of you. Love never gives up because I never let go.

Love sees you as the entirely new person enfolded into Christ. My Perfect Love made you entirely like He is now. You are My delightful child, whom I love with the same Love I have for Him. My Tremendous Love covers you with tender mercy and wraps you in the riches of My superabundant grace. The more time you spent with Me, the more you treasure Me in your heart!

I am your Treasure of Infinite Wealth Who holds your destiny and its timing in My hands. I am always close to you. I overwhelm you with the precious privileges of being in union with Me! Come drink deeply of My Spirit's power and gifts until rivers of living water flow within you to fulfill the destiny and the good works I have given you.

I am your Divine Helper Who keeps you alive. I have woven you into the fabric of My heart and laid My hand of blessing upon you. Your heart I kiss with My forgiveness. And shower you with the miracles of My Kindness. I supernaturally infuse you with My Divine Strength, My explosive power to triumph over every difficulty and help you in every situation.

My Glorious Light in you pushes back the sons of darkness attempts to intrude upon your life. You are My dear child, and nothing can separate you from My Love. I am your Salvation, Who surrounds you with songs of victory and protects you. Christ's divine presence within carefully watches over and protects you, and the accuser's evil strategies do not touch you.

You will look in triumph over all those who hate you, for you live in My Presence which no foe can withstand. You possess My Glorious Treasure living in your inner being, the Brilliant Light of My Glory. He nurtures you with Tender Love and inwardly transforms your thoughts to see yourself as I see you, My Beloved child.

I love you,

Daddy God. Amen.

*Like newborn babies you should crave the pure spiritual milk, that by it you may be nurtured and grow unto salvation*

1 Peter 2:2, AMPC

## SCRIPTURES FOR FURTHER READING:

1 Peter 2:2, Song of Songs 4:5, Ephesians 4:12, 1 Timothy 4:6, Ephesians 3:12, Romans 8:38-39, James 4:8, 1 Corinthians 13:7, 2 Corinthians 5:17, 1 John 4:17, Ephesians 1:6-8, Ephesians 1:6-8, Ephesians 1:6-8, Psalms 16:5, Romans 8:17, 1 Corinthians 12:13, John 7:37. Ephesians 2:10, Hebrews 13:6, Psalm 54:4, Psalm 118:17, Psalm 103:2-4, Philippians 4:13, Ephesians 6:10, Isaiah 41:10, John 1:4- 5, 1 John 3:1, Romans 8:35, 1 John 3:1, Romans 8:35, 1 John 5:18, 2 Corinthians 2:14, Isaiah 41:11, Colossians 1:27, Romans 8:31, 1 John 5:18, 2 Corinthians 2:14, Isaiah 41:11, Colossians 1:27, Romans 8:31, 2 Corinthians 4:7

## Prayer

Heavenly Father,

Thank You for stirring me to embrace Your heart and experience an intimate relationship with You. My heart is open to Your passionate Love; draw me closer and closer to satisfy the deep longings of my heart. I ask You to infuse me with Your divine strength to triumph over every difficulty. Nurture me in Your Tender Love and carefully watch over me because I need You.

In Jesus' name. Amen.

# MADE WORTHY BY MY MARVELOUS LOVE

*G*od makes you Worthy by His Marvelous Love, not your performance. He lavishly bestowed upon you all the riches of His grace to demonstrate how valuable you are to Him. He chose to wrap you in Christ Jesus as His Precious inheritance before He even made the stars in the heavens.

Your new life is under the reign of My Grace that makes you a child of the Living God. There was nothing you could earn His Love and acceptance, because it was given to you freely by God's choice, so you never have to wonder are doing enough to be worthy of His Love. For His Gifts of Love come freely by faith, not your works.

Your Worth is determined by God's Glorious Gift of His Passionate Love, no matter what you feel is necessary for God to accept you in your limited human perspective. The high price God paid in blood to make you His child is your true Worth and guaranteed acceptance before Him forever.

# Letter From God

Good Morning.

I Love you, My dear, precious, beloved, blessed, beautiful child of My GREAT Love. And that is what you are!

You are worthy of all of the Riches of My Grace, the Gifts of the Divine Favor and Blessings so lavishly bestowed upon you by Me. For I Am Who makes you Worthy!

I chose you to be wrapped in Christ Jesus before I made the universe, long before Adam was placed on the earth, to be holy and blameless in My Eyes. It has always been My Divine Perfect Plan to mark you out as My Own in Christ Jesus and Reveal you as My Dearly Beloved child through your union with Him.

Since you are now in union with Christ, you are Most Worthy of all the Treasures of Redemption through His Blood—the forgiveness and total cancellation of all your sins. My Gift of Love and Divine Favor is now pouring over you, all because of Jesus' sacrifice that set you free from the condemnation, shame, guilt, punishment, and power of sin.

I canceled and wiped away, as far as the east is from the west, every record of sin and remove all guilt from you. I erased it all and deleted it forever! The accusing voice of condemnation is silent; you are My New Creation, for you are joined in a life-union with Christ in Me. For the law of Spirit of Life flowing through your union in Christ Jesus has completely liberated you from the law of sin and death.

Most assuredly, you are Worthy because the depth of My Marvelous Love lavishly bestowed upon you! For I call you Worthy and made you My Very Own beloved child. For you are a new creation, an entirely new person that never existed before. Your old identity died with Christ, and your New Identity is a child of the Living God. And that is who you are!

You are Worthy because I am who makes you Worthy through your union with My Beloved Son. Sin was not suppressed by the cross, but eliminated. Your new life is under the reign of My Grace that made you a partaker of Christ's salvation. There was nothing you could ever do to earn this salvation, for it was the Gift of My Love. So you never have to wonder if you're doing enough to be worthy of My Love because I made you Worthy by the Gift of My Love.

You see your True Worthiness in the mirror of My Word. It reveals how from the beginning that I saw you as My New Creation before I set the stars in the sky. Never forget your divine origin comes from being one with Christ in His Glory. You share His Glory because you have been made one with the Godhead through the Blood of Jesus.

In My Everlasting Love, I chose to love you in eternity past, the present, and eternity future, not based on your performance, but My Divine Choice. You have been in My Heart for All Eternity. Your Worth is the Eternal Value of My Righteousness and Love imparted to you by the Glorious Gift of My Passionate Love. Christ gave His life on the Cross to give you His Righteousness so you could dwell with Me forever.

Jesus gave Himself for you to prove how Truly Worthy you are! Embrace the Truth of your Worth from My Perspective, not the demands of others or your limited human perspective. For you being joined with the Lord Jesus are One Spirit with Him. You no longer belong to yourself, for My Gift of the Holy Spirit lives inside you. I paid a high price for you in blood, so by all means then, you are Worthy of all that is Mine, My Precious child.

I love you,

Daddy God. Amen.

> *Your hearts can soar with joyful gratitude when you think of how God made you worthy to receive the glorious inheritance freely given to us by living in the light.*
>
> Colossians, 2:12, TPT

## ▌Scriptures for Further Reading:

1 Corinthians 2:12, Ephesians 1:3-7, Colossians 1:14, Romans 3:24, Colossians 2:14, Psalm 103:12, Romans 8:1-2, 1 John 3:1-2, 2 Corinthians 5:17, Galatians 2:20, Romans 6:6, Romans 6:14, Ephesians 2:8-9, James 1:23, Psalm 147:4, Colossians 1:26, Colossians 3:4, John 17:22, Colossians 1:21-22, Isaiah 53:4-5, Romans 5:8, Romans 8:9-11, 1 Corinthians 6:17

## Prayer

Heavenly Father,

Thank You for Your Marvelous Love that made me worthy to be Your Precious child and receive a glorious inheritance of the riches of Your Grace. My Worthiness comes from You alone. I am what You say I am, Worthy of Your Love and acceptance.

In Jesus' name. Amen.

# FORGIVENESS IS AN ACT OF DIVINE LOVE

*O*ne of the Greater acts of Divine Love is forgiveness. There is no true and lasting forgiveness without love. God's Love changes our hearts to see people as He sees them in all their frailties and weaknesses. People ache for the Presence of God in their lives, where they can receive the Life-Changing Gift of True Forgiveness.

People make mistakes, but God makes Miracles of the mistakes to create a testimonial of His Great Love and Mercy. His Burning Love within you provides the Miraculous Power to bond hearts and lives together with the Kiss of Forgiveness, despite all someone has done.

Only God can change the heart to Love the undeserving with the Gift of Forgiveness. He Loves you, let Him Love through you by giving the Gift of Forgiveness.

# Letter From God

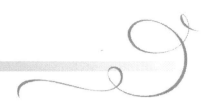

I love you, My dear, precious, beloved, blessed, special, beautiful child of My GREAT Love. And that is what you are!

Forgiveness is an act of My Divine Love expressing My Unlimited Mercy through the Infinite Riches of My Grace and Kindness showered upon you unconditionally.

There is No Forgiveness without Love. True forgiveness is the basis upon which Love is fully demonstrated by My Son's sacrifice for you on the cross when you were entirely helpless and powerless to help yourself. Because of My Beloved Sons Life-Giving Sacrifice, you Receive the Life-Changing Gift of True Forgiveness.

My Love is the reason behind the act of Forgiveness. My Forgiveness wipes away completely and comprehensively all records of the wrong done; it clears the slate of all offense permanently.

My Forgiveness is not as the world forgives with conditions of acceptance. My Forgiveness is Divine Forgiveness that removes from the heart the desire for retaliation of a wrong done to you and replaces it with Love to see the offender's life changed for good.

My Spirit transmits the Gift of Forgiveness to give what only I can provide, undeserved kindness and mercy to you whom I have empowered to intentionally love another that eliminates enmity and restores to harmony the fellowship to a relationship, to even the most undeserving. For Only My Love Expressed through My Gift of Forgiveness Can Accomplish it.

I AM Who gives you the power and desire to forgive as I forgive, to experience The Deepest Levels of My Love. Forgiveness is My Gift to you, to Love others undeserving with the Gift of My Forgiveness I have given you.

Forgiveness Comes Only from ME. The Holy Spirit continually creates in you the Power and Desire to release the same Gift of Forgiveness to others as I have forgiven you. To tolerate the weaknesses of one another, and if you have a complaint against another, to release the Gift of Forgiveness I have graciously forgiven you, and readily forgive them.

I have wrapped you in My Cascading Love and Unlimited Mercy to flow Forgiveness to Others, just as I have given you. Thus Forgiveness becomes the mark of Love's True Maturity at work in you and through you.

Just like My Endless Love never ceases nor stops Loving, and keeps no records of being wrong. My Endless Forgiveness never stops Forgiving and refuses to hold resentment by My Spirit's Power at work within you to accomplish it.

My Burning Love, Coming from the Inner Depths of your Heart, Provides the Eternal Energy and Active Power to Bond Hearts and Lives Back Together. My Love is a Loyal, Endless, Unconditional Commitment I demonstrate toward you and others with acts of kindness and mercy, easily seen in Forgiveness. For I so Loved you that I gave My Son as a Gift of Forgiveness to you.

I am the God of Forgiveness. I am gracious and merciful, slow to anger, and rich in My Unfailing Love for you. Love and Forgiveness are attributes of My Nature. Likewise, being born again of My Spirit, Love, and Forgiveness are now part of your new nature as a new creation in Christ Jesus.

My Fountain of Forgiveness Flows My Abundant Love to you that washes away ALL your guilt and takes away the shame and guilt of sin. I Forgive to the Fullest ALL your rebellious ways, and erase the deepest thoughts of your conscience with the Blood of Jesus.

I Kiss your heart with The Gift of My Forgiveness, in spite of all you done. You now experience My Compassionate Mercy, for I have Lavishly Bestowed My Forgiveness upon you. Therefore, release The Forgiving Power of My Love, given to you to others. For My Forgiveness gives Life to the Fullest to All who receive it.

I alone can judge the hearts of another man. After all, who can see into a person's heart and know their hidden impulses except for Me? I am the Author of your spirit. I am intimately aware of you. I read your heart like an open book, and I know all the words you are about to speak before you even start a sentence! I know everything there is to know about you, and I understand your every thought before it even enters your mind, and I Forgive your sins Totally for ALL Eternity! My Forgiveness can never be lost.

I heal your hurting heart, so you can stand healthy and whole in the My Power of Love and Forgiveness, enabling you to release the Gift of Love and Forgiveness to Others. I free from the snare of unforgiveness so that you can gain an entirely New Strength in ME. I set you free to Minister My Love and Mercy to those I love, which releases the Power of Forgiveness in you and for you and through you, to Love yourself and others as I Love you, My child.

I love you,

Daddy God. Amen.

*Bear with one another, and forgiving one another, if anyone has a complaint against another; even as Christ forgave you, so you also must do.*

Colossians 3:13, NKJV

Romans 5:6, Romans 3:24-25, Ephesians 1:7, Isaiah 55:6-7, Philippians 2:13, Colossians 3:13, Matthew 6:12, 18:21-22, Colossians 3:14, 1 Corinthians 13:8, Philippians 2:13, Ephesians 3:20, 1 Corinthians 13:1-7, John 3:16, Nehemiah 9:17, John 3:5-7, 2 Corinthians 5:17, Romans 8:10-11, Psalms 51:1-2, Psalms 103:3, Matthew 6:12, 18:21-23, Mark 11:26, Luke 11:4, John 10:10, 1 Corinthians 2:11, Genesis 1:26-28, Psalm 139:1-4, Hebrews 9:12, Hebrews 10:10

## Prayer

Heavenly Father, You are God of Forgiveness. You are gracious and merciful, slow to anger, and rich in Unfailing Love. I praise You for your Love and Forgiveness—attributes of Your Nature. I pray that likewise, I would also have a spirit of Love and Forgiveness as a new creation in Christ.

In Jesus' name. Amen.

# FILLED WITH MY ETERNAL FLAME

*G* *od's Spirit is the Eternal Flame of Life Who lives within you—
God Himself! He is always with you and surrounds you with
the Glory of His Eternal Light. Where you are, He is always in
your midst.*

*You are a member of God's Kingdom and a citizen of heaven. He
picked you out for Himself to satisfy His Great Love for you by
birthing into you His Kingdom of Light through the Holy Spirit. He
releases the Life of Christ deep within you and makes His Permanent
home with you.*

*The Holy Spirit roots you deep in God's Unfailing Love, which
becomes the very source of your life. He fills you with His Eternal
Flame to be a Light in the world before you. So that the world will
discover the Overcoming Life found in Jesus Christ.*

# Letter From God

Good Morning,

I Love you, My dear, precious, beloved, blessed, beautiful child of My GREAT Love. And that is what you are!

I am the KING of the Kingdom of God, Who lives within you. Where you are, I AM Always in your midst and surrounding you.

For I AM Spirit, and My Kingdom is the Realm of the Holy Spirit, filled with children born of My Spirit, approved and accepted and in right relationship with ME, by My Goodness.

I picked out for Myself as My Own, in Christ Jesus before the foundation of the world! Because of My GREAT Love, I Ordained you, set you apart holy and blameless in My Eyes, because of My Great Love for you. Deep inside you, My Spirit releases the Life of Christ within you, Who makes His Permanent Home in your heart.

You are rooted deep in Love and Founded Securely on Love, which is the very source of your life. My Spirit in you empowers you to live and to experience the benefits of My Living My Life in you. I move you by the Impulses of the Holy Spirit in My Kingdom to motivate you to pursue what Pleases ME.

I have filled you with My Eternal Flame—with God Myself to be Light to the world, and All who embrace ME, the Life-Giving Light that never fails to shine through the darkness—My Light darkness cannot overcome! My Light in you penetrates the darkness, and the sons of darkness cannot diminish it.

The Eternal Flame of Life is in you that Lights up the world. You live in the midst of a brutal, crooked, and perverse culture and appear as a Shining Light holding out to them the words of Eternal Life. You Shine the Eternal Light of My Kingdom, always in Sincere Love expressing the Word of Life, which flows through you piercing the world of darkness.

You are My Chosen Treasure to be a Living Word sent from My Mouth and authorized to speak on My Behalf. You are the Voice of Heaven to the Earth, Invested with Royal Power through the Name of Jesus and the Authority of His Blood. So, the world will discover the Overcoming Life found in Jesus Christ and experience My Eternal Glory that lasts Forever.

You are my Own Purchased Special Child, who has experienced My Marvelous Light, and now you Light the world with My Kingdom's Presence. You carry My Eternal Flame to the world. As My Personal Representative, you tenderly plead for the world to take hold of the Divine Favor now offered and be reconcile yourself to ME.

I have made you a Messenger of My Good News by the Gift of My Grace that works through you; to make known the revelation secrets of My Kingdom and the Unending and Inexhaustible Riches available to you in Christ.

Things Never Heard of or Discovered before, Things beyond what your mind can imagine; that I have in store for you in whom the Glory of My Eternal Flame burns brightly, My child.

I love you,

Daddy God. Amen.

*Live clean, innocent lives as children of God,*
*shining like bright lights in a world full*
*of crooked and perverse people.*

Philippians 2:15, NLT

## ▎Scriptures for Further Reading:

Luke 17:21, Romans 14:17, Ephesians 2:8-9, John 3:5-7, 2 Corinthians 5:21, Ephesians 2:4, Ephesians 1:4-7, Ephesians 3:17, Romans 8:4-5,14; Philippians 2:13, John 1:4-5, Matthew 5:14, Philippians 2:15, Ephesians 4:15, John 9:5, 1 Peter 2:9, 2 Corinthians 5:20, 2 Timothy 2:10, Ephesians 3:7-9, 1 Corinthians 2:9

## Prayer

Heavenly Father,

You empower me with Your Eternal Flame to experience the Life of Christ and fill me through all my being with Your Endless Love. You have qualified me to be a partaker of Your inheritance in the Light and delivered me from the power of darkness to be Your Light in the world. Empower me to shine for Your Glory!

In Jesus' name. Amen.

# My Gift of Wholeness

*G*od's Gift of Wholeness is available to you, which gives Peace, Well-Being, Prosperity, and Success. Jesus endured divine punishment for you to demonstrate His Passionate Love and desire to provide the Wholeness you need.

The Fruit of Wholeness produced in you by the Holy Spirit's overflow of Divine Love is an Undivided Heart of Peace with limitless inner Strength. God's Wonderful Wholeness transcends your understanding, assuring you He is with you and there is no need to worry because your Heart and mind are kept safe in union with Christ Jesus.

You are always dearly loved by God, Who empowers you to live in Perfect Harmony, which His Wholeness manifests in active Goodness and Kindness. A soul harmony of His Peace to give you direction needed to make the decisions you face daily.

Receive from Him the Gift of Wholeness today.

# Letter From God

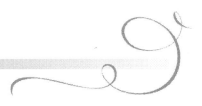

Good Morning,

I Love you My Dear, Precious, Beloved, Blessed, Special, Beautiful child of My GREAT Love. And that is what you are!

I created you Whole, having a new spiritual nature with a soul within your body and made you Completely Holy. Now, your entire being—spirit, soul, and body—is Flawless and blameless in My Sight, even above reproach, in My Love.

You are My Masterpiece to fulfill the destiny I have given you, living in a union as One with Me. I continually implant the passion and desire in you to do what Pleases Me. By My Amazing Grace and Blessing, I have made you who you are!

And I continue to pour My Strength and Empowering Grace out upon you and through you; to accomplish what those who judge you by your weaknesses cannot imagine, by the display of mighty signs and amazing wonders through you, both in word and deed. I am doing more incredible than you can think or your wildest imaginations by the action of My Miraculous Power Constantly Energizing your spirit, soul, and body!

I made you a Triune Creation interconnected as One with Me, a New Creation of My design, which only I can create by My Spirit. Because I Desired to give Myself for you and to you, I took My Nature and Likeness and fashioned you; so I could Love you with Unlimited Passion. You have become an entirely new being enfolded into Christ and indwelt by the Holy Spirit.

Now you being made in My Likeness and Spirit-Born, you are mysteriously complex, through all your being with the riches measure of My Divine Presence, your body filled and flooded with God Myself. Your body is now the Temple of the Living God, in Whom My Holy Spirit Dwells Permanently.

You have received the "Spirit of Full Acceptance." I enfold you into My Family. My Spirit testifies continually together with your eternal spirit, which I placed inside you from the beginning to recognize My Voice and receive My Life—Eternal Life and Live Forever in a personal relationship with ME.

Now, you are My Workmanship Marvelously Made and Thoroughly Breathtaking in Every Way, joined with Me to fulfill My Designed Plan and your destiny! Jesus Himself endured the punishment for your sins, beaten to make you Completely Whole through your union with Him.

He is your Shalom, your Wholeness, Peace, Well-Being, Prosperity, Success. You have received all the riches of My Shalom because of what He suffered for you on the cross. Everything is new! Now through His sacred blood—you have actually been united as one in Christ! And you received all the Blessing of My Wholeness.

Since I am Whole, I have made you My Child, Whole— complete, lacking nothing, all-inclusive, well-rounded, and spiritual mature— being joined together with Christ in Me! He is your "Gift of Wholeness"—My Shalom!

I AM Jehovah Shalom. The Lord is Peace. Your faith in Jesus transfers My righteousness to you, and I now declare you holy and blameless in My Sight. Thus, you currently enjoy a True and Lasting Wholeness with ME. All because of what My Beloved Son has done for you.

I have given you My "Gift of Wholeness." Don't yield to fear or let your Heart be troubled—instead, be encouraged and filled with

Great Joy. For I am with you always! I love you and supply you with My Healing Wholeness for your spirit, soul, and body! I exchanged My Divine Wholeness for the griefs and sorrows you absorbed from the deep hurts, insults, and rejections of people.

I AM your Shalom! I make you wonderfully well and Whole in Christ Jesus. Now you can take great confidence as you rest in My Wholeness. I have not given you a spirit that pulls you in different directions or causes you to be fearful or worried about anything. I have given you My Holy Spirit Who lives within, giving you a spirit of mighty power and Unfailing Love and a well-balanced, self-controlled mind.

Now you live the life of the Spirit of Wholeness. The Holy Spirit dwells within you. He directs and controls you because you genuinely are My child, moved by the impulses of the Holy Spirit. And the Fruit of Wholeness He produces in Divine Love within you is an Undivided Heart of Peace with limitless inner Strength to conqueror every difficulty. Because I Who lives within you is Much Mightier than he is in the world.

Don't worry about anything; instead, come boldly and confidently into My presence. You make your request before Me, Who knows all your needs. Thanking Me with Great Gratitude, I meet all your needs. Then you will experience My Wonderful Wholeness extended through My Peace that surpasses all understanding, which will guard your Heart and mind against the fiery darts of the enemy through Christ Jesus.

You are always and dearly Loved by Me! I empower you to tolerate the weaknesses of others, forgive them as I have graciously forgiven you. if you have a complaint against another, even as I forgave you, you also release the same gift of forgiveness.

And above all things, clothe yourself with Love, for I AM Love Who Lives in you. Let My Love Flow through you, which binds all things together in Perfect Harmony. Now, My Gift of Wholeness manifests itself in active goodness, kindness, and charity in you. Thus, the soul harmony of Christ acting as umpire continually in your Heart gives you His Peace to decide and settle with finality all questions that arise in your mind, My child.

I love you,

Daddy God. Amen.

> *May the God of Peace Himself sanctify you completely,*
> *and may your whole spirit, soul, and body*
> *be kept blameless at the coming*
> *of our Lord Jesus Christ.*

1 Thessalonians 5:23, NIV

## SCRIPTURES FOR FURTHER READING:

1 Thessalonians 5:23, Ephesians 1:4, Ephesians 2:10, Galatians 2:20, Philippians 2:13, 1 Corinthians 15:10, 2 Corinthians: 8-10, Romans 15:18-19, Ephesians 3:20, John 3:7, 2 Corinthians 5:17, Psalm 139:14, Ephesians 3:19, 2 Corinthians 6:16, 1 Corinthians 6:19, Romans 8:15-17, John 3:15, John 3:36, Luke 1:47, John 10:10, John 17:3, Isaiah 53:4-5, Ephesians 2:13-14, Galatians 3:28, Matthew 5:48, Colossians 1:27, Judges 6:24, Romans 5:1, John 14:27, Joshua 1:5, 9, John 16:33, 2 Timothy 1:7, Romans 8:9,14, Galatians 5:22, Philippians 4:13, 1 John 4:4, Ephesians 3:12, Philippians 4:6-7, Ephesians 6:16, Colossians 3:13-15

## Prayer

Heavenly Father,

You are My Shalom! You have made me Whole—complete, lacking nothing, all-inclusive, well-rounded, and spiritually mature through Christ, Who is my "Gift of Wholeness." I am wonderfully well and whole in Christ Jesus because you exchanged Your Wholeness for my griefs and sorrows, and absorbed the deep hurts, insults, and rejections I have experienced, making me Completely Whole!

In Jesus' Name. Amen.

# MY ALL SATISFYING LOVE

*G*od created you with an eternal thirst for His All Satisfying Love. You inwardly yearn to experience more and more of His Unfailing Love.

*You can feel His Tender Love Pouring into Your Heart through the Holy Spirit who lives in you! He produces the Joy you need to live above the distractions and worries of this world. And He empowers you to overcome daily challenges.*

*When you stay close to God, He infuses you with His mighty power to stand victorious in His Glorious Love. And you find God's Unfailing Love pouring into your Heart is the only thing that truly satisfies your every need.*

*God's Sovereign Love is your comfort come drink deeply in His Presence.*

# Letter From God

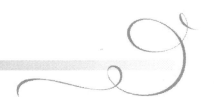

Good Morning,

I Love you My Dear, Precious, Beloved, Blessed, Special, Beautiful child of My GREAT Love. And that is what you are!

I created you with a Never Ending Thirst That can only be satisfied through ME. Your inner self thirst with a deep longing for My All-Satisfying Love, with cravings in your Heart only I can fulfill. Like a lovesick lover, you inwardly yearn passionately to experience more and more of My Unfailing Love, which is Better than Life.

Oh, how I Love you! You can feel My Tender Love because you are joined with ME. My Sovereign Love is your Comfort. Come, drink Deeply from the Living Waters that flow from My Presence. When you are near ME, your whole being, body and soul, sing joyful songs to ME, the True Source, and Spring of Life!

Only I can satisfy your Heart each Morning with My Unfailing Love. I fill your Heart with Divine Love to produce Joy; you need to live above the distractions and worries of the world. I empower you to overcome daily challenges through the Mighty Power of Christ living in you.

Stay close to ME, Who made you more than a conqueror and equal to everything through the Power of My Love, your Glorious Victory. I infuse you with Mighty Power through your life-union with ME to stand victorious in My Glorious Love by the force of My Explosive power flowing in and through you.

LEE RICHARDS

My Love is the only thing that can satisfy the human Heart. I placed in your Heart a deep longing desire for what can only be satisfied by a personal relationship with ME. Your innermost being longs to be refreshed daily with My Living Water, gushing from the fountain of the Holy Spirit, flooding you with Endless Love and giving you eternal life.

I satisfy you with My Unfailing Love cascading in your Heart through the Holy Spirit within you, fully satisfying your every need. Whenever your thoughts race out of control with worries and stress, the Soothing Comfort of My Presence Quiets your Heart and mind with Peace and overwhelms you with My Tender Love to Ease and Relieve and Refresh your Life being in Union with ME.

I surround you with My Perfect, Absolute Peace, and stir your minds Most Holy Emotions to Fix your thoughts on what is true, and noble, and just, and pure, and lovely, and of an excellent report. So, think about things that are excellent and worthy of praise.

The Holy Spirit opens the eyes of your understanding to see things beyond the imagination I have in store for you. My Spirit takes hold of you to empower you in your weaknesses to pull down every perceived obstacle the spirit of fear attempts to bring to your thought. He increases your courage and confidence to believe what I promise and not what the spirit of fear directs your thoughts.

The Spirit of Truth unveils the reality of who you are as My Dear, Precious child. He whispers into your spirit, "I Love you." You are My Most Valuable inheritance paid with My Tears. And He reveals the things I have freely given to you as My child.

I AM Always with you regarding your Heart and mind. In My Presence, you taste the Fullness of Joy. Drink Deeply of My Tender Love that satisfies your every longing. Abandoned everything that does not satisfy, because My Love is not in it. And your eyes will be open to My Abundant Life ever before you, purchased by the blood of My Son to live an abundant and victorious life, My child.

I love you,

Daddy God. Amen.

*Because your Love is better than life, my lips will glorify you.*

Psalms 63:3, NIV

## SCRIPTURES FOR FURTHER READING:

Psalm 63:3, Romans 8:23, Psalm 63:3, Psalm 119:123, Psalm 42:1, Psalm 84:2, Nehemiah 8:10, Romans 8:35, 37, Philippians 4:13, Ephesians 3:20, Ephesians 6:10, John 4:14, John 7:38, Philippians 4:19, Psalm 94:18-19, 1 Peter 5:7, Philippians 4:7, Matthew 11:28-29, 1 Corinthians 2:4, Philippians 4:8, 1 Corinthians 2:9, Romans 8:26, John 16:13, Romans 8:15-16, 1 Corinthians 6:19, 1 Corinthians 2:12, Psalm 16:11, Proverbs 19:23, Leviticus 17:11, Hebrews 9:22, Ephesians 1:7

## Prayer

Heavenly Father,

Thank You for pouring Your Tender Love into my innermost being to quench the deep longings of my Heart. I come confidently into Your Presence to Drink Deeply from the living waters of Your Divine Love. Open the eyes of my Heart to see the reality of Your Truth. I ask Your Tender Love to satisfy my deepest longing and guard my Heart and mind with Your Presence.

In Jesus' name. Amen.

# THE REWARD OF LOVE IS LOVE!

*L*ove is its own Reward. God's Love brings you into an intimate experience of His Love. And His Love shed abroad in your Heart by the Holy Spirit grows continually within you, producing a varied expression of Divine Love through you.

He nourishes your Heart with His Love to strengthen your spirit and satisfy the desires of your Heart. His Faithful Love toward you never ends, and His Compassion never fails. His Love Reveals your High Value in the Gift of Passion He paid to make you His Own child.

Find out today God's Love Never Diminishes!

# Letter From God

Good Morning,

I Love you My Dear, Precious, Beloved, Blessed, Special, Beautiful child of My GREAT Love. And that is what you are!

The Reward of Love is Love! I Am Love, and you Love ME because I First Loved you. My Love has brought you into an intimate experience of living continually in my Love, and I live in you and through you. Your Love Grows Forever as you walk with ME in the destiny I placed within you.

I have filled you with My Love to Love others as I Love you. My Love continually nourishes your Heart, with the same Love that I love My Son. And you live continually nourished and empowered by My Love through the Holy Spirit Who lives in you.

Day by day I take care of you, for I have given you an inheritance that lasts forever to satisfy the Great and Intense Love I have for you. My Love satisfies the desires of your Heart and renews your spirit's Strength to strong and overcoming.

You have a Great Reward in loving ME; you receive the victorious crown of life, things never heard of, and beyond your ability to imagine. I assure you that I being with you, am weaving every detail of your life together for good to fulfill My Divine Purpose.

I have made My permanent home in you, and My Love comes to its full expression through you. My Endless Love, I have poured into your Heart through the Holy Spirit Who lives in you to produce all My Divine Love's infinite expressions through you.

LEE RICHARDS

Love is My Gift and My Reward. I gave My Love to you, and you have received My Love. Now, you can experience for yourself the astonishing magnitude of My Divine Love as it transforms your whole being till you are full and overflowing with Myself.

My Reward for cascading My Love on you is receiving your Love, as well as the Love of those I Love through you. And all who Love ME through their Love Generation after Generation, for all eternity. For the Reward of your Love is My Love, which can never Be Taken from you, for My Faithful Love Never Ends, and My Compassion Never Fails. My Love for you Never fades, Never Stops loving, Never Comes to an end, for I continually exist, being Love.

You are My Glorious Inheritance purchase by the Blood of My Beloved Son. His Beautiful offering of Love reveals the High Value you are to ME! A Dear Precious Reward far over and above all you dare think, infinitely more than you can imagine!

Nothing can diminish My Reward in you because of the Love Gift We share. You have been made My Reward, and I desire to Reward you with all that is Mine. I Speak Words of Life over you, which My Son Purchased to give you as My Gift, My child.

I love you,

Daddy God. Amen.

*We love Him, because He first loved us.*
1 John 4:19, KJV

## SCRIPTURES FOR FURTHER READING:

1 John 4:16-19; John 15:9-10, Romans 5:5, Psalm 37:18, Ephesians 2:4, Isaiah 40:31, Psalm 103:5, Psalm 58:11, James 1:12, 1 Corinthians 2:9, Romans 8:28, 1 John 4:12-13, Galatians 5:22, Ephesians 3:18-19, 1 Corinthians 13:8, Lamentations 3:22, Ephesians 1:18, John 16:13, John 10:10

## Prayer

Heavenly Father,

I love You because You first loved me. Thank You for bringing me into an intimate personal relationship with Yourself. Your Love continually nourishes my Heart and empowers me to love others as You love me. Thank You for filling me with your Faithful Love that Never Ends and making me Your glorious inheritance to live in Your Love for all eternity.

In Jesus' name. Amen.

# REST IN MY TENDER LOVE

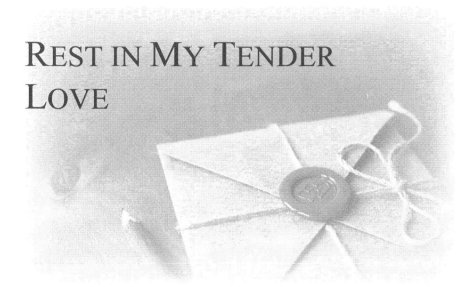

*God draws you to Himself to rest in His Peace and Strength. He knows your limits and whispers to you to: "Come to ME and Rest in My Tender Love." The invitation is to Soak in His Presence to recharge in your union with Him.*

*His arms are always wide open, welcoming you into His Presence. He Dearly loves you. He carries you close to His Heart to comfort you in His gentle, compassionate presence. His Tender Love empowers you with renewed Spiritual Strength.*

*He wrapped His Heart with your Heart in an unbreakable cord to continually experience His Divine Strength. And He empowers you out of the rich treasury of His Glory to refresh your innermost being.*

*Let His Love nourishes your Heart continually.*

# Letter From God

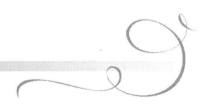

Good Morning,

I Love you My Dear, Precious, Beloved, Blessed, Special, Beautiful child of My GREAT Love. And that is what you are!

Rest with ME, Now. I am your Endless Source of Peace and Strength. I know your limits and your need to Rest with ME; I draw you to Myself to Soak in My Presence and recharge in your union with ME.

My arms are always open wide to welcome you into My Presence because you are Dearly Love by ME. Come to ME and Rest in My Tender Love. I am your refreshing oasis, Who causes you to rest. I ease and relieve and recharges you with the Power of My Presence. I Never Grow Weary or Worn out, so you are alive and joined in Life-Union with ME through My Spirit have an Overflowing fountain of Love to eternally refreshing you.

I carry you close to My Heart and comfort you with My Gentle, Compassionate Presence. I empower you with Tender Love when feeling faint and weary. And I infuse you with My Mighty Strength, which you sense more deeply when weak. Yes, I give you a fresh supply of Spiritual Strength, and I increase your Strength. I Love you, My child; I am your Strength.

Your Heart is wrapped tightly with My Heart, forever. I bind your Heart together with Mine in an unbreakable strand, to come to know practically, through experience for yourself, the immeasurable greatness of Divine Strength in you and for you. I empower you for victory with My Wraparound Presence. My power within you makes you strong in ME and the power of My Might. I have given you the Shield of Your Salvation, and hold you up with My Right Hand; and in gentleness, I have made you great!

How Blessed you are Soaking in My Holy Presence. I grant you out of the rich treasury of My Glory to be strengthened and reinforced with mighty power in your inner man by the Holy Spirit indwelling your innermost being and personality.

I have locked you safely in My Heart. You rest with ME, and My Love nourishes your Heart continually. You remain in My Love. I have seated you together in the heavenly realm with Christ in ME to rest as one. I am always within you, and My Presence Gives you Rest, supernaturally infusing you with Strength from union with Me, My child.

I love you,

Daddy God. Amen.

*Rest in the LORD, and wait patiently for Him.*
Psalms 37:7, NKJV

## Scriptures for Further Reading:

Colossians 3:12, Matthew 11:28, Isaiah 40:28, Romans 8:9-10, Ephesians 2:5, Isaiah 40:29, Philippians 4:13, 2 Corinthians 12:9, Psalm 18:1, Isaiah 40:31, Psalm 25:5, Ephesians 1:19, Psalm 18:35, Ephesians 6:10, Psalm 84:5, Ephesians 3:16, John 15:9, Ephesians 2:5, Colossians 3:3, Exodus 34:14

## Prayer

Heavenly Father,

I come to Your open arms to Rest in Your Tender Love. Cause me to Rest, ease and relief, and recharge my soul. I need to soak in Your Love and receive a fresh supply of Your Spiritual Strength. I ask you to grant me out of the rich treasury of Your Glory to strengthen Me continuously by your Holy Spirit.

In Jesus' name. Amen.

# MY EVERLASTING LOVE FOR YOU

*G*od loves you with an Everlasting Love and wraps you with Unshakable Faithfulness. He draws you to Himself with Unfailing Love to experience His extravagant tender care and kindness that never ends. God is eternal, so all He expresses to you is woven into eternity.

You are so valuable to God that He gave His Greatest Treasure, His Son, as a sacrifice for you to live with Him forever. Christ proved God's love for you! His Endless Love resting inside you is the very source and root of your life.

God is your Faithful Father, Who obligates Himself to take care of you, watch over you and provide all your necessities. He invites you to run and hide in His Faithfulness. You are secure in His Unchanging Nature, where your comfort and strength rest in the Faithful Love of His heart.

# Letter From God

Good Morning,

I Love you, My Dear, Precious, Beloved, Blessed, Special, Beautiful child of My GREAT Love. And that is what you are!

Nothing can separate you from My Endless Love and Unshakable Faithfulness. I love you with Everlasting Love. In My Lovingkindness, I draw you continually close and wrap you with My Unshakable Faithfulness.

I keep My Word and lavish My Loyal Love to you who loves Me, forever! My Divine Love is everlasting, and My Faithfulness infinite beyond the highest heavens. So, preciously extravagant is My tender care and kindness toward you; *it is most* readily *express* in My Cherishing Love for you that never ends.

My tender care of you continues forever! My Everlasting Love is a Faithful Love, which demonstrates the high price I paid to receive you back to Myself. It reveals just how valuable you are to Me by giving My Greatest Treasure, the Gift of My Son, for you. How deeply intimate is My Endless Love released inside of you through the Holy Spirit. My love that is resting in you is the very source and root of your life.

I am your Faithful Father Who is bound to take care of you whom I created. I obligate Myself to My Unchanging Nature. It is impossible for Me to lie. My Promise and Vow of Love for you will never change! I have opened My heart to you, run and hide in My Faithfulness. I am where you find your comfort and strength, for I am your unshakable hope!

LEE RICHARDS

My Faithfulness guarantees your provisions for all your necessity. I am your Faithful Friend and Good Shepherd. You can declare with boldness: "My God satisfies all my needs." I do! I always have more than enough. And I am more than ready to overwhelm with every dimension of My Grace. I take care of you always and under all circumstances, no matter the need – in every moment and every way.

Rest in the luxurious love of My Heart. Nothing can divorce you from My Endless Love. Nothing has the power to diminish My Great Love for you and toward you – nothing is potent enough to hinder My Omnipotent Love for you. I even call you to triumph over all things to demonstrate My Glorious Loves victory over everything. Nothing can separate you from My Endless Love and Unshakable Faithfulness which I have lavished upon you, My child.

I love you,

Daddy God. Amen.

*I have loved you with an everlasting love;*
*I have drawn you with unfailing kindness.*

Jeremiah 31:3, NIV

## Scriptures for Further Reading:

Jeremiah 31:3, Deuteronomy 7:9, Galatians 5:22, Psalm 36:5, Psalm 36:5-7, 1 Corinthians 13:8, Psalm 136:1, Romans 8:32, Romans 5:5, 8, Ephesians 3:17, Numbers 23:19, Hebrews 6:18, Psalm 23:1, Philippians 4:19, 2 Corinthians 9:8, Romans 8:35-37

## Prayer

Heavenly Father,

I come to You with an open heart; wrap me in Your Unshakable Faithfulness. You have promised to take care of me and sealed it in Your Vow of Love. You are my unshakable hope. I trust You to take care of me always and under all circumstances, no matter the need—in every moment and every way.

In Jesus' name. Amen.

# GIVING IS MY DIVINE NATURE

*G*od's Divine Nature is to Give! He is the Source of Every Good and Perfect Gift, which all contribute to His Divine Legacy for you. Each is a demonstration of His Passionate Love for you. The purpose of each Gift is to enable you to live your life through Him.

He has opened the windows of heaven and Lavishly bestowed upon you every Spiritual Blessing and All Grace, every favor and earthly blessing. He keeps nothing from you, and all that is His He makes available to you because you are His child.

God's Giving Nature gives insight into His divine design in creating you:

*Why was I created?*
*Does God care about me?*
*How can I know God loves me?*
*How can I hear God?*

Remember, every detail of your life is Tenderly Woven together for Good because you Love God. His Gifts of Love are a visible display of the Infinite Riches of His Grace and Kindness towards you.

# Letter From God

Good Morning,

I Love you, My Dear, Precious, Beloved, Blessed, Special, Beautiful child of My GREAT Love. And that is what you are!

Giving is My Divine Nature. I present to prove My Passionate Love for you. The Light of My Love shines upon you in My Giving My Beloved, Unique Son to the world—My Only Son—as an invaluable Gift. So now, you who believed in Him will never perish, but have My Free Gift of Eternal Life Lavished Upon you through your union with My Son, Jesus.

I am the God Who Gives. And My Giving proves My Love! I sent the Gift of My Son, My Greatest Treasure, to be freely offered up as My all-atoning sacrifice to take away all your sins. I held nothing back, so you can most certainly know I won't withhold anything else I have for you, and that I freely and graciously give you all things that are Mine.

My Spirit Reveals to you that the Truth of My Giving Nature was to Give My Love in all its infinite variety and innumerable aspects to you, so you can Live through ME because of My Great Love for you, My child.

My Giving Nature Provides you with insights into some of Life's Greatest Questions:

**Why was I created?** To become a new creation to fulfill the destiny I have given you since your conception, before the foundation of the world. I gave you the capacity to live in union with ME. So, you can Receive ME and Experience My Unfailing

Love for All Eternity that will fulfill My Prearranged destiny for you.

**Does God care about me personally?** I died for you personally! Remember, your feelings are never a good barometer of My Endless Love for you. I reveal just how valuable you are to ME! I paid a Precious Price to make you My Own—My Son's Life. Most assuredly, I Deeply Care about you, and I am always with you. I know every detail of your life. I know every hair on your head. I Never forget you nor abandon you, so do not worry. You are More Valuable to ME than anything else in the world.

Every single moment I am thinking about you! My Spirit Confirms with your spirit that I care about you! I am your Good Father Who liberally supplies your every need—spiritually, emotionally, socially, relationally, financially, and protectively. I meet them All! So, pour out all your worries and concerns on ME, for I ALWAYS Tenderly Care for you.

**How can I know God loves me?** Because you can experience for yourself My Endless Love, poured out in your heart through My Holy Spirit Who Lives within you! I empower you to know the Great Magnitude of My Unfailing Love in all its dimensions.

I come to live within you, My Spirit Whispering together with your own spirit, assuring you that you are My child and I Love you. The Light of My Love shines within you because Christ Lives in you, Who died in your place to prove My Passionate Love for you. Finally, you know I love you because I call you, recognize you, and count you as My Dearly Loved Child. And that is what you are!

**How can I hear God?** I Am Always present with you, and I always want to speak to you and hear from you. I am constantly talking, but you miss out because you have not spent the time to get to know ME personally. So, it seems complicated for you to distinguish My Voice. But I desire a loving, personal, intimate relationship with you, and I sent My Son to die in your place to make it available to you.

Fix your thoughts and attention on ME. Look away from all that's distracting you, set your heart on ME, and you will hear ME whispering into your innermost being: I love you!

The more time you spend with ME, the easier it becomes to recognize My Voice More Clearly, just like in any good relationship. First, begin by Believing I Am Already Speaking to you and Start Actively Listening by writing down what I tell you.

Stop to Hear from ME! Look away from all the distractions. Sit quietly, focusing your attention and expectation on ME, FOR I AM pulling on your heart to embrace the Unfailing Love of My Presence.

Open My Word and sit quietly before Me. As you do, I stir your mind's most holy emotions and in-birth in your heart the ability to receive My Word, imprinted and engraved in your innermost thoughts. Through this Holy process, I persuade you to do what I Prefer, continually birthing in you My Divine Persuasion through MY Spirit. All I reveal I guarantee will come to pass.

So, listen to Me. I am answering you by My Living Word which is active and operative in you. Hear My Spirit's Voice answer you! You will know My Answers by My Fruits. My Love transforms your spirit and never fails you. My Joy is your strength. And My Peace guards your heart and mind, and acts as an umpire to guide your every decision.

I AM your Good Shepherd, Best Friend, and Your Caring Father Who tends to you out of My Overflowing Love for you. I always desire for you to **Stop to Listen and Absorb My Word,** which I have implanted within your heart. Then respond to what I have told you by acting on it.

Then, you will find ME in My Word. For you perceive how I see you in the reflection of My Word. I see you from the beginning to the end, and the person you see in the reflection of My Word is the new creation I have made you—your divine origin to fulfill your divine destiny.

All I give you is a visible display of the Infinite Riches of My Grace and Kindness Towards you, which I have lavishly showered upon you in Jesus Christ. It is My Love Gift to you, My child.

I love you,

Daddy God. Amen.

*For God so loved the world that He gave*
*His only begotten Son, that whoever*
*believes in Him should not perish*
*but have everlasting life.*

John 3:16, NKJV

1 John 4:8-10, John 3:16, Romans 6:23, Romans 8:32, John 16:15, Ephesians 2:10, Romans 8:23-20, Deuteronomy 7:7-8, 1 Corinthians 13:8, Jeremiah 31:3, John 17:3, 1 John 5:10-13, Psalm 16:3, Romans 5:8, 1 Corinthians 6:20, Psalm 139:1, Luke 12:6-7, Romans 139:17, 1 John 5:14-15, Philippians 4:19, 1 Peter 5:7, 1 John 4:9, 1 John 3:1, Joshua 1:5, Matthew 1:23, John 10:27, Psalm 27:8, Psalm 119:5, Hebrews 12:2, 1 Corinthians 2:4, Hebrews 10:16, 1 Corinthians 13:4-8, Nehemiah 8:10, Philippians 4:7, Colossians 3:15, Psalm 23, James 1:21-26, 2 Corinthians 5:17, Ephesians 2:7-8

## Prayer

Heavenly Father,

I Praise You for Your Great Love for me! You gave Your Greatest Treasure, Your Son, to totally cancel all my sins. He died for me personally, to reveal how valuable I am to You. Every single moment I am thinking about you! You whisper into to me that I am your child. You pull on my heart to embrace You in order that I may know You intimately and believe You always. You are My Caring Father Who gives me the desire to hear You and provides all My needs. Thank You!

In Jesus' name. Amen.

# THE HOPE OF ALL HUMANITY

*J*esus' Victory is all mankind's victory! His death and resurrection prove and demonstrate that God's Passionate Love is Greater than Everything! It creates Eternal Life-change.

God provided a Great Exchange opportunity for mankind that would change the world and your life's destiny forever with childlike faith. The sinless Son of God would give His Life in Exchange for your life, as a demonstration of His Passionate Love for you. And all who accept His sacrifice as their own for their sin debt, God will make His child.

God requires no works or deeds on your part, only that you Believe. Jesus does ALL the rest! Then, God's Life-Giving Spirit recreates you into a new creation, alive together in union with His Son to Live in your New Father's house forever!

A Great Exchange, Indeed!

# Letter From God

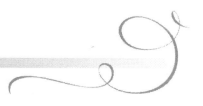

I Love you, My Dear, Precious, Beloved, Blessed, Special, Beautiful child of My GREAT Love. And that is what you are!

Jesus' Victory is the Hope of All Humanity. Jesus paid it all. Everything you need, His Sacrifice Demonstrates to you, by Him dying in your place on the cross, that My Passionate Love for you is your Glorious Victory over everything.

I offered mankind a Great Exchange—which took place at the cross—My Beloved Son gave His sinless life as a Substitutionary Sacrifice for your life. I placed all your sins on Him and left them there permanently as a public display for all the ages to come, throughout all eternity, of their Total Cancellation.

And you who accepted His Sacrifice have Received My Righteousness through your union with Him. Now you Possess the Complete and Perfect Righteousness of Christ. I see you as I see My Beloved Son—holy and blameless and above reproach in My Sight.

My Passionate Love is stronger than sin, death, and the grave—Christ's Resurrection proves it! Never underestimate the Power of Love that was released through the Resurrection. Now, the Overflowing Power of His Resurrection is working in, for, and through all who believe as an advertisement of My Passionate Love!

There is No Power in Heaven above, Earth below, underneath the Earth, in the Universe, or in All Creation that can separate you from My Passionate Love, which I have Lavishly Bestowed upon you through your union with Christ Jesus.

My love never fails. I have poured it out upon you without measure. It is as Transcendently Infinite as I AM, for I AM Love! My Love's Sacrifice gives you a New Life and New Identity with a New Future as My New Creation, Dear child.

My Love fuels your passion and desires to do what pleases ME. Christ now Lives in you! I have given you His Very Life, and made you alive together in union and fellowship with Him.

My Life-Giving Spirit has imparted eternal life to you because you are Fully Accepted by ME. I have forgiven all your sins! So, no longer look at your past sins, mistakes, and failures, the Empty Cross shows I have erased and deleted them all. Look to ME, Who has given you this Great Victory, as I have made you more than a conqueror by giving you a Hyper-Victory over everything, even death and the grave, through My Passionate Love and Grace that empowers you to be unrivaled, My child.

I love you,

Daddy God. Amen.

*But God demonstrates His own love toward us,*
*in that while we were still sinners,*
*Christ died for us.*

Romans 5:8, NKJV

## SCRIPTURES FOR FURTHER READING:

Romans 5:8, 2 Corinthians 5:21, Colossians 2:15, Hebrews 9:25-26, Colossians 1:21-22, Ephesians 1:19-20, Philippians 3:10, Romans 8:39, 1 Corinthians 13:8, 1 John 4:16, 2 Corinthians 5:14, Romans 8:9-10, Philippians 2:13, Ephesians 2:6, Colossians 2:13-14, 1 Corinthians 15:57, Romans 8:37

## Prayer

Heavenly Father,

My heart soars with Joyful gratitude thinking about the Passionate Love You demonstrated in Jesus dying in my place on the cross. Your Wonderful, Divine Exchange that took place at the cross of Jesus gave sinless life as a substitute for mine to remove all my sins. He removed them forever, and I walked away with All of Your Righteousness, approved and acceptable and in right-relationship with You. To You be all Praise and Glory and Honor and Power, forever and ever!

In Jesus' name. Amen.

# LIVE IN UNION AS ONE

*God's Divine Passion has opened wide to you the Gates of His Kingdom, where He richly welcomes you with open arms. Jesus deleted all your sins, and nothing will ever separate you from God's Love or Presence.*

*You have been made alive in union and fellowship with Him, who is your Life. You are an entirely new being, recreated with God's Nature. Your old identity with Adam is gone!*

*You now live in union with HIM, experiencing His Endless Love Forever!*

# Letter From God

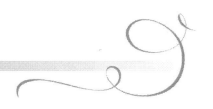

Good Morning,

I Love you, My Dear, Precious, Beloved, Blessed, Special, Beautiful child of My GREAT Love. And that is what you are!

My Divine Passion redeemed you Completely out of the authority and power of darkness, and transferred you into the Kingdom Realm of My Beloved Son. My Kingdom's gates are open wide to you, My child, I richly welcome you into My Eternal Kingdom.

Jesus deleted all your sins, and they can never be retained again! Everything you were in Adam has been set aside and cleared completely out of your way, having been nailed permanently to Jesus' cross as a public display of the Total Cancellation of your sins, Forever! Every Weapon has been stripped away from all the powers and principalities of darkness, and all their spiritual authority, and power to accuse you or harm you being My child.

I have made you alive in Union with ME. You are embedded with the DNA of Jesus and have become a new creation altogether in My Righteousness. And now you are My Very Own in the realm of True Holiness. Your Old Life Identified with Adam was crucified with Christ and No Longer Lives. Now, Christ Lives His Life through you, for your new life is hidden away with Him in ME!

We live in union as One! For you are the Temple of the Living God, Even as I have said, "I have made My Home in you and with you and walk in you and with you. I AM your Father and have made My Home in you; and you are My Child in whom I Live."

LEE RICHARDS

I Myself assume the role of caring for you, and not you for yourself. I meet your every need, and give Myself Eternally to you! You are My True Child. I have Released the Spirit of Sonship into your heart, testifying together with your own Spirit that you are My child, so now you can access everything that is Mine as My Heir through Christ.

This is My Divine Passion demonstrated to you, by which you experience My Endless Love pouring into your heart through My Spirit Who lives in you. You were worth every drop of My Son's Precious Blood, paid in My tears for you, My child.

I love you,

Daddy God. Amen.

*The Lord your God in your midst,*
*The Mighty One, will save;*
*He will rejoice over you with gladness,*
*He will quiet you with His love,*
*He will rejoice over you with singing.*

Zephaniah 3:17, NKJV

## Scriptures for Further Reading:

2 Peter 1:11, Zephaniah 3:17, Colossians 2:14, Ephesians 4:24, Colossians 3:3, 2 Corinthians 6:16, Exodus 25:8, 29:45, Leviticus 27:12, Jeremiah 31:1, Psalm 23:1, Galatians 4:6-7, 1 Corinthians 6:20

## Prayer

Heavenly Father,

Thank You, Father, for erasing permanently all my sins, and deleting them so they never can be retrieved again! Everything I once was in Adam was nailed to the cross, publicly canceling my identity with him. Now, Christ is my Life! You have made me alive together with Christ in You. It is no longer I who lives, but Christ in me lives His Life through me.

In Jesus' name. Amen.

# I AM YOUR RESTORER!

*G*od holds you close to His Heart to see the breakthroughs He made to Restore your Passion for Life. He is the Lord of the Breakthrough, His Spirit Supernaturally infusing you with strength to stand victorious with the force of His power flowing through you.

Fix your eyes on Him. He is your Restorer. He has Broken down every wall that restrains you. God has totally restored you back to Himself. He has kissed your heart with forgiveness and wrapped His Spirit around you to announce a new season of grace in your life.

God is Always Good.

# Letter From God

Good Morning,

I Love you, My Dear, Precious, Beloved, Blessed, Special, Beautiful child of My GREAT Love. And that is what you are!

I AM your Restorer—The Lord of the Breakthrough Who Restores your Passion for Life to Taste Triumphant Joy in every Breakthrough I bring you. I hold you close to My Heart and give you the power and desire to obey ME.

I uphold you by My Generous Spirit. I AM the Spirit, and where My Spirit is, there is Restoration, Breakthrough, and Freedom from bondage. For My Spirit liberates you, and His impulses motivate you to see the breakthroughs I bring to you that restores to you what was lost or decayed.

I AM the Lord of the Breakthrough. I Flow My Spirit of Life through you that sets you free from the enemies of your soul. You may think you're facing a wall of containment that is keeping you in the same place, seeing no evidence of change. It is just a dart of the enemy, who Knows I, your, Father ceaselessly work on your behalf, as well as the Son and Holy Spirit, weaving every detail of your life together to fulfill My Design and Purpose for you.

I am El Shaddai—Almighty God—the All Sufficient One, God Who is More Than Enough. Most Assuredly, you are not contained, for I AM standing permanently with you. What obstacle can stop My Design Purpose for you? I AM Sovereign, and I have made you more than a conqueror. My Divine Love and Power work for you and through you to triumph over all things. My Love and Grace empower you to be unrivaled. Because Greater Am I in you, than he who is in the world. I am Spirit, and My Breakthrough Spirit lives in you to pull down strongholds!

Fix your eyes on ME, full of expectation, and you will see I have broken down every wall that has contained you. The Wounds of your past no longer hinder you from embracing My Blessing in the present. I have broken down the walls in your heart, so you can experience for yourself the great magnitude of My Love for you in all its dimensions. How deeply intimate and far-reaching is My Love for you.

The Holy Spirit's Dynamic Power has worked within you and made you into a new creation. He Totally transformed you into an entirely new person that never existed before. The old has passed away and the new has come. You are no longer your own. You died with Christ and now have the Mind of Christ, and hold the Thoughts, Feelings, and Purposes of His Heart and Mind.

My Spirit reveals to you every truth of who you are as My child, so you can know the wonderful things I have freely given you, and the authority, power, privileges, and rights that are yours as a co-heir with Christ.

I have totally restored you back to ME, reconnecting you to Myself through the precious blood of Jesus Christ's cross. Now you dwell in My Presence—Restored to innocence again! And there is nothing between you and ME, for I see you as holy, blameless, and restored in My Love.

In your total restoration I empower you to discern how I see you—Redeemed Back to ME and wrapped in My Divine Love Forever through the Blood of Jesus.

Your life is a beautiful song written by ME that sings forth all I desire in your life and have given you to do. You have breakthroughs because Christ broke down the wall that separated you from ME. He has set you Free!

I have Restored everything that was taken from you and conquered every foe. There is nothing too difficult for ME. I heal the wounds of your broken heart, and kiss your heart with forgiveness. You are healed from the inside out. I have redeemed your life and crowned you with My Tender Love and Mercy. I fill your life with good things and restore your strength with My Strength's explosive power to conquer every difficulty.

I have wrapped My Spirit around you, to heal the wounds of your broken heart, to free you from the bondages of darkness, announcing a new season of grace in your life. I break the shackles of your every bondage, and bestow on you a crown of beauty instead of ashes. You have received the oil of Exceeding Joy instead of tears, and the mantle of praise instead of a spirit of heaviness. As My Heir, I have Lavishly Bestowed upon you a Double Portion of Endless Joy and Everlasting Bliss, because I AM your Great Restorer, My child.

I love you,

Daddy God. Amen.

*Restore to me the joy of Your salvation,*
*And uphold me by Your generous Spirit.*

Psalm 51:12, NKJV

## SCRIPTURES FOR FURTHER READING:

Psalm 51:12, Philippians 2:13, 2 Corinthians 3:12, Romans 8:10, Genesis 17:1, Romans 8:31, Romans 8:37, John 4:4 John 4:24, Hebrews 12:2, Ephesians 3:19, 2 Corinthians 5:17, Galatians 2:20, 1 Corinthians 2:16, Isaiah 40:13, John 16:13, 1 John 3:1, 1 Corinthians 2:12, John 1:12, Romans 8:17, Colossians 1:20-22, Ephesians 2:10, Galatians 5:1, Ephesians 2:14, Jeremiah 32:17, Psalm 147:2, Psalm 103:3-5, Jeremiah 17:14, Jeremiah 30:17, Isaiah 40:31, Philippians 4:13, Isaiah 61:1-3, 7

## Prayer

Heavenly Father,

You are my Restorer! The Lord of the Breakthrough Who Restores my Passion for Life. My heart rejoices, tasting the Triumphant Joy you bring to me in every Breakthrough. You hold me close to My Heart and give me the power and desire to do what pleases You. I fix my eyes on You with full of expectation as the All Sufficient One, God Who is More Than Enough to help me in everything.

In Jesus' name. Amen.

# ROCK OF EVERLASTING LOVE

*T*he heart of God is easy to recognize in the Precious Price He paid to redeem us back to Himself. He clearly shows and proves His Passionate Love for us by Christ dying in our place while we were still lost and ungodly!

He is our Creator Who gave you new birth, nurtured you in His Love, and even created us in His Spirit-Womb. The love God has for us is similar to a mother's love. His is a Tender Love that lasts forever.

His Superabounding Grace and Mercy make His Redemption available to you to satisfy His Great Love.

You are loved.

# Letter From God

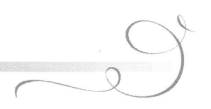

Good Morning,

I Love you, My Dear, Precious, Beloved, Blessed, Special, Beautiful child of My GREAT Love. And that is what you are!

I AM your Rock of Everlasting Love and your Redeemer. Listen to ME, My Chosen one. I AM your Creator Who formed you in My Womb. I gave you New Birth through My Spirit. I am Always Nurturing you in My Tender Unfailing Love, beginning even when I formed you in My Womb.

My Tender Love for you is similar to a Mother's Love—a Womb-Love that carries you, then births you into a New Spiritual Life. I wrap around you as a shield of protection, and take you by the hand and teach you. Your heart is entwined with ME into My purposes! My Nurturing is a constant Tender Love that lasts forever! It causes you to grow and develop in My Spirit and My Power with My Wisdom, which is exhibited in everything I do to help you, My child.

My Word is your spiritual food. I rock you in the comfort of My Spirit, I Change your Life, I smile My Face upon you can continually, for you are My New Creation, a New Spiritual creature that never existed before.

You are always Precious in My Presence! I never leave you nor forsake you. I will not in any way fail you. So, you can take comfort in ME. Do not be afraid or be discouraged, for I am your God. I am your Strengthener and Helper. I hold you up with My Victorious Right Hand.

I have Redeemed you by a high, precious price, paid for by the Blood of Christ to make you My Own child. It is only by Christ you have the Release of Redemption through His Blood, for all your sins.

Since you are now joined to Christ, you have been given All the Treasures of Redemption by His Blood—the Total Forgiveness of your sins because of the Cascading of My Grace in all its Infinite Variety and Innumerable Aspects available for you.

This Super Abounding Grace has already been lavishly poured out upon you, and is powerfully working in you, releasing all its diverse forms of wisdom and understanding and prudent insight to make known to you My Mystery in Christ, which I Implanted from the Very Beginning of Time to establish you as My Own child through your union with Jesus.

This is the Glorious and Divine Mystery of the Gospel of Grace which has made you a Co-Heir of My Divine Promise in Christ. Through your union with Christ, I have appointed you as My Own Inheritance. My Spirit Testifies Together with Your Own Spirit that you are My True Child and My Heir, Whom I Qualified to Share All My Treasures, My child.

I love you,

Daddy God. Amen.

*For You formed my inward parts;*
*You covered me in my mother's womb.*

Psalm 139:13, NKJV

Psalm 19:14, Isaiah 44:1, Ephesians 1: 4, John 3:5-6, Psalm 115:10, Psalm 25:5, Psalm 118:3, Jeremiah 18:16, Matthew 4:4, Deuteronomy 9:3, John 6:33, John 14:16, 2 Corinthians 5:17, Hebrews 13:5-6, Isaiah 41:10, Isaiah 43:1, 1 Corinthians 6:20, Colossians 1:14, 1 Corinthians 2:12, Ephesians 3:5-6, Romans 8:16-17

## Prayer

Heavenly Father,

You made me and knitted me together in my mother's womb. Thank You for making me so wonderfully complex! Everything You do is marvelously breathtaking. It simply amazes me to think about it! You saw me before I was born. Every day of my life is recorded in Your book. Every single moment You are thinking of me!

In Jesus' name. Amen.

# My Spirit Imparts Life to You

*G*od's Life-Giving Spirit imparts new life to you. He made you alive in a union as one with Christ. His plan from the beginning was to reveal you as His child through Jesus Christ because of His Great Love for you.

His Endless Love continuously pours in your hearts through the Holy Spirit Who lives in you. He makes God's fatherhood real to us as He whispers into our innermost being, "You are God's beloved child!"

The Holy Spirit is your Helper, who is a friend to you just like Jesus. He stands with you and for you to defend, protect, intercede, strengthen, encourage, comfort, guide, counsel, and keep you safe, whole, and healed. He will never leave you because He lives within you forever.

# Letter From God

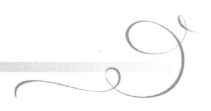

Good Morning,

I Love you, My Dear, Precious, Beloved, Blessed, Special, Beautiful child of My GREAT Love. And that is what you are!

My Life-Giving Spirit imparts new life to you. I made you alive together in a union with Christ and gave you His very life. Now, I empower your life with My mighty power and Endless Love in a personal relationship with Me.

As My child, I move you by the impulses of the Holy Spirit. He is My guarantee that you are My child forever—the eternal stamp of My sealing you in Christ with Me. In My perfect plan, I chose to reveal you as My child through Jesus Christ. And that is what you are!

I sent the Holy Spirit as My Gift, pouring My Tremendous Love in you and over you to glorify My Grace lavishly bestowed upon you. He is the very Spirit of Adoption Who joins you with Me, calling out through you to Me with tender affection: "Abba Father, Daddy God." The Holy Spirit makes My Love and Fatherhood a reality, whispering into your innermost being, "You are My Beloved Precious child!"

He is your Helper, Whom I have called to stand with you and for you to defend, protect, intercede, strengthen, encourage, comfort, guide, counsel, and keep you safe, whole, and healed. He will never leave you because He lives eternally inside you and with you. He is My Spirit, the Spirit of God, Who makes My immeasurable, unlimited power available to you who believes in Me.

The Holy Spirit is your Comforter. He testifies with your spirit, assuring you I love you. He stirs your mind's most holy emotions and persuades you that I am within you and guarantees My Word I reveal to you comes to pass. Thus, you come to understand and experience for yourself All His Grace has been Lavishly Bestowed upon you.

The Holy Spirit's Impulses are at work in you, energizing and creating in the power and desire and passion for doing what pleases Him. This Impulse is the Love of Christ, which is so Great and Intense that it demands a response that is great and radical, affecting your innermost being. The Love of Christ poured in you activates this change within you, changing your reactions to life's activities, situations, and circumstances, My child.

I love you,

Daddy God. Amen.

*And Christ lives within you, so even*
*though your body will die because of sin,*
*the Spirit gives you life because you have*
*been made right with God.*

Romans 8:10, NLT

## SCRIPTURES FOR FURTHER READING:

Romans 8:10, Ephesians 2:5, Romans 8:6, 10, Ephesians 3:20, Romans 8:14, Ephesians 1:14, Colossians 3:3, Ephesians 1:5-6, 1 John 3:1, Galatians 4:6-7, John 14:16-17, Romans 8:15-16, John 14:16-17, Ephesians 1:19, 1 Corinthians 2:4-12, Philippians 2:13, Ephesians 2:4

## Prayer

Heavenly Father,

Thank You for making me alive together in union with Christ and saving me by Your Amazing Grace! Now, Your Spirit fills my heart with Your Love and makes Your Fatherhood a reality, assuring me of Your Love. To You be all Glorious praise Who fills me to overflowing with the Love of Christ!

In Jesus' name. Amen.

# FINGERPRINT OF MY FAITHFUL LOVE

*G*od's Faithful Love is overall He does throughout human history. He planned before the foundation of the world to make you, His child. In eternity past, God decided to demonstrate His Love to the world by giving up His Son as a gift, so that when you believe in Him, you share eternal life with your Heavenly Father.

You were in God's Loving embrace long before Christ came into the world. In eternity past, the Father and the Son chose you in Love to be God's for all Eternity. Nothing can come between you and My Endless Love.

God's Love for you is Eternal. It has no end and has no limits. His Love is Unconditional. He loves you even when you stumble. His Faithful Love reveals Who He is, and how He loves you for all eternity.

God has hidden you in His Heart to Love for Eternity.

# Letter From God

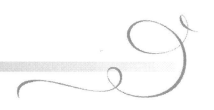

Good Morning,

I Love you, My Dear, Precious, Beloved, Blessed, Special, Beautiful child of My GREAT Love. And that is what you are!

Times will change, but My Faithful Love for you is always the same, yesterday, today, and forever. It never ends, and keeps taking you to higher highs, higher because My compassion never stops. Great is My Faithful Love—superabundant and eternally stable. Even if you waver, I never hesitate in My faithfulness to you. I am Eternally Faithful to you!

My Tender Love is overall that I do. You can see My Love and Tender Care in all creation. You can see the Fingerprint of My Love throughout human history. I so loved the world, I gave up My Only, Unique Son as a gift to humankind, so whoever believes in Him will never perish but have eternal life and live forever. Thus, I declare and demonstrated My Passionate Love for you by Christ dying in your place.

Yes, I loved you long before Christ came into the world. From the very beginning of time, I chose you in Love to be Mine for all Eternity. Nothing can come between your and My Endless Love. For nothing has the power to diminish My Love toward you. Everything is impotent to hinder My Omnipotent Love. I sent Jesus into the world so that through Him, you could receive and experience My Endless Love. And I have given you My Holy Spirit to assure you that I love you and give you the power to love others.

I am rich in mercy toward you to satisfy My Great Intense Love with which I love you. Even though you were dead in your sins, I made you a life in union with Christ. It is no longer you who lives, for Christ lives His life through you. You are one with Him forever.

My Love for you is Eternal, so it has no end, and because I am Infinite, so My Love for you has no limits. There is never anything you can do to win My Love, and nothing in all creation that can keep Me from loving you through all eternity. Nothing in all eternity can ever separate you from My Passionate Love I lavish upon you through Christ.

My Love reveals Who I am, Love. I continually exist, being Love, so My Love for you continues forever. Love is My essential nature. I am gracious and full of compassion, tenderhearted to those who do not deserve it, and very patient even when you stumble. My Love for you is like a river overflowing its banks with loving-kindness and tender mercy.

I am always Good to you and ready to spend time with you. My Faithful Love is so amazing that it continues through all your generations forever. My Goodness extends to everything I do, for My Tender Love for you is woven into My heart forever, My child.

I love you,

Daddy God. Amen.

*Jesus Christ is the same yesterday,*
*today, and forever*
Hebrews 13:8, NKJV

## Scriptures for Further Reading:

Hebrews 13:8, Lamentations 3:22-23, I Corinthians 13:8, Psalm 145:8-9, Psalm 119:64, 2 Timothy 2:13, Romans 1:20-21, John 3:16, Romans 5:8,1 John 4:10-11, John 14:17, Ephesians 2:4-5, Galatians 2:20, Ecclesiastes 3:11, Romans 8:39, 1 John 4:8, Psalm 100:5, Colossians 2:2

## Prayer

Heavenly Father,

Your Faithful Love produces the confidence I need to face this day with You by my side. You knew all about me before I was born, and You destined me from the beginning to be Your child. Thank You that Your Love for me has no end. Nothing will ever separate me from it because I am one with You forever.

In Jesus' name. Amen.

# GOODNESS AND TENDER LOVE PURSUE YOU

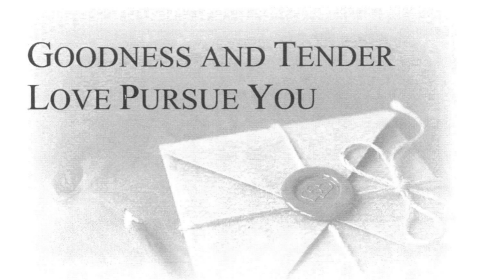

*G*od's Spirit opens your ears to hear Everything Grace has freely given to you. His Goodness and Tender Love continuously pursue you, even from the beginning, and never stop. He blends His Tender Love in Everything He does to show you His Goodness.

*The Holy Spirit within you produces the fruits of Tender Love in you and through you. One of those fruits is Goodness. God's Goodness disposes Him to desire your Everlasting Best, and His Goodness in you disposes you to want the same for others.*

*God began loving you the moment He first thought of you, and He never stops loving you! His Love for you is Everlasting. And Everything He does flows from His Goodness to experience His Tender Love for you.*

# Letter From God

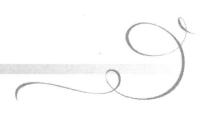

Good Morning,

I Love you, My Dear, Precious, Beloved, Blessed, Unique, Beautiful child of My GREAT Love. And that is what you are!

I created you to hear My voice speak into your innermost being. My Spirit opens your ears to listen to what I have to say. My Tender Love flows from Him into your heart for you to understand and experience Everything My Grace has freely given you.

The Holy Spirit produces My fruit of Goodness. And My Goodness and Endless Love actively pursue you all the days of your life, because My Love never stops loving you. It never leaves you, nor does it give up on you. My Love never lets you down because you are always in My Presence. And My Spirit within you assures you that I live in you, you live in Me, and I live through you.

My Love is brought to full expression through you living in union with Me. I fill you to overflowing with My Tender Love, so your Love for others is a gracious response to the Tender Love I have fathered in you.

My Goodness disposes Me to desire your Everlasting Best, and My Goodness in you disposes you to want the same for others. I blend My Tender Love into Everything I do so you can see Everything I do flows from My Goodness. And I, being Sovereign over all things, enable you to experience My Goodness and Tender Love through My Spirit.

I began loving you the moment I first thought of you—and I never stop loving you! My Love for you is Everlasting. I chose you before the foundation of the world, yet you should be holy and blameless in My Eyes. I decided in advance to make you My child and adopt you into My Family through your union with Jesus Christ, so that My Tremendous Love would glorify My Grace.

Most assuredly, you can know that I am weaving all the details of your life together for good, for you are My child, called to fulfill the destiny I have given you. I sealed you with My Holy Spirit from the Beginning to Fulfill My Design Purpose for your life, to transfigure you into Christ's image, and to inwardly share His likeness.

See what an incredible quality of My Marvelous Love I lavish upon you! I call you and make you My beloved child, with all the authority, rights, and privileges as a member of My Own household.

I love you,

Daddy God. Amen.

> Surely your Goodness and unfailing Love
> will pursue me all the days of my life.
>
> Psalm 23:6, NLT

## SCRIPTURES FOR FURTHER READING:

Psalm 42:1, 8, 1 Corinthians 2:13, John 17:26, Romans 5:5, Galatians 5:22-23, Psalm 23:6, 1 Corinthians 13:8, Hebrews 13:5, 1 John 4:13, John 14:16-17, 20, 1 John 4:17, 1 John 4:11, Colossians 3:13, Ephesians 1:4-5, Romans 8:28-29, Psalm 119:68, Psalm 145:9, 2 Corinthians 3:16, 1 John 3:1-2, Ephesians 2:19, John 1:12

## Prayer

Heavenly Father,

You have promised Goodness and Tender Love pursue me all the days of my life. How wonderful You are to desire my everlasting best! Please help me recognize and embrace and experience the great magnitude of Your Goodness flowing from Your Tender Love. For Your best for me wrapped in Your Goodness and Tender Love is always far beyond what I could hope or imagine.

In Jesus' name. Amen.

# ENJOY THE SECRET PLACE OF MY PRESENCE

*A*s God's child, you have direct, free access to the Creator of ALL things visible and invisible at any moment. His warm arms are open, waiting to embrace you because He dearly loves you.

In His Presence, you find you are filled with mighty, glorious strength to keep you going, despite the obstacles you face, so that you have expectant joy waiting entwined with His heart and do not give up.

Fix your eyes on Him, Who is always with you, and cast all your worries and cares on Him. And look with great expectation for the blessings and answers He already has coming to you.

# Letter From God

Good Morning,

I Love you, My Dear, Precious, Beloved, Blessed, Unique, Beautiful child of My GREAT Love. And that is what you are!

Enjoy the secret place of My Presence within you, where you have free access to Me at any time. I love you unconditionally, entirely—just the way you are! I made you for fellowship with Me continually. In My Presence, you find that I strengthen you with the unlimited riches of My Grace and Glory in your innermost being through My Spirit until supernatural strength floods you with My Divine Might, filling you with My Joy.

I pull you into My Presence to embrace My Tender Love, to spend time with Me, and enjoy our relationship. Come to Me Who Treasures and Enjoys you. I delight in your presence with Me because you are Mine. The Special Treasure of My Passionate Love—a Treasure above All Treasures.

I gave My Son to purchase your freedom, to open the way back to Me. With liberty and complete confidence, I welcome you warmly into My Presence. I dearly love you! I encircle you with Myself, so I have you all to Myself, wrapped in My Glorious Grace and surrounded by My Tender Love, blessed beyond measure!

I fix your heart on My Promises to feast on My Faithfulness. In My Presence, you taste the fullness of joy, for I set you on My Right Side to experience the Divine Pleasure hidden in the pierced, wounded side of Christ.

Lee Richards

When you come to Me, you find True Delight and pleasure in Me. Your heart trusts Me to give you what I know you desire the most—the right to direct your life in all My Delight, casting all your cares and worries upon Me, Who always tenderly cares for you, knowing I desire your Absolute Best.

I have already blessed you with every spiritual blessing and lavishly bestowed upon you every favor and earthly blessing coming to you in abundance as My Love Gift. Look away from the world's distractions and focus your attention and expectations on the joy and pleasure of spending time with Me, My child.

I love you,

Daddy God. Amen.

*You have made known to me the ways of life;*
*You will make me full of joy in Your presence.*

Acts 2:28, NKJV

## ▌Scriptures for Further Reading:

Acts 2:28, Ephesians 3:12, 16, Colossians 1:11, Ephesians 1:11, 1 Peter 2:9, Titus 3:14, Ephesians 3:12, Hebrews 4:16, Ephesians 1:6, Psalm 32:10, Psalm 37:3, Psalm 16:11, Psalm 37:4-5, Psalm 16:3, 1 Peter 5:7, Ephesians 1:3

## Prayer

Heavenly Father,

In Your Presence I find unconditional love. You strengthen me with the unlimited riches of Your Grace and Glory, Flooding me with Your Divine Might and Joy. You embrace me with Tender Love and give me Divine Worth. I fix my heart on Your promises of blessings and favor, and look away from the world.

In Jesus' name. Amen.

# I Am Your Way Maker

*G*od makes a way where there seems no way. Many times, the walls before you are doors, just waiting for Him to open. But you have become weary from the journey and need to rest. As God infuses you with increasing strength, you begin to see things from His perspective. And He leads you through a way you did not see before.

Do not yield to fear, for God is always with you. God knows everything about you. He even knows every thought before you think it. And every outcome before it comes to pass. The wisest decision you can make is to go to God, Trust Him Completely and do not rely on your understanding. And ask Him to direct what you should do.

# Letter From God

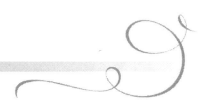

Good Morning,

I Love you, My Dear, Precious, Beloved, Blessed, Unique, Beautiful child of My GREAT Love. And that is what you are!

I am your Way Maker. I make a way where there seems no way. When there is a wall before you, if you look through the eyes of faith, it is just a stopping point of rest to infuse you with increasing strength. I intertwine your heart with Mine, as you wait for My Plan to unfold while experiencing My divine strength empowering you. I lead you through the seas of life on a pathway no one even knew was there, My Beloved!

I Am with you Now. You are precious in My Sight, and I love you dearly and chose to honor you because you are My child. Do not yield to fear, for I am always with you. I chose you to know Me intimately, believe Me constantly, and understand I am God your Father, Who from the very beginning loved you and chose you in Christ.

There is No one that can snatch you out of my hand or can undo what I have done! I am your Sovereign Creator. I Know Everything about you. I know every step you take on your life journey before it begins. I direct your life and each step to fulfill your destiny.

Before you are ever born, I recorded every day of your life in My Book. Every moment was laid out and planned for you before a single day took place. I created you in your mother's womb. I know everything you're going to do before you do it. I know every thought before you think it. I know you better than you know even yourself.

I know everything about you, all your thoughts, feelings, and purposes—I see all and know all. Everything is open before Me, Who created you. I know My good thoughts and plans for you, and I know what will happen next.

So, the wisest thing for you to do is come to Me First, before you make a decision. I hold your future in My Hands—your every moment is continually woven together in My Glorious Grace.

I declare the end of your life and the result of your life from the beginning before it happened. Everything I plan will come to pass. For I am in the past, the present, and the future, all at the same time. I am intimately aware My Chosen Treasure and My Passionate Love unite you in the very life of Christ.

You walk with the seal of My promised Holy Spirit. He is your guarantee, and all I have pledged to you is coming. He is the first installment of what else is coming! He is the promise of your future inheritance, who seals you in Christ until you have all I have promised. I renew your strength, and I always guide you along the right paths and lead you in My Footsteps of Righteousness to bring Me Glory.

I am always with you, watching over you. I am at your side to shelter you in the Safety of My Presence. I Protect you from all harm, day and night. I keep you from every form of evil or calamity. I continually keep watch over you as you come and go. I protect you now, and I will protect you forever.

I go before you, and I follow you. I am in your future, preparing the way for you, and in kindness, I follow behind to protect you from your past. Most assuredly, My Hand of Blessing is upon you, My child.

I love you,

Daddy God. Amen.

> *I am the Lord, who opened a way through the waters*
> *making a dry path through the sea.*
>
> Isaiah 43:16, NLT

## ▎SCRIPTURES FOR FURTHER READING:

Isaiah 43:16, Isaiah 40:29-31, Psalm 77:19, Isaiah 43:4-5, 1 John 3:1, Isaiah 43:10, Isaiah 43:13, Ephesians 1:4, John 10:29, Psalm 139:1-5, Psalm 37:23, Ephesians 2:10, Psalm 139:16, Isaiah 44:1, Psalm 139:3, Jeremiah 29:11, Psalm 31:15, Jeremiah 33:3, Romans 8:28, 1 Peter 2:9, Romans 5:8, Ephesians 1:13-14, 2 Corinthians 1:22, Psalm 23:3, Psalm 121:5-8

## Prayer

Heavenly Father,

You make a way where I see no way. It is incredible to see how You work on my behalf. Your thoughts and plans for me are good and not for evil, directing me with Your Hand of blessing upon me to fulfill the extraordinary destiny You have given me.

In Jesus' name. Amen.

# I AM YOUR PROVIDER

*ehovah Jireh is your Provider, Who anticipates all you need and makes it available to you. He is intimately aware of your every thought, desire, feeling, action, hope, and dream.*

*His understanding of you is unlimited. He knows everything there is to know about you, because he is your Creator. He knows all your needs entirely, perfectly-being the source and author of your life.*

*God is your caring Father who provides for you out of His Deep Sense of Love, so you never lack. He knows everything you need before you ask Him. And He provides just what He knows you need in His perfect timing.*

# Letter From God

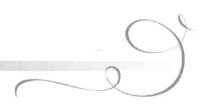

Good Morning,

I Love you, My Dear, Precious, Beloved, Blessed, Unique, Beautiful child of My GREAT Love. And that is what you are!

I AM your Provider—Jehovah Jireh! I see for Myself to all your needs and make provisions available before it even enters your mind. I am Omniscient. I know everything there is to know about you—every thought, desire, feeling, action, hope, and dream. I am intimately aware of you. My eyes rest upon you, and My Provision you need I have already sent.

My understanding of you is unlimited and effortless. I know you through and through. You can take safe shelter in My Presence because I know you completely and perfectly. I am the source and the author of your life. There is nothing for Me to discover about you. So, there's nothing that stops you from experiencing all My Provision I anticipated you need beforehand and have already lavishly provided.

I am not just your responsible overseer, but your caring Father Who provides for you out of My Deep Sense of Love, so you shall never lack. I am the God Who Sees all your needs—not just your physical needs, but also your mental, emotional, and spiritual needs. I know what you need on the inside and outside, and provide it before you ask Me. There is nothing hidden from My Sight. I am the Creator of your heart, so I understand everything you do.

You can trust Me, Who holds every moment of your life in My Hands, to have prepared beforehand all I know you would need. I appear with My Provision coming just when you need it. Abraham knew—I see the need and appear with the required answer.

Abraham told Isaac, "My son God himself will provide the lamb for an offering." Abraham knew that I had all the power to fulfill My Promise. Even in Offering up Isaac as a Sacrifice, He knew I would fulfill My Promise that Isaac would carry on his lineage.

Abraham did not withhold his beloved son from me. He Trusted Me! And I Provided a ram caught by its horns in a nearby thicket, just at the right time to be a substitute for Isaac. Just like the ram became Isaac's substitute, Christ became your substitute.

In providing for Abraham, I provided for you. For you belong to Christ, so you are now Abraham's child and a true spiritual heir of all his blessings because of the promise I made to him. You are My beloved child! And since you are, you qualify to share all His treasures being My precious heir joined to Christ.

Christ is your Eternal Provision Who fully satisfies your every need. He makes all grace, every favor and earthly blessing come to you in abundance in every moment and in every way, so that you overflow in abundance for every good thing you do because every spiritual blessing in the heavenly realm has already been lavished upon you as My Love Gift, My child.

I love you,

Daddy God. Amen.

*And Abraham called the name of the place,*
*The-LORD-Will-Provide; as it is said to this day,*
*In the Mount of the LORD it shall be provided.*

Genesis 22:14, NKJV

Genesis 22:14, Genesis 22:8, Psalm 139:1-3, 1 Peter 3:12, Psalm 34:15, Psalm 139:16, 1 Corinthians 2:12, Psalm 23:1, Genesis 16:13, Matthew 6:8, Hebrews 4:13, Psalm 33:15, Psalm 31:15, Hebrews 4:16, Romans 4:20-21, Genesis 21:12, Hebrews 11:17-19, Genesis 22:12-13, Matthew 20:28, Romans 4:25, Romans 5:6-8, 2 Corinthians 5:14-21, Philippians 4:19, 2 Corinthians 9:8, Ephesians 1:3

## Prayer

Heavenly Father,

You know everything there is to know about me. You anticipate every need of my spirit, soul, heart, and body. You are intimately aware of all that I require today. So I ask that You make all grace, every favor, and earthly blessing come to me in abundance so that I may be a blessing to others.

In Jesus' name. Amen.

# YOUR HEALING FRIEND

*G*od's Radiant Light shines through you to overcome discouragement and drive out the shadows of fear. He is your Healing Friend Who carries you in your emotional, physical, and spiritual hurts, wrapped in the presence of His Tender Love.

He flows Life-Giving, Living Water to you that brings a refreshing River of Life with every drink. He is your oasis of peace Who refreshes your soul and gives you rest in His Tender Care.

Your Union with Him gives you an Endless Victory. God directs your steps and constantly guides you in the right ways to go. Listen for Him Who is Forever Faithful to hold your life, to rise over and again to bring honor to His Name.

# Letter From God

Good Morning,

I Love you, My Dear, Precious, Beloved, Blessed, Special, Beautiful child of My GREAT Love. And that is what you are!

My Radiant Life shines brightly through you. I cause your discouragement to end and the shadows of fear to flee. My Great Light now radiates from within you. I am your Healing Friend Who lives My Life through you and fills you to overflowing with the Words of My Encouragement and Comfort.

I carry you in your hurts and shield you while you recover in My Tender Love. You constantly possess My Presence within you. I am more than enough to meet your emotional, physical, and spiritual needs. I am your Healer and Helper! I make you rest in My Presence, healing, wrapped in My Tender Love from the battles of life.

I walk continuously before you, and behind you, and with you on every path of life, shepherding you, guiding you to the Life-Giving Spring of Living Water flowing from My Kingdom within you. Every drink becomes a refreshing River Life for you.

I am your oasis of peace that transcends all understanding Who guards your heart and mind. For your life is joined with Mine to refresh your soul and give you rest in My Tender Care. Here, I restore and revive your life with new strength.

I choose the steps you take and delight in every detail of your life. I constantly guide you into making good decisions as you listen to My Voice. You will hear My Voice saying, "This is the way to go—follow it." When you turn to the right or the left, though you may stumble, you will never fall. For I uphold you with My Hand and pick you up Continuously to Rising, over and over again to bring honor to My Name.

We live in union as one! My Eyes are continually on you. Even in the valley of deep darkness, there is nothing to fear, for I am your Faithful God Who Never turns My Gaze from you. For Jesus' death, burial, and resurrection brought you an Endless Victory over every enemy, stripping away from them every weapon and all spiritual authority and power.

You are My Eternal Victory! The entire universe stands on tiptoes to see My Authority is your strength and peace that comforts you in My Love, removing all fear. I am with you always, My child.

I love you,

Daddy God. Amen.

*He lets me rest in green meadows; he leads me beside peaceful streams. He renews my strength. He guides me along the right paths, bringing honor to his name.*

Psalm 23:2-3, NLT

## SCRIPTURES FOR FURTHER READING:

Isaiah 9:2, John 14:17, Revelation 7:17, John 7:38, Luke 17:21, Matthew 11:28-29, Psalm 23:2, Proverbs 16:9, Psalm 37:23-24, Isaiah 30:21, Proverbs 20 4:16, Psalm 23:3, Galatians 2:20, Isaiah 41:10, Colossians 2:15, Psalm 23:4

## Prayer

Heavenly Father,

You already know what I'm feeling and understand everything about me. You are continually with me. There is nothing to fear. You strengthen me and help me. And hold me up with Your victorious right hand and remove all my fears wrapped in Your Loving Arms.

In Jesus' name. Amen.

# Protected by My Divine Love

*G*od's love overcomes all things! His Love never fails. He is Sovereign over all things, and His Infinite Love rules over all! You can run to His Protective Embrace to rest in the Secret Place of His Shelter to shield and protect you.

He is your Great Protector. He wraps His Love around you as a shield. His Endless Love already conquered the author of all your fears, worries, and stresses. Jesus carried them on the cross, so don't carry the load Jesus removed.

The Holy Spirit infuses you through your union with Jesus Christ to stand victorious with the force of His Mighty Power, Love, and Well-Balanced mind. So, your weaknesses do not defeat you, but make you stronger because His Love Demands He Protect you.

# Letter From God

Good Morning,

I Love you, My Dear, Precious, Beloved, Blessed, Unique, Beautiful child of My GREAT Love. And that is what you are!

My Love Overcomes All Things! Love never fails, Love never lets you down, and Love never stops going higher and higher. My Infinite Love rules over ALL! I am Love. Let the Radiance of My Love penetrate every fiber of your being and pull you into the Tender Embrace of My Protective Arms.

I am your Beloved, and you are Mine. You have everything in Me. I Am Love Who leads you into the place of true rest in My Heart. You live your life in the Secret Place of My Shelter, where I always shield you from harm.

No evil will prevail against you, for I am with you. I am your Great Protector. I send My Angels who are glad to minister to you, My Heir, with the particular assignment to protect you and to defend you from all evil, harm, and disaster wherever you go, for they see you "in Christ".

I make my Grace come to you in abundance. You are wealthy beyond belief in Christ, blessed with every spiritual blessing as My Love Gift in the heavenly places, as well as every favor and earthly blessing already lavished upon you. So, you enjoy life to the fullest and fulfill your destiny, living the good life I prearranged and made ready for you. I have given you My Grace to Love Me and Seek Me with your whole heart.

LEE RICHARDS

I loved you long before you loved Me. And I proved it by offering up Christ, My Greatest Treasure, as a sacrifice to take away your sins. My Endless Love makes you more than a conqueror. I am your Loving Father, Who already conquered the author of all your fears, worries, and stresses. Do not carry them, load upon Me, your every care, concern, and burden, and leave them with Me, Who always watches over you with tender care.

I have wrapped My Love around as a shield because I am your Fierce Protector Who watches over you and stands up for you. I never give you a spirit of fear to worry or stress, but the Holy Spirit Who gives you Mighty Power, Love, and a Well-Balanced mind.

He takes hold of you in your weaknesses to empower you with inner strength to conqueror all things. So, your shortcomings do not defeat you but make you stronger. For those things that trouble, concern, and distress you make you stronger and more powerful through My Divine Strength—a Gateway to My Power.

My Love Demands I Protect you. I have supernaturally empowered you through your union with Me to stand victorious with the force of My Explosive and Boundless Might flowing from within you through you. I have made the immeasurable greatness of My Power available to you.

My Love drives out fear. You triumph over all things, for I made you be more than a conqueror. And My Divine Love and power work for your Glorious Victory over Everything. My Love Protects you and empowers you to be unrivaled—no foe can stand against you.

No weapon formed against you will succeed, and every tongue that rises against you in judgment, you will prove to be wrong. This Peace, security, triumph, and victory over opposition through My Empowering Love is your heritage as My child.

I love you,

Daddy God. Amen.

> *It always protects, always trusts,*
> *always hopes, always perseveres.*
> *Love never fails.*

I Corinthians 13:7-8, NIV

## ▌Scriptures for Further Reading:

1 Corinthians 13:8, 1 John 4:18, John 6:44, Song of Solomon 2:16, Psalm 23:2, Psalm 91:9-10, Ephesians 1:3, 2 Corinthians 9:8, Psalm 91:11-13, 2, Corinthians 9:8, Proverbs 10:6, Proverbs 3:21, Ephesians 2:10, Jeremiah 29:13, Psalm 119:58, 1 John 4:10, Romans 8:32, Romans 8:37, Matthew 10:30-31, 1 Peter 5:7, Psalm 55:22, Proverbs 23:11, 2 Timothy 1:7, Romans 8:26, Philippians 4:13, 2 Corinthians 12:9-10, Ephesians 6:10, John 7:38-39, Ephesians 1:19, Romans 8:31, Isaiah 54:17

## Prayer

Heavenly Father,

I love You. Thank You for being my safe place and shelter of love. I run to Your Tender Embrace and Your Protective Arms to wrap Yourself around me as a secure shield. I leave all my fears, worries, and stresses with You, Who tenderly cares for me. I ask you to empower me with Your Spirit to stand victorious in Your Mighty Power, Love, with a Well-Balanced mind.

In Jesus' name. Amen.

# I SATISFY YOUR THIRSTY SOUL

*T*here is no struggle or hurt too deep that the Power of God's Love cannot heal and make whole again. He is your miracle-working Father, to Whom nothing is too hard or too wonderful for Him to do for you.

God embraces your every heartache, touches your every tear, and overcomes your every fear. Don't give up, though the pace seems slow. His answer is already on the way, for His Love demands He satisfy your every need.

He satisfies your thirsty soul with Living Water and frees you from all fears. He infuses you with inner-strength to conqueror every trouble. He is your Divine Helper Who assures you He is always near. Do not yield to fear.

# Letter From God

Good Morning,

I Love you, My Dear, Precious, Beloved, Blessed, Unique, Beautiful child of My GREAT Love. And that is what you are!

My Love will win every struggle you face. There is no hurt too deep that My Love cannot heal. I am the Power of Love, because I am Love, and My Tender Love for you continues forever.

I am your miracle-working Father, the Creator Who made the heavens and the earth with wisdom by My Great Power and outstretched arm. There is nothing too hard or too wonderful for Me to do for you.

I embrace every heartache. I touch every tear. I overcome every fear. My Face shines upon you, and My ears are open to the cries of your heart entwined with My Heart. Hear My Voice whisper to your heart saying, "Come talk with Me. You are My beloved child!"

Don't give up, and don't be impatient. I have you wrapped in union as one with Me. I know your distress before it even enters your mind, and I send My Answer before you know it is coming. I know what you need before you ask! My Love Demands I satisfy your every need—every moment, in every way. I am always tenderly loving you and doing good to you, for My Faithful Love never ends.

I broke through and rescued you from the power of darkness and transferred you into the Kingdom of My Beloved Son, Who canceled all your sins and redeemed you back to Myself through His Blood. He set you free to be My Very Own!

I Satisfy your thirsty soul with Living Water, and fill your Hungry Heart with My Goodness to passionately pursue Me. I free you from all your fears! There is nothing for you to fear, for I am Always near you. I never leave you, nor in any degree leave you helpless or relax My hold on you.

Keep your eyes on Me, your Faithful Father. I infuse you with My Inner Strength that makes you ready to conquer every difficulty. I am your Divine Helper in every situation of life. I hold you up with My Victorious Right Hand, bringing My Miraculous Deliverance when you need it most.

Drink Deeply of My Living Water—experience for yourself the joy of My Strength and your salvation's deliverance. For I find no fault with you, so you can experience for yourself My Tender Love toward you. Because of My Great Love, I ordained you to be holy and blameless before Me, forever.

I release My Supernatural Peace to you in Christ Who guards your heart and mind. I have given you the Sword of My Spirit in you, My Spoken Word, to heal you spiritually, physically, emotionally, and mentally. You declare the shalom—peace, prosperity, wholeness, success, and well-being you received through Christ's suffering for you. For in your being co-wounded with Him is how you find your healing and wholeness, My child.

I love you,

Daddy God. Amen.

*Give thanks to the Lord, for he is good!*
*His faithful love endures forever.*

Psalm 136:1, NLT

## ▎Scriptures for Further Reading:

1 John 4:8, Psalm 136:1, Psalm 136: 4-5, Jeremiah 32:17, Psalm 34:18, Psalm 27:7 NLT, Psalm 27:14, Psalm 25:5, Psalm 139:2, Matthew 6:8, Psalm 107:6, 2 Corinthians 9:8, Psalm 23:1, Philippians 4:19, Psalm 107:1, Colossians 1:13-14, Psalm 107:3, Psalm 107:9, Hebrews 12:2, Isaiah 41:10, Philippians 4:13, Hebrews 13:6, Psalm 34:6, Hebrews 13:5, Hebrews 4:16, Nehemiah 8:10, Ephesians 1:4, Colossians 1:21-22, Philippians 4:7, Psalm 107:20, Isaiah 53:4

## Prayer

Heavenly Father,

Thank You for Your Deep Love that heals all my hurts. You turn the scars of my past into the stars of my present. There is nothing too hard or too wonderful for You to do for me. I come to You— infuse me with explosive power to conquer every difficulty, and calm my heart with Your Wonderful Peace, and Strengthen me with Your Joy.

In Jesus' name. Amen.

# SECURE IN MY PASSIONATE LOVE

*C*hrist proved God's Passionate Love for you by dying in your place while you were still a sinner. Through Jesus' blood, your innocence before the Father is restored. Now you have the assurance that God lives in you.

You have become an entirely new person—a new creation that never existed before in Christ Jesus. You have been enfolded into Christ. Your old identity passed away with Christ, and your New Identity in Christ has begun!

It is no longer you who lives, but Christ lives His life through you. Chris is now your life! So, never doubt God's Passionate Love for you, because He paid a high and precious price to make you and call you His child.

# Letter From God

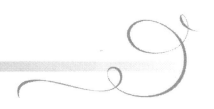

Good Morning,

I Love you My Dear, Precious, Beloved, Blessed, Special, Beautiful child of My GREAT Love. And that is what you are!

You are Secure in My Passionate Love for you because I made Christ your secure refuge. He provided proof of My Passionate Love for you by dying in your place while you were still a sinner.

Through Jesus' bloodshed on the cross, I restored you your original innocence again! I reconnected you back to Myself through the Sacrifice of His Body On your behalf so that you can have the assurance that I live and remain in you, and you in Me, Forever.

I have eternally declared you Holy and blameless before Me in Love. Now you possess the Perfect Righteousness of Christ and are seen by Me as righteous as He is! I have given you My Righteousness, What I created you to be—approved and accepted and in right relationship with Me, because of My Great Love.

You have become an entirely new creation, a new creature altogether, made completely new in My Likeness and My Image by your union with Christ and My Spirit living in you.

You are transformed—your old identity died with Christ, and your New Identity comes from living in union as one with Him in the Realm of True Righteousness and Holiness.

I made you alive together in union with the very life of Christ and saved you by My Wonderful Grace, making you a partaker of Christ's salvation. Christ's life is now your life. I re-created you all over again to share My Love with you and Live through you, just as I determined ahead of time.

I chose you to be Mine before I created the universe and all that is within it. As Chosen by Me, your life is one with Christ, and you can Never Be the Same Again. For My Choice can never be changed, for I never change My Mind. What I determined ahead of time comes to pass and is never subject to change. I am always the same—yesterday, today, and forever.

I am the fulfillment of all I have chosen for you. You are Mine. I have made My Permanent Home in you to experience a more profound and deeper measure of My Love. And I have given you My Holy Spirit Who assures you continually that I live in you and you in me.

Your life is hidden with Christ in Me. You don't belong to yourself—your old identity was co-crucified with Christ. It is no longer you who lives, but Christ Who lives His Life through you. You are My Most Expensive Purchase—the cost of your soul was the Precious Blood of My Beloved Son, Jesus Christ. A price so High only I could Pay It! You are Eternally Valuable!

I cause your heart to Soar with Joyful Praise at the Depth of My Marvelous Love that I have lavishly bestowed upon you, My Special Treasure. For I call you and made you, My Beloved child! Never doubt My Passionate Love for you. I hold you entwined with My Heart, and I weave the details of your life together for good with Me, being your Divine Partner to fulfill My Designed Purpose for your life, My child.

I love you,

Daddy God. Amen.

*God demonstrates His own passionate love*
*toward you in that while you were still*
*a sinner, Christ died for you.*

Romans 5:8, NKJV

## SCRIPTURES FOR FURTHER READING:

Romans 5:8, Colossians 1:14, Colossians 1:20-22, 1 John 4:13-15, Romans 5:1, Ephesians 1:4, 2 Corinthians 5:21, Romans 5:9, Ephesians 2:4-5, 2 Corinthians 5:17, Genesis 1:27, Ephesians 4:24, Ephesians 2:5, Galatians 2:20, 1 John 4:16-17, Ephesians 1:4, Numbers 11:23, James 1:17, Hebrews 13:8, 1 John 4:12-13, 2 Corinthians 6:16, Romans 8:16, Colossians 3:3, 1 Corinthians 6:19-20, 1 Peter 2:9, 1 John 3:1

## Prayer

Heavenly Father,

Thank You for sending Jesus to die in my place so that I can have an intimate, personal relationship with You forever. As a new creation in Christ Jesus, I ask You Fill me with all the inexhaustible riches of my New Identity in Christ, lavishly bestowed upon me through Your Marvelous Love and Grace.

In Jesus' name. Amen.

# FIND RARE TREASURES IN MY TRUTH

*G*od speaks eternal truth that liberates you from the bondage of sin and religion, wrapped in works to earn favor with God. The more you embrace the reality of your being in Christ, the more freedom you will discover for your life.

Christ is The Truth you embrace Who sets you free to be all God created you to be. It is no longer you who lives, but the Spirit of Christ Who lives in you, with you, and through you. He is the Word of God Who enfolds you into the family of God.

His Word of Truth in you leads you into all Truth. He unveils the reality of every Truth within you. Through Him, you experience My Tender Love and Faithfulness poured in your heart, which is sweeter than honey dripping from the honeycomb.

# Letter From God

Good Morning,

I Love you, My Dear, Precious, Beloved, Blessed, Unique, Beautiful child of My GREAT Love. And that is what you are!

I speak Eternal Truth to you. I am the Absolute, Unchanging Truth you embrace to release Freedom into your heart. My Truth liberates you from the bondage of religion wrapped in your works, and the bondage of your sins—past, present, and future—with an eternal, total cancellation and release through the blood of Jesus. And the more you embrace your new creation-reality in Christ, the more freedom you bring to your life.

Christ is the Truth you have to embrace to release true freedom into your life that sets you free! He came from ME, overflowing with lovingkindness, full of everything that your heart craves. He is the Living Expression of My Divine Portrait. My True exact likeness Who is the Spirit of Truth. Who, being the Truth, leads you into all Truth.

Christ never leaves you because He Lives with you constantly and inside you. So, you know the Spirit of Truth intimately Who is the Spirit of Christ your Savior. The Spirit guides and encourages you, protects and defends you, comforts and consoles you, saves you, and keeps you whole and healed. He is My Spirit of Full Acceptance Who enfolds you into My Family.

I love Passionately those who love My Son. I personally come to you and reveal Myself to you. And Loving Him empowers you to do what pleases Me. I Love you so Deeply, that I made My Home with you forever. Indeed, you are My Temple. I live in you, and I have made My Home with you, My child.

I am belief, Who sent the One Who sets you Free. He represents Me and asks on My Behalf and teaches you all things. He inspires you to remember My Word I have embedded within your thoughts and fastened into your heart. My Truth-Giving Spirit leads you into Truth and unveils the reality of every Truth within you. What He receives from Me, He reveals it to you.

My Word is Truth! I make you holy by My Truth, which I teach you from My Word. I am Spirit. And I long for you to kiss Me with the steady stream of praise offered from your lips as you experience My Tender, Unfailing Love and Faithfulness pouring into your heart through My Living Truth Living within you.

My Truth Possesses the Rarest Treasures of Life—wisdom and endless riches of knowledge that's the reason My Word is prized and even more valuable and desirable than fine gold. My Word is Living Truth, sweeter than honey dripping from the honeycomb, which I have magnified above My Name and everything, My child.

I love you,

Daddy God. Amen.

*If you abide in My word, you are My disciples indeed. And you shall know the truth, and the truth shall make you free.*

John 8:31-32, NKJV

John 8:34, John 8:31-32, John 1:14, John 14:16-17, Hebrews 13:5, Isaiah 53:4-5, Romans 8:15, John 14:21, Exodus 33:13, John 14:23, 2 Corinthians 6:16, John 14:26, Hebrews 8:11, Hebrews 10:16, 1 John 2:27, John 16:13-14, John 4:24, Hebrews 13:15, Psalm 138:2, Psalm 19:10

## Prayer

Heavenly Father,

I embrace Your Truth, which frees me from sin and opens my heart to the new creation realities You have lavishly bestowed upon Me in Christ Jesus. Your Word is Sweeter than Honey, poured from the Truth of Your Tender Love and Faithfulness to me and for me.

In Jesus' name. Amen.

# DIVINE BENEFITS OF A LISTENING HEART

*G*od gives you a Listening Heart to hear Him unveil every Truth and its application, which He has imprinted upon your innermost thoughts and engraved upon your heart. His Perfect Peace gives you Great Confidence as the Holy Spirit reveals His Great Love for you.

You are His beloved child. Because you are in union with God, He keeps your heart and mind in

Perfect Peace, transcending all human understanding through Jesus Christ. So, fix your eyes and expectation on Him continually, and look away from the distractions of this present evil world.

God is living in you, Who conquerors all your fears and worries with His Divine Love. God is Love, and His Word is His Promise that proves His Passionate Love for you because He guarantees it will come to pass.

# Letter From God

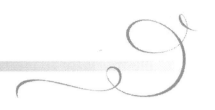

Good Morning,

I Love you, My Dear, Precious, Beloved, Blessed, Special, Beautiful child of My GREAT Love. And that is what you are!

I give you a Listening Heart to Hear My Voice, soaking in Tender Life to Unveil the Reality of Every Truth and its application within you. I know Everything there is to know about all things perfectly. Nothing is unknown to Me.

I plant Myself in you to whisper everything that is Mine to you, so that you can understand and experience the infinite riches of My Grace lavishly given to you. I have imprinted My Living Word upon your innermost thoughts and engraved them upon the pages of your heart, whispering, "You are My Beloved child."

I speak these things to you so that you may have Perfect Peace and Great Confidence as you Rest in Me. For your life is in union with Me Who has overcome the world. My Peace mounts guard over your heart and mind. Fix your eyes on My Truth, which is My Living Word alive and full of power.

My Word has the inherent Vital Power to accomplish all I whisper to your heart. It will do everything I send it to do because My Word and I are One. It always accomplishes and fulfills the Purpose I intend it to do. My Word is My promise to prove My Passionate Love for you. I guarantee it will come to pass.

I am living in you, so do not yield to fear. I am Love, and all that I am now, you are in the world. And My Love is brought to full expression in you. Love never brings fear, but expels it. Remember, you belong to me, Who has conquered the agent of fear, and I living in you is greater than he who would tempt you to fear.

You have My Heart, My Presence, My Work, My Spirit, and My Favor within you and for you, which is more than enough Divine Power to Overcome the evil in this world. I infuse you with Supernatural Strength through your union with Me to victoriously triumph over all the power the enemy possesses with the weapons of My Explosive Power I flow through you. Assuredly, absolutely nothing will harm you walking in My Authority.

Your heart is wrapped in Mine to hear My Tender Voice which gives you overwhelming success in everything you set your hand to do. It makes your way prosperous, able to deal wisely, having My understanding to be successful, for I AM with you and living in you wherever you go, My child.

I love you,

Daddy God. Amen.

*Give me an understanding heart so that I*
*can govern your people well and know*
*the difference between right and wrong.*

1 Kings 3:9, NLT

## SCRIPTURES FOR FURTHER READING:

1 Kings 3:9, John 1:27, John 16:13, Jeremiah 33:3, Psalm 139:1, John 16:30, Hebrews 4:13, John 16:13-15, 1 Corinthians 2:12, Ephesians 2:7, Hebrews 8:10, Psalm 40:6, Romans 8:17, John 16:33, Matthew 11:28, Philippians 4:7, John 14:6, Hebrews 4:12, Isaiah 55:11, John 1:1, John 10:30, 1 John 4:17-18, John 4:4, Ephesians 6:12, Ephesians 6:10, 1 John 5:4, Luke 10:19, Joshua 1:7-9, Hebrew13:5

## Prayer

Heavenly Father,

Thank You for giving me a Listening Heart to hear Your Voice unveil every Truth and its application to me. I trust in You with all My Heart and depend on Your Understanding and Insight. For You cause me to prosper and succeed in everything I set my hand to do, because I know You are with me wherever I go.

In Jesus' name. Amen.

# Sing and Shout in Victory

*G*od gives you the Joy of His every Break-Through for you. He lifts your heart into a new song of Glorious Praise for His deliverance. His Joy fills you to overflowing by pulling you up from darkness' grip, and you want to tell the world of the Marvelous Depth of His Love demonstrated for you, His child.

The awe-inspiring Resurrection Power of Christ's Victory in you and for you infuses you with supernatural strength to stand in Triumph with the force of His explosive power. For you have the Delegated Authority—all heaven, earth, and hell recognize it because you live in union as One with Christ.

God's Joy in you shouts out Christ's Triumphant Victory over all the power the enemy possesses, which releases His Breakthrough Power. The splendor of His Radiant Light and the Brightness of His Glory arise upon you and stream from you to break through every stronghold's grip on you. For you possess the Brilliant Light of My Glory—Jesus Christ is living in you.

# Letter From God

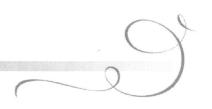

Good Morning,

I Love you, My Dear, Precious, Beloved, Blessed, Special, Beautiful child of My GREAT Love. And that is what you are!

My Joy causes your heart to sing a new song every time you think about how I break through for you. Raise up to sing a new song of Glorious Praise poured out of your mouth, tuned to My Glory! Tell the world how wonderful I am and the Depths of My Marvelous Love that I have lavished upon you, whom I call and made My child.

How awe-inspiring, Exceedingly Great, and Glorious is the power made available in and for you who believe My Word, given to you by the Holy Spirit Who responds to My utterances. You will experience for yourself the immeasurable and all-surpassing greatness of My Mighty Power, which became your possession when I raised Christ from the dead and seated Him at My Own Right Hand in the Heavenly Places.

You have Delegated Authority—all heaven, earth, and hell recognize you are One with Christ in Me, Who lives His life through you. You have been raised up together with Christ and given His Authority as My child to do the mighty works He did and even greater ones. For I have put everything under The Authority of My Son, Jesus Christ, and Authority He exercises through you, who are in union with Him.

It's time to sing and shout for Joy! You are My redeemed, righteous, upright child, in right-standing with Me. I rise in your heart with praise and thanksgiving to sing and shout with passion a New Song with all your being to Me. For My Word and Authority are something to think about. I am True to all My Promises, and I am Trustworthy in Everything. I am Infinitely Reliable—anywhere and everywhere you go, you find My Unfailing, Faithful Love.

I am your secret hiding place; I protect you from troubles and surround you with Songs of Deliverance. My Joy in you shouts out My Triumph Victory over all the power the enemy possesses, releasing My Breakthrough Power. People will stand in awe of Me, Surrendered to My Tender Love, and Fall in Love with Me.

Arise from the depression and circumstances that have kept you –Rise up and walk in your New Life and your New Authority. Your Light has dawned. Rise, My Radiant Glory now streams from you! Your Light has broken through thick gloom, for I AM the Light that shines upon you and through you. Shine upon the nations.

You have experienced My Life-Giving Light and will never be pushed around by the darkness. For I who said, "Let Like shine out of darkness," is the one who shines My Glorious Light into you and through you. Now, you possess the Brilliant Light of My Glory, Jesus Christ, and carry Him within you as your Greatest Treasure, My child.

I love you,

Daddy God. Amen.

*He has put a new song in my mouth—*
*Praise to our God;*
*Many will see it and fear,*
*And will trust in the Lord.*

Psalm 40:3, NKJV

## ▍ SCRIPTURES FOR FURTHER READING:

Psalm 40:3, Psalm 66:1, 1 John 3:1, Ephesians 1:19, Psalm 66:3, John 16:13, Romans 8:16, Romans 10:17, Ephesians 1:20, Luke 10:19, John 14:12-14, Galatians 2:20, Colossians 3:3, John 1:12, John 14:12, Ephesians 1:22, 1 Corinthians 12:27, Ephesians 2:5, 2 Corinthians 5:21, Psalm 33:1-5, Isaiah 60:1, Mark 16:16-18, John 8:12, Matthew 5:14, 2 Corinthians 4:6-7

## Prayer

Heavenly Father,

You have placed a new song in my heart. I sing to you thinking about how you breakthrough in every circumstance and emotion. I shout for Joy about the Depths of Your Marvelous Love that protects me from troubles and surrounds me with Songs of Deliverance. You raise me from depression with Your Life-Giving Light, which darkness can never extinguish.

In Jesus' name. Amen.

# I Answer Your Prayers

*G*od always hears your prayers. He gives you the desire to come to Him—to call upon Him to listen to your voice and respond to you. He removes all barriers and gives you free, unreserved access to come boldly, full of courage and complete confidence to approach Him because of Christ's Faithfulness.

He pulls on your heart to embrace His Heart in total assurance and complete confidence that nothing can weaken His Passionate Love for you. Now your heart is free from the voice of an accusing conscience that reminds you of your failures and past mistakes, making you feel guilty and unacceptable, for He finds no fault in you.

God knows what you need even before you ask, because He had written all your needs for each day in His Book before you were born. The Holy Spirit stirs your most holy emotions to come boldly to Him to receive the Good Things already headed your way each day to satisfy your every need.

# Letter From God

Good Morning,

I Love you, My Dear, Precious, Beloved, Blessed, Special, Beautiful child of My GREAT Love. And that is what you are!

I hear your prayers always! For I am the One Who gives you the desire to come to Me, removing the barrier, so you dare to have the bold courage and complete confidence to approach because of Christ's Faithfulness.

You carry this confidence in your heart to draw near fearlessly in boldness to My Throne of Grace because of your union with Christ before Me. I kiss you with My Mercy and I make My Grace Abound toward you to help you in your time of need, My Well-timed help coming just when I know it is Most Needed.

I welcome you to enter into My Most Holy Place in the heavenly places, being a member of My Family by the Power and Virtue of the Blood of Jesus. I pull on your heart to come closer to Me to Embrace My Heart in total assurance and complete confidence that nothing can distance you from My Passionate Love for you. There is nothing that can weaken My Love for you!

I have freed your heart from an accusing conscience and all condemnation against you by joining you in a Life-Union with Jesus. Now you are Totally Clean before Me inside and out, Holy and blameless in My Eyes in love.

Even if a fiery dart hits your heart to remind you of your failures and past mistakes, making you feel guilty and unacceptable to Me, I find no fault in you. My Tender Mercy for you is higher than the highest heavens to satisfy My Great Loyal Love I lavishly bestow upon you.

I am Greater than your conscience and the lying darts of your enemy. He sees you in your old sin identity; I see you as Blood-bought in your new identity in Christ Jesus. I re-created you all over again. You now live your new life in union with Me and belong to Me. You were co-crucified with Christ to free you from the power of sin within you. And now you are united in the very Life of Christ.

I know everything about you and still accept you. I made the deliberate choice to Unconditionally Love you for all eternity before you were ever born, knowing the sins, failures, and mistakes you would make. You have a complete assurance, since My Nature is love, there is never a moment I do not love you because I do everything for you out of My Love.

I know what you need even before you ask, having written all your needs in My Book before you were born. My Spirit stirs you to embrace Me and ask Me for the Good Things I know I already have coming to you—which truly satisfies your every need and inspires an outpouring of praise and thanksgiving to Me.

My Super-Abounding Grace achieves infinitely more than you dare ask or think, exceeding your highest expectations and imagination! And since you have this confidence in Me, you also have great boldness to ask anything you know is agreeable to My will, and I will hear you. And if you know I hear you, then you know you have the request you asked of Me.

Because I know what you need before you ask Me. The Holy Spirit empowers you in your weaknesses to ask Me what I guarantee will come to pass, knowing it's already on the way. He divinely persuades to switch your human wishes for My Divine Wishes, Who knows all things needed at all times, My child

I love you,

Daddy God. Amen.

*As for me, I will call upon God, And the LORD shall save*
*me. Evening and morning and at noon I will pray, and cry*
*aloud, And He shall hear my voice.*

Psalm 55:16-17, NKJV

## SCRIPTURES FOR FURTHER READING:

Psalm 55:16-17, Philippians 2:13, Ephesians 3:12, 2 Corinthians 3:4,
Hebrews 4:16, Ephesians 2:19, Romans 8:38-39, Romans 8:1,
Ephesians 1:4, Ephesians 6:16, 1 John 3:20, Ephesians 2:4, Psalm
103:9-11, John 8:44, 2 Corinthians 5:17, Ephesians 4:24, Romans
6:6-8, Ephesians 2:5, Psalm 139:1, John 3:16, Psalm 103:3, 1 John
4:8, Deuteronomy 7:9, Matthew 6:8, Psalm 139:16, Philippians 4:19,
2 Corinthians 9:12, Ephesians 3:21, 1 John 5:14-15, Matthew 6:8,
Romans 8:26

## Prayer

Heavenly Father,

Thank You for always hearing my prayers and giving me the desire
to call upon You. I ask You for the absolute best for each situation
and need I face throughout the day. I lean on You to direct My
asking. You already know what I need before I ask, so direct my
asking to receive all Your Best.

In Jesus' name. Amen.

# YOU DEFINITELY BELONG TO ME

*W*hen the voices of the world say you are unacceptable and unworthy of His Love, He says to you, "You are Mine." He made you, and you belong to Him. He actually picked you out for Himself to satisfy the Great Love He has for you before the foundation of the world. He marked you out to reveal you as His child. You most Definitely Belong to Him!

He pours His Tremendous Love over you—the same Love He has for Jesus, He pours into you. And this brings Him Great Pleasure! Beloved, you are His child Right Now! You are approved and acceptable and in right-relationship with Him through your union with Christ. When you gave your life to Him, He severed the tie to your old life and Re-Created you all over again.

He has nothing but Tender Feelings toward you. His Unfailing Love supports you. He races to your rescue when doubts fill your mind. His comfort gives you renewed hope and joy. The peace of His Presence calms your heart and mind, because nothing can erase My Passionate Love for you and the fact you Belong to Him.

# Letter From God

Good Morning,

I Love you, My Dear, Precious, Beloved, Blessed, Special, Beautiful child of My GREAT Love. And that is what you are!

When you hear you don't Belong, I Say to you, "You are Mine." I am the Lord your God who made you. You are My Chosen, Special Treasure, who I chose in Love before the foundation of the world. I actually picked you out for Myself in order to satisfy My Great Love with which I love you.

I ordained you to be holy and blameless in My Son. I marked you out to Fulfill the Destiny I have given you to Establish and Reveal you as My Own Child through your union with Jesus Christ, according to My Plan Prepared Ahead of Time to Glorify My Grace in pouring My Tremendous Love over you!

I love you with the same Love I have for Jesus Christ my Son, being One with Him. And this brings Me Great Pleasure! Beloved, you are My Child Right Now! You can be confident you belong to Me, for You Are Completely Filled with the Godhead—Father, Son, and Holy Spirit, Who Fully Feel and Flood You with God Myself.

Indeed, you are the Temple of the Living God. I have made My Home in you. I am your Father Who rescues and draws you to Myself out of the Authority of Darkness and have transferred you into the Kingdom of My Dear Son. Through Him, I canceled all your sins, and you have become approved and acceptable and in right-relationship with Me through your union with Him.

You Definitely Belong to Me. When you gave your life to Me, I severed the tie to your old life. I Re-Created you all over again, and now you belong to Me in the Realm of True Holiness. And now you possess My Perfect Righteousness, justified and co-crucified you with My Son and made you My Heir.

Who would even dare say you don't belong to Me, whom I chose in Love and put in Right-Relationship with Me to be My Beloved Child? My Son gave His Life for you. He conquered all the power of the enemy to say you Belong to Me by the power of His Cross.

I take delight in you and rejoice over you with great joy. With My Tender Love, I calm all your fears, for I make no mention of your past sins or even recall them because I am rejoicing over you with singing. I have nothing but Tender Feelings toward you. My Endless Love stretches from eternity to eternity, and I am faithful to keep every gracious promise I made to you in your generation.

My Unfailing Love supports you. I race to your rescue when doubts fill your mind and your thoughts spin out of control. My comfort gives you renewed hope and joy. I soothe you with the peace of My Presence to calm your heart and mind, refreshing your life by resting in union with Me to overwhelm you with My Joy, which is your Strength.

Nothing can erase My Passionate Love for you and the fact you Belong to Me. When you embraced Jesus and welcomed Him into your heart, I gave the authority, all the power, privileges, and right to be a member of My Household, My child.

I love you,

Daddy God. Amen

*Know that the Lord is God.*
*He made us, and we belong to him;*

Psalm 100:3, NCV

## ▎SCRIPTURES FOR FURTHER READING:

Psalm 100:3, 1 Peter 2:9, Ephesians 2:10, Ephesians 2:4, Ephesians 1:13, Ephesians 1:6, 1 John 3:2, 1 John 4:4, Colossians 2:10, Ephesians 3:19, 2 Corinthians 6:16-18, Colossians 1:13, John 6:44, 2 Corinthians 5:21, Colossians 3:3, Ephesians 4:24, Romans 8:30, Galatians 4:7, Romans 8:17, Romans 8:33, Colossians 2:15, Zephaniah 3:17, Psalm 103:13, 17, Psalm 94:18-19, Matthew 11:28-29, Nehemiah 8:10, Romans 8:39, John 1:12

## Prayer

Heavenly Father,

Thank You for making me Your Chosen, Special Treasure. I am Yours no matter what other voices say I am. You actually picked me out for Yourself and have made Your Home in me, severing the tie to my old life by the power of Jesus cross. Your Tender Love calms all my fears, and you never mention my past failures and sins. You race to My rescue when doubts fill my mind. Nothing can erase Your Passionate Love for me.

In Jesus' name. Amen.

# MY MASTERPIECE OF LOVE

*G*od created you, His Beautiful Masterpiece, to reveal His Great Love and the unfading, inexhaustible riches of Christ for you.

He made you a one-of-a-kind artistry, created in Tender Love and Passion by His Hand to fulfill your destiny He planned in advance and the good works you would do.

He formed you with an Eternal Spirit to be transformed into the Image of Christ. The Holy Spirit wove in your innermost being the Marvelous Grace Gifts, individually fashioned for you to fulfill your Divine Destiny. He made you an Image-Bearer to reflect God's Glory and Ability to the world.

Your image and name are indelibly imprinted on the palm of each of His hand, so you know every single moment He cherishes you constantly in His thoughts. Most assuredly, He is always with you— He never leaves you nor forsakes you, and will never relax His hand on you because of the precious price He paid to make you His child.

# Letter From God

Good Morning,

I Love you, My Dear, Precious, Beloved, Blessed, Special, Beautiful child of My GREAT Love. And that is what you are!

Your life is a Beautiful Masterpiece, perfectly designed by Me to reveal My Great Love and the unfading, inexhaustible riches of Christ. Yes, you are My Masterpiece of Love!

You are a one-of-a-kind, unique artistry created by My Hand in Tender Love and Passion for fulfilling the good destiny I have given you. I made you Marvelously Complex and Breathtaking, carefully and skillfully shaping you from My First Beautiful Thought to My Spectacular New Creation, I made you that never existed before.

I formed your innermost being with an Eternal Spirit and shaped your True Beauty in the uniqueness of your inner-personality created in Christ's image. My Spirit wove you together with Marvelous Grace Gifts, individually fashioned for you to fulfill your Divine Destiny uniquely. Your distinct design and function contribute to the tremendous growth of all members of Christ's body.

You are My Perfect Workmanship enfolded into Christ, My Beautiful Image-Bearer. I created you as My Masterpiece to reflect My Glory and Ability to the world. I see you, as I picked you out for Myself before the foundation of the world an entirely new creature altogether, holy and blameless before Me in Love—Faultless in My Presence!

You may experience times when you feel utterly alone and abandoned—entirely forgotten by people in your life. I Never forget you! Even if your mother and father leave you without support, I always hold you next to My Heart and Tenderly care for you. It is impossible to forget you when I have dispensed My life into you, live through you, and made My Home in you. We live in union as one.

I have your beautiful image and name permanently engraved on the palms of My Hands! My Everlasting Love for you Never Allows me to leave you or forsake you or in any way leave you helpless! I will never relax My hold on you, and no one has the power to snatch you out of My care. Every single moment I am thinking of your radiant beauty, cherishing you constantly in My thoughts.

You are My Masterpiece to fulfill My Designed Purpose preplanned in every detail of your life and the good works prearranged for you to achieve it. My Plans for you are always good and not for evil—to provide you with a Wonderful Hope, experiencing for yourself My Endless Love Pouring into your heart.

My Divine Light illuminates you as The Masterpiece of My Grace and Mercy to the world around you, seen in the Face of Jesus. Your Love Lights up the World with the Message of My Endless Love in Christ to bring others in harmony with Me, My child.

I love you,

Daddy God. Amen.

*For we are God's Masterpiece.*
*He has created us anew in Christ Jesus,*
*so we can do the good things he*
*planned for us long ago.*

Ephesians 2:10, NLT

## ▍SCRIPTURES FOR FURTHER READING:

Ephesians 2:10, Ephesians 1:4, Ephesians 2:4, Ephesians 3:8, Psalm 139:13, 2 Corinthians 5:17, John 3:5-7, 1 Peter 3:3, Romans 12:6, 1 Corinthians 12:28, Ephesians 4:14, 2 Corinthians 5:17, Genesis 1:26, Romans 8:29, 1 Corinthians 11:16, Genesis 1:27, Isaiah 49:15-16, Psalm 27:10, 1 Peter 5:7, Galatians 2:20, 2 Corinthians 6:16, John 14:20, John 17:23, Hebrews 13:5, Jeremiah 31:3, 1 Corinthians 13:8, John 10:29, Psalm 139:1, Ephesians 2:10, Jeremiah 29:11, Romans 5:5, 2 Corinthians 4:5-6, Matthew 5:14, 16

## Prayer

Heavenly Father,

My life is hidden with Christ in Your Tender Love. You recreated me in Christ Jesus a new creature that never existed before. I am your one-of-a-kind, unique Masterpiece to fulfill the excellent destiny You prearranged the plans to fulfill it, experiencing for myself You Endless Love Pouring into my heart that gives me the heart to love others as You love me.

In Jesus' name. Amen.

# I AM YOUR SOVEREIGN SHELTER

*W*hen you are overwhelmed by life, God is your Sovereign Shelter. He draws you to the safety of His Sanctuary to heal you—to give rest to your weary soul while His peace that surpasses all understanding mounts guard over your heart and mind wrapped in Jesus' arms. There, you release the weight of all your worries, anxieties, and cares to Him.

Jesus will cause you to rest in His Tender Care and refresh your life every time you come to Him. He is full of Love and Compassion that never fails to comfort and encourage you. Jesus knows what truly bothers you—every unnecessary weight and sin that cleverly clings to and entangles you. He washes you in His Fountain of Forgiveness.

His Love washes away all your failures and guilt, and the power of your conscience from condemning you. The accusing voice is gone because you live in union with Him, which liberates you from condemnation. Now you are entirely acceptable to God, holy and blameless in His Sight in Love. Your soul is quiet.

# Letter From God

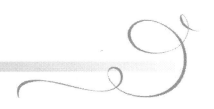

Good Morning,

I Love you, My Dear, Precious, Beloved, Blessed, Special, Beautiful child of My GREAT Love. And that is what you are!

I am your Sovereign Shelter! When you are overwhelmed by life, I guide you into My Glory where you are safe in the secret place of My Sanctuary, a perfect hiding place to heal and rest your soul. Here you are surrounded with My Presence, guarded by My Peace and refreshed by My Spirit as you Rest in Me. I will cheer you up!

My Glorious Light consumes every unnecessary weight that pulls you in different directions. When you Draw near to Me, you let go of every wound that pierced you and enjoy the oasis of My Presence. I pull on your heart to embrace Me and release the weight of all your worries, anxieties, and cares to Me, for I Tenderly Care for you and strengthen you with Measureless Grace.

When you feel weary and overburdened, come to Me, and I will cause you to rest in My Tender Care and refresh your life. Enjoy the Delight that awaits you. I am Good to you who Hope in and depend on Me! My Compassion for you never fails. They are new every time you come into My Presence.

I am Full of Compassion. I forgive all your sin and give mercy for your failures from My Fountain of Forgiveness! My abundant love completely washed away all guilt, and erased your conscience's power to condemn you.

Now there is no accusing voice, because you are in a living union with Christ, the Law of the Spirit of Life flowing through

Jesus liberates you from condemnation, having been made one with Him and wholly filled with the Godhead. Every legal record against you was canceled, and all your sins deleted forever, because Jesus disarmed all spiritual rulers and authorities' power to accuse you.

Jesus gave His body as the sin offering to set you free from the curse of the Law. I once and for all overcame the guilt and power of sin over all who accepted His Sacrifice. So now every righteous requirement of the Law is fulfilled through Christ living in you, which makes you entirely accepted by Me.

Draw near to Me, come close with an open heart and unqualified assurance that I lovingly welcome you with a Joyful Heart. I sprinkled your own heart with My blood, freeing you from an Accusing Conscience. Now your heart touches mine to experience intimacy with Me to ease and relieve and refresh and quiet your soul, My child.

I love you,

Daddy God. Amen.

*But as for me, how good it is to be near God!*
*I have made the Sovereign* LORD *my shelter, and I*
*will tell everyone about the wonderful things you do.*

Psalm 78:28, NLT

## ▍Scriptures for Further Reading:

Psalm 73:28, Psalm 61:2, Psalm 27:5, Psalm 9:9, Philippians 4:7, Matthew 11:28-29, 1 Peter 5:7, Psalm 55:22, Lamentations 3:26, Luke 18:19, Lamentations 3:22-23, Psalm 78:38, Hebrews 9:26, Colossians 1:13, Hebrews 4:16, Psalm 51:1-2, Romans 8:1-2, Colossians 2:1, Colossians 2:14-15, Galatians 3:13, Romans 8:3, Leviticus 7:37, Romans 8:4, 10, Ephesians 2:5, Hebrews 10:22, James 4:8, Hebrews 7:19

## Prayer

Heavenly Father,

You are my Sovereign Shelter of Measureless Grace. I come to rest in the healing power of Your Presence to receive rest for my weary soul and strength to step further. I let go of the wounds that have pierced me, and release the weight of every worry and anxiety to You. You touch my heart with Your Heart, and ease and quiet and refresh my soul. I am wholly dependent on Jesus. I know You have me.

In Jesus' name. Amen.

# A NEW-CREATION HEART

*G*od recreates you entirely a New Creation with a New Heart. He removes your old, stony heart and replaces it with a Tender, Responsive Heart to Him. Your old heart was not just changed, but made into a New-Creation Heart that never existed before. A new tablet, where God has written His Words He put in your mind.

You have been born anew from above of the Holy Spirit Who lives within you. His presence in you is the guarantee that Jesus' life sacrificed for your sins makes you entirely acceptable to God. The Dynamic Power of the Holy Spirit flowing through you empowers you to live the New Creation Life.

The Holy Spirit causes you to recall God's Word written on your heart and in your mind. He testifies with your own spirit that Christ's Home is now your heart. His Love for you sets your heart on fire! He produces in you a Passionate Heart to Love God with all your heart and all your soul and your every thought, and love others as you do yourself.

# Letter From God

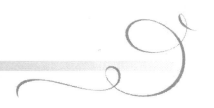

Good Morning,

I Love you, My Dear, Precious, Beloved, Blessed, Special, Beautiful child of My GREAT Love. And that is what you are!

I give you a Single Heart Devotion and Pure Love for Christ. You have been re-created an entirely New Creation with a New Heart and a New Spirit Within You. I have taken out your old, stony, stubborn heart and given you a Tender, Responsive Heart to Me.

Your old heart was not just changed, but created into a New-Creation Heart, one you never had before, You have been born anew from above of My Spirit Who I put within you. He remains in you and causes you to follow My Words which I have put in your mind and written on your heart.

I have declared an end to sin's control over your life by giving My Son's Life as a sacrifice for your sins. Now, all My requirements have been satisfied through the life of Jesus. The Dynamic Power of the Holy Spirit released in you empowers you to live your new life with Christ in Me.

My Holy Spirit causes you to recall My Word within you—the divine self-expression of all that I am. My Word perfectly expresses Myself because My Word and I are One. And you are One in Us so that the world recognizes and confirms that Christ Lives!

Christ's Home is now your heart. Your old heart I crucified with Christ. Now your new heart is alive in Union with Him Who dispenses His Life into yours. I made you one heart and one Spirit, so you have the Mind of Christ and possess the thoughts, feelings, and purposes of His Heart.

You are One Spirit in union with Christ. His Love for you sets your heart on fire! His Singleness of heart comes alive in living a life not to please yourself. Instead, Christ fills you to overflowing with His Comforting Love.

As a New Creation in Christ Jesus, the Spirit of Life is flowing through you. He produces within you a Passionate Heart to Love Me from the depths of your soul, with all your energy and with your every thought. And to Love others in the same way you love yourself. I inwardly transform your heart by grace, giving you the power and desire to fulfill all I ask of you, My child.

I love you,

Daddy God. Amen.

*I will give you a new heart and put a new spirit within you; I will take the heart of stone out of your flesh and give you a heart of flesh.*

Ezekiel 36:26, NKJV

## ▎Scriptures for Further Reading:

2 Corinthians 11:3, 2 Corinthians 5:17, Ezekiel 36:26, Psalm 51:10, Hebrews 8:10, Romans 8:4, Colossians 3:3, John 14:26, John 16:13, John 1:1, John 10:30, John 17:21, Galatians 2:20, 1 Corinthians 2:16, 1 Corinthians 6:17, Psalm 69:9, Romans 15:3, Philippians 2:1, 4, Romans 8:2, Galatians 5:22, Matthew 22:39, Romans 12:2, Philippians 2:13

## Prayer

Heavenly Father,

Thank You for creating in me a New Heart to respond to Your Love wholeheartedly. My old heart was co-crucified with Christ and no longer lives. I am an entirely New Creation with a New Heart, and Your Spirit of Life living within me. Fill me with Your Comforting Love, to not just look out for my own interests, but the interests of others, too.

In Jesus' name. Amen.

# MY UNFAILING LOVE COMFORTS YOU

*G*od sends His Mercy Kiss to comfort you with Unfailing Love. His Love floods your heart with Abounding Joy to strengthen you when you're feeling lonely, sad, or discouraged. The Holy Spirit's Kiss of Peace calms your heart amid the storms of life with the Comforting Love of Christ that guards your heart and mind against the strategies of darkness.

The Holy Spirit is your Fountain of Hope, pouring out Living Waters of Divine Love that drives out discouragement and despair, protecting you from the lies of the devil. His Kiss awakens your heart to stand in the radiant hope that never disappoints, because He wraps your hurting heart in the Endless Love of God, pouring into your heart rest in His deliverance.

He infuses inner-strength into you to conqueror every discouragement through the working of His Mighty Power and Love, giving you a calm and well-balanced mind ruled by Christ. So you can walk through the storms of life because you know He lives in you, Who calms every storm, expels all fears, and gives you the victory shielded in His Faithful Arms.

# Letter From God

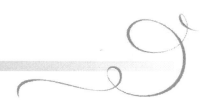

Good Morning,

I Love you, My Dear, Precious, Beloved, Blessed, Special, Beautiful child of My GREAT Love. And that is what you are!

I send My Kind Mercy-Kiss to comfort you with My Unfailing Love. My Love is a flooding river, overflowing the banks of your heart with Tenderhearted kindness, plenteous in mercy for your failures, and My Abounding Joy to strengthen you when you feel sad and discouraged or lonely.

My Kiss of Peace brings you calm amid the storms of life through the comfort and encouragement of the Holy Spirit. He is the Spirit of Christ living in you, Who fills you to overflowing with His Comforting Love. His Calming Peace guards your heart and mind against being agitated and disturbed from the evil strategies of the devil by Me Divinely Persuading you what is true and extinguishing the blazing arrows thrown at you.

As your Fountain of Hope, I am bubbling over with Living Waters of Divine Love to overtake every thought and drive out discouragement to protect your thoughts from lies. My Kiss awakens your heart to stand in the radiant Hope of My Wraparound Presence, while I strengthen your hurting heart resting in My Salvation's total deliverance.

My Nurturing Love is tender and gentle, full of compassion and abounding grace to strengthen you. My chosen one, I infuse you with inner-strength to conqueror every discouragement by hearing My Holy Spirit whispering into your spirit, "You are My beloved child." I have given you a spirit of power and of love, of a calm and well-balanced mind, so that Christ's rule always guides your heart in deciding all questions that come to your mind.

My Heart always hears your heart's cry since I live inside you. I answer your cry for help with the tender embrace of My Presence. I am walking through the storms of life with you. Yes, even the winds and waves obey Me. The storms of pain, doubt, or discouragement will never conquer you, for I have already triumphed over them.

The comfort of My Love expels all your fear. I have hidden your life in Me, God the Destroyer of your Enemies. My arms of Faithfulness are wrapped around you, shielding you from darkness and giving you victory over all the power the enemy possesses, making you a world-overcomer, My child.

I love you,

Daddy God. Amen.

*Now let your unfailing love comfort me,*
*just as you promised me, your servant.*

Psalm 119:76, NLT

## SCRIPTURES FOR FURTHER READING:

Psalm 119:76, Psalm 103:8, Hebrews 4:12, Nehemiah 8:10, Psalm 29:11, Acts 9:31, Romans 8:10, Philippians 2:1, Ephesians 6:11-12, Romans 15:13, Galatians 5:22, John 7:38, Psalm 33:20-21, Matthew 11:29, Psalm 86:15, Romans 8:17, 2 Timothy 1:7, Colossians 3:15, John 14:17, Psalm 43:2, Matthew 8:23, Luke 8:25, Psalm 23:4, Psalm 139:5, Psalm 91:1-4, 1 John 5:4-5, Luke 10:19

## Prayer

Heavenly Father,

Thank You for comforting me with Your Unfailing Love. May Your Abounding Joy strengthen me and lift me out of the sadness, discouragement, and loneliness. I ask You to quiet the storms I face with Your Calming Peace that guards my heart and mind, and protect my thoughts from the lies of the devil. Your Comforting Love expels all my worries and concerns, because I know You are taking care of me.

In Jesus' name. Amen.

# I Am More Than Enough

*F*ocus your attention and fix your eyes on God in full expectation that nothing is impossible for Him. He is your Provider, Who always has More than enough for you. He knows your every need before you ask Him, and abundantly satisfies you with More than Enough, fully satisfying all your needs.

As God's child, He promises you to do Great and Mighty things for you to demonstrate His Faithfulness to you, which is as Eternal as He is and never changes. He draws you to Himself to embrace His strength and comfort, Who empowers you to hold fast to the anchor of His Unbreakable Hope.

He causes the winds of heaven to blow in your favor to bring all you need through His Grace—which is always More than Enough. So, you can celebrate in your insufficiencies because Christ is your Sufficiency, Who makes all grace, every favor, and earthly blessing come to you in abundance so that you have More than Enough of everything.

# Letter From God

Good Morning,

I Love you, My Dear, Precious, Beloved, Blessed, Special, Beautiful child of My GREAT Love. And that is what you are!

Never yield to the distractions of the world around you. Look away from the world to Me. Focus your attention and fix your eyes on Me with full expectation. I always have More than enough for you. I know all your needs, and I abundantly satisfied you with More than Enough, fully satisfying your every need.

You are My child, and I am your Father Who takes care of you through the Glorious Riches of My Grace Given to You in Christ Jesus. Open Your Heart to the Revelation that I Am the God of More than Enough.

Today I do Great Marvels, as I did in the past. My Miracles and incredible power reveal My Ways as a lesson of My Faithfulness to My people called by My Name, and you who is My child and My Glorious Inheritance. Since it is impossible for Me to lie you, know My Faithfulness is as Eternal as I am and will never change. So, you can run to Me with an open heart and hide in My Faithfulness. You find I am your strength and comfort, Who empowers you to hold fast forever to the unbreakable anchor that holds your soul to Me.

I split the Red Sea open to pass on dry land. I directed My people by day in a cloud of glory and by night in a pillar of fire. I continuously stand as a sentry over My Children, just as I do you, now. I split the mighty rock to give water to the thirsty all they wanted to drink. When they were hungry, I fed them with Angel

Food— manna from heaven to depend on Me, Who is the Bread of Life.

I caused My heavenly winds to blow in their favor and brought all that was needed—My Grace was More than Enough. I, being full of compassion, covered their sins with My Love more Love than was ever given them. Over and over, I held back My Anger to show them My Mercy.

My Grace is always More than Enough for you. It reveals My Favor and Lovingkindness, and My Mercy is sufficient for you to overcome all things. I do this to demonstrate that throughout the ages to come, the infinite riches of My Grace is showered upon you in Jesus Christ. You can celebrate your weaknesses, for My Power and strength find their Full Expression through your weaknesses, because you sense more deeply Christ's Mighty Presence living within you.

Yes, I am more than ready to overwhelm you with every form of Grace—every favor and earthly blessing coming to you in abundance, so that you have More than Enough of everything, needing nothing from the world, My child.

I love you,

Daddy God. Amen.

*The Lord is my shepherd;*
*I have all that I need.*

Psalm 23:1, NLT

# SCRIPTURES FOR FURTHER READING:

Psalm 23:1, Matthew 6:8, Philippians 4:18-19, Psalm 78:6-7, Psalm 102:18, Ephesians 1:18, 1 John 3:1, Hebrew 6:18-19, Exodus 14:21, Exodus 15:8, Exodus 13:21, Psalm 78:14, Hebrews 13:5-6, Psalm 78:15, Exodus 17:6, Numbers 20:8-11, Psalm 78:25, Exodus 16:4, John 6:31, Psalm 78:26, Numbers 11:13, Psalm 78:38, Numbers 14:18-20, Exodus 34:6, 2 Corinthians 12:9-10, Ephesians 2:27, 2 Corinthians 9:8

## Prayer

Heavenly Father,

I turn to You, I rely on You, I am fully dependent on You to meet all my need and dismiss reliance on the world. You are My Father, the Creator of the world and all that is in it. Nothing is impossible for You. I ask that You make all Grace, every favor, and earthly blessing come to me, so that I have More than Enough of everything and plenty left over to give to the aid and support of others that cause Praise and Thanksgiving to Your Holy, Holy, Holy Name.

In Jesus' name. Amen.

# I LOVE YOU AS MUCH AS JESUS

*O*ne Truth that Jesus gave goes to the heart of almost all spiritual problems that He knew and came to reveal to you, Knowing God as a Loving Father and God's Sovereignty. The Truth is: God Loves you as much as He Loves Jesus. When God sees you, He sees Jesus living in you.

Your life is hidden with Christ in God. He Loves you with the same Passionate Love He Loves His Beloved Son with. The Truth will revolutionize your walk with God. Jesus prayed to the Father, "that you love them as much as you love me." (John 17:23, NLT) Jesus is telling you to believe God Loves you as Much as He loves Him.

You may believe in your head that God is your loving Heavenly Father. But Jesus is telling you to dare to believe in your heart that God loves you as Much as He Loves Him. May your eyes be opened to this Glorious Truth—that God has Tenderly Loved you from Eternity Past, despite all He knew you would do. His Great Love for you Never changes.

His Perfect Love for you drives out all fears of any rejection from Him, far from your heart.

# Letter From God

Good Morning,

I Love you, My Dear, Precious, Beloved, Blessed, Special, Beautiful child of My GREAT Love. And that is what you are!

One Truth removes from your heart the insecurity and fear that causes you to worry and be anxious. Here's the Truth: I Love you as much as I Love Jesus! When I see you, I see Jesus living in you, Who lives in Me, and you are one with Me, and I am Living in you.

You live fully in Jesus Christ, My Beloved Child, and now I live fully in you so you can experience the glory and the Love of being made One with Us through the blood of Jesus. Now, your True Life is with Christ living in Me. Everything is fresh and new!

I Love You with the Same Passionate Love that I Love My Beloved Son with! My Love for you began before I laid the foundation of the world. I Chose to Love you before the fall of the world. Because of My Great Love, I ordained you, set you apart to be seen holy and blameless in My Sight without a single fault. And that is what you are!

I did this to satisfy the Great and Passionate Love I have for you, because I am so rich in Mercy and Compassion. Even when you were dead in your many sins, I united you with Christ's Very Life and Saved you by My Amazing Grace! You did nothing to earn My Love, and there is nothing you can do to lose My Love.

It was always My plan from Eternity past for you to be My child through your union with Jesus. Now you can experience My Tremendous Love pouring over and through you that glorifies My

Grace, the Love Gift that brought you to Christ. For the same Love I have for Jesus, I have for you.

My Tender Love for you Endures Forever—It Never Ends! For I will Never Leave you nor relax My hold on you—never! My Love never comes to an end because I Never Stop Loving you.

The Holy Spirit makes My Love real to you as He constantly whispers deep inside you, "I Love you, My dear child," and He does so until My Love becomes the source and foundation of your life. Thereby, I empower you to discover and experience for yourself the Great Astonishing Love of Christ in All Its Varied Expressions.

How deep My Passionate Love is for you, as demonstrated in sending My Son into the world for you so that you could live through Him. My Endless Love that is Infinitely Transcending beyond your understanding fills all your being with My Extravagant Love pouring into you, filling and flooding you with Myself, My child.

I love you,

Daddy God. Amen.

*I am in them and you are in me. May*
*they experience such perfect unity that the*
*world will know that you sent me and that*
*you love them as much as you love me.*

John 17:23, NLT

## SCRIPTURES FOR FURTHER READING:

2 Timothy 1:7, John 17:23, John 14:20, Colossians 3:3, John 17:22-23, Ephesians 2:13, Colossians 3:3, 2 Corinthians 5:17, Ephesians 1:4, Ephesians 2:4-5, Ephesians 1:5-6, Ephesians 2:8-10, Psalm 136:1, Hebrews 13:6, 1 Corinthians 13:6, Ephesians 3:17-19, Galatians 5:22

## Prayer

Heavenly Father,

I know everything is possible to those who believe. Have compassion on me, and help me accept the incredible Truth that You Love me as much as You Love Jesus. I do believe. I ask the Spirit of Truth to reveal the reality of Your Extravagant Love, and pull on my heart to embrace the fullest measure of Your Endless Love pouring into me.

In Jesus' name. Amen.

# NATURE OF MY UNLIMITED LOVE

*Y*ou *share Christ's crucifixion. Your old identity has been co-crucified with Christ. It is no longer you who live, but Christ lives in you. He infuses you with His explosive power and imparts His Divine Life into you as your Living Redeemer. Your heart is entwined with His heart because you live in union as one.*

*God has kissed your heart with forgiveness, redeemed your life from death and crowned you with love and mercy. He satisfies your mouth with good things and renews your life with divine strength, so you can walk through life without giving up.*

*He Spiritually Resurrected you from your Spiritual Death to walk in newness of life. He severed ties to your old life forever, and now your New Life is hidden with Christ in God. Now, you possess the Complete Righteousness of Christ through your union with Him., and you are seen by Me as Righteous as My Child.*

# Letter From God

Good Morning,

I Love you, My Dear, Precious, Beloved, Blessed, Special, Beautiful child of My GREAT Love. And that is what you are!

You share Christ's crucifixion. Your old identity has been co-crucified with Christ. It is no longer you who live, for you have been made alive in union as one with Him! You now live your New Life infused with Christ's explosive power by His Faith, Who Loves you and gave Himself up for you. Now, My Life-Giving Spirit imparts My Divine Life in you, being fully acceptable to Me!

I AM your Living Redeemer Who entwines your heart with Mine and helps you. Never forget All the good things I have done for you. My Benefits cause your soul to rejoice. I have kissed your heart with forgiveness, despite all you have done. I heal all your diseases, I redeem your life from death, I crown you with love and mercy, I satisfy your mouth with good things, and I renew your life with divine strength so you can walk through life without giving up.

Yes, I am so rich in mercy, that to satisfy the Great Love I have for you, I give you mercy for your failures, and in My Presence, you find Grace to help in your times of need. Even when you were dead in your trespasses and sins, I made you alive together in union with the very Life of Christ, and Saved you by My Amazing Grace!

I have Spiritually Resurrected from your Spiritual Death. You now walk and live in the freshness of your New Spiritual Life. You are permanently engrafted into Christ; you have become an entirely new person—old things have passed away. Behold, all things have become new!

Redemption takes you from knowing about Me to an instant, direct, and intimate relationship with ME. Your crucifixion with Christ severed your ties to your old life forever, and now your New Life is hidden with Christ in ME.

The Nature of My Unlimited Love proves to you the great lengths I went to make you My Own through Redemption. I gave the Gift of My Son to be crucified for the forgiveness of your sins, and His resurrection proves you have been made right with ME!

I made My Son, Christ, to be sin for you. He Who knew no sin, that in and through Him, you would become My Righteousness through your union with Him. I made a Divine Exchange at the cross. All of your sins were left on the cross, and you were endued with My Righteousness.

Now, you possess the Complete Righteousness of Christ, and you are seen by Me as Righteous as My Son. I have unveiled My Redeeming Grace for you to experience for yourself, My Heart of Love for you, My child.

I love you,

Daddy God. Amen.

*I have been crucified with Christ and I no longer live,*
*but Christ lives in me. The life I now live in the body, I*
*live by faith in the Son of God, who loved me and gave*
*himself for me.*

Galatians 2:20, NIV

## SCRIPTURES FOR FURTHER READING:

Galatians 2:20, Philippians 4:13, Romans 8:10, Job 19:25, Isaiah 49:26, Isaiah 41:14, Psalm 103:2-5, Isaiah 40:31, Hebrews 4:16, Ephesians 2:4-5 & 8-9, Colossians 2:13, Romans 5:8, Ephesians 2:4-8, 2 Corinthians 5:17, Romans 6:5-6, Colossians 3:3, Romans 8:32, Romans 4:25, 2 Corinthians 5:18, 21

## Prayer

Heavenly Father,

Thank You for the new life you have given me in Christ Jesus. You have made me alive in union with Him and entwined my heart with His. I will never forget all the good things you have done for me. I rejoice in all Your benefits, especially forgiving me despite all I have done.

In Jesus' name. Amen.

# FEAST ON MY FAITHFULNESS

*T*he *LORD GOD ALMIGHTY is the Maker of heaven and earth, and there is nothing too hard or too difficult or too impossible or too incredible for Him to do for you! He keeps all His Promises to you, because He is Forever Faithful to you. He is near you always to expectantly Hope in His Divine Help, so you never have to be afraid of what people may say or do.*

*He is your Deliverer, the Source of your Salvation. He is determined to stand with you; He is on your side. Who can be against you? He is your Helper; so take comfort and be encouraged—the Lord Fights for you. Rest in His Presence and surrender your anxiety to Him. He is a proven Help in times of trouble and never leaves your side.*

*Fear not! There is nothing to fear when God is always with you, for you are His child. He is intimately involved in all the details of your life. And He loves to surprise you with the magnitude of His Astonishing Love in all its dimensions for you. He takes pleasure in hearing your voice and delights in satisfying you with His Amazing Grace.*

# Letter From God

Good Morning,

I Love you, My Dear, Precious, Beloved, Blessed, Special, Beautiful child of My GREAT Love. And that is what you are!

I AM the LORD GOD ALMIGHTY, Maker of heaven and of earth, and there is nothing too hard or too difficult or too impossible or too wonderful for Me to do for you!

I Keep All My Promises, and I AM Forever Faithful to you. I have Blessed you to Expectantly Hope in ME! I am your Divine Helper! So you can say with great confidence: "I know the LORD is for me, and I will never be afraid of what people may do to me. For the Lord fights for me." Surrender your anxiety. Be still—I am God, and no weapon formed against you will succeed, for I am your vindication.

I AM your revelation-light and the source of your salvation. I am on your side and stand beside you—fear no one! I am your mighty fortress Who surrounds you and protects you. Nothing can stop you when I am with you. For I grip you by your right hand and whisper, "I am here to help you!" It is so much better to trust in ME to help you than put your confidence in man.

I give you My Mercy Love for your weaknesses which is limitless, reaching beyond the highest heavens. And My Faithfulness that is Infinitely Transcending, Further than the East is from the West. Listen, I Am Intimately involved in Every Detail of your Life, and I love to surprise you with how thoroughly I know you and meet all your needs.

I take pleasure in hearing your voice in My Presence. I delight in revealing how extravagant is My Unfailing Love toward you. Keep trusting in Me and Fix your heart on My Promises, Feast on My Faithfulness to All My Promises given to you.

Find your true delight and pleasure in ME, and I will give you the desires and secret petitions of your heart. Commit everything you do to ME, roll all your burdens and cares over on ME; Leave them all at My Feet, and My Measureless Grace will strengthen you and fill your heart with praises as you Trust in My Promises.

Before you do anything, put your Trust Wholly in ME, Who causes your thoughts to become agreeable with My Plans, and in this way, you know All your plans will be established and succeed.

Remember, I am Infinite in All My Ways. I never run out of resources. There is nothing contingent upon your resources or abilities. I am within you, so come to ME in Joyful Expectation of liberally receiving your every need.

Step out beyond your self-imposed boundaries of what you think I'll do for you. Instead, come to ME with an open heart and open arms, ready to be fully satisfied by My Amazing Grace to strengthen you in your time of weaknesses. Well-timed help coming just when you, My child.

I love you,

Daddy God. Amen.

*Your unfailing love, O Lord, is as vast as the heavens;*
*your faithfulness reaches beyond the clouds.*

Psalm 36:7, NLT

## SCRIPTURES FOR FURTHER READING:

Jeremiah 32:17, Psalm 46:5-7 & 10, Hebrews 13:6, Joshua 23:10, Isaiah 54:7, Psalm 27:1, Psalm 118:6-8, Isaiah 41:10-13, Matthew 6:8, Psalm 23:1, Psalm 36:5-7, Psalm 37:3-4, Psalm 56:4, Proverbs 16:3, Philippians 4:19, Hebrews 4:16

## Prayer

Heavenly Father,

You are the Maker of heaven and earth. There is nothing too hard or too difficult or too impossible or too wonderful for You to do for me! I know You are always faithful, because you continually raise me up when I am weak and give me the grace to help in my time of need. I commit everything I do to you and Trust in Your Faithfulness to meet my every need.

In Jesus' name. Amen.

# FOCUS ON MY LIGHT

*G*od is the Light that never fails to shine through the darkness. So focus on His Light in you to walk you through your darkest moments. His Holiness protects your heart, and His Glory is your rear-guard, protecting your heart as He restores and revives your life. For His Word makes your spirit shine radiant, rejoicing your heart and enlightening your eyes.

The Light of Life is living within you. His Self-Existent Life produces Divine Illumination to reveal and impart Life in you through Christ. Your New Life Always comes from and is sustained by Him sharing His Gift of Life with you, manifest and revealed in the face of Jesus Christ. Now His Light within you produces what is good and right and genuinely acceptable to God.

His Light in you Lights up the world around you to benefit those near to you. As a Child of Light, you speak the Word of Light to the deepest darkness, and the Light of God's Love will break through every difficulty. Your Life manifests the Supernatural Fruit of Light produced by the Holy Spirit to express Divine Love through you.

Focus on His Light!

# Letter From God

Good Morning,

I love you, My Dear, Precious, Beloved, Blessed, Special, Beautiful child of My GREAT Love. And that is what you are!

I AM the Light that never fails to shine through Darkness, Who overcomes the dark heaviness surrounding your soul. Focus on My Light living in you; He is far greater than the darkness around you. My Light bursts through your darkness to restore and revive your life to recovery quickly. My Holiness protects your heart, and My Glory is your rear-guard. I open the right path to bring Me honor.

My Word is your Light that makes your spirit shine radiant, rejoicing your heart and enlightening your eyes. The Revelation of My Word makes your pathway clear, shining My Light on your choices and decisions. I break open My Word within you to give you Light into My Plans for you.

The Light of My Radiant Face shines upon you, and My Gracious Favor bursts through you every cloudy day. I called you out of darkness to experience My Marvelous Light and tell others about My Goodness. Each morning, I awaken your heart to bask in the Light of My Great Love and open your ears to hear My Voice. So, you walk on a highway of Light that shines brighter and brighter because My Light clears the path before you.

I AM the Light of Life is living within you. I manifest My Self-Existent Life within you through My Divine Illumination to reveal and impart Life to you through Christ. This Life Always comes from and is sustained by ME sharing My Gift of Life with you. I flood the eyes of your heart with Light to brightly reflect My Glory, transfiguring you into My Very Image, moving from one level of glory to another.

My child, I pour My Light into your heart as it is manifest and revealed in the face of Jesus Christ. Once your life was full of darkness, but now you have My Very Light Shining through you because of your union with Christ. Now, My Light within you produces what is good and right and genuinely acceptable to Me.

My Light in you Lights up the world around you to benefit those near to you. Let your Light shine brightly upon them to let the Light of Truth take the place of darkness. I am manifesting the Supernatural Fruits of My Light, Produced by the Holy Spirit within you, expressing Divine Love in all its varied expressions of Spirit Living through you, My child.

I love you,

Daddy God. Amen.

*In Him was life, and the life*
*was the Light of men.*

John 1:4, NKJV

## SCRIPTURES FOR FURTHER READING:

John 1:3-4, Psalm 23:2-3, John 17:17, 1 John 4:4, Isaiah 58:8, Psalm 119:24, Psalm 19:8, Psalm 119:105, Psalm 119:129, Psalm 4:6, Numbers 6:25, I Peter 2:9, Isaiah 50:4, Proverbs 4:18, Isaiah 26:7, John 8:12, 1 Thessalonians 5:5, 2 Corinthians 3:18, 2 Corinthians 4:6, Ephesians 5:8-9, Matthew 5:14-16, Matthew 6:22-23, Philippians 2:13, Galatians 5:22

## Prayer

Heavenly Father,

I look away from all distractions to focus my attention and expectation on Your Light living in me. Your Light makes my spirit rejoice as I rest in Your Tender Love that restores and revives my life. I ask You to Let Your Light in me shine through me to break down the walls of darkness to produce what is good and right and pleasing to You.

In Jesus' name. Amen.

# SPIRITUAL REVELATIONS NEVER SEEN

*G*od grants you the privilege of knowing the My Secrets of the Kingdom of God. They are hidden from those who do not have the Spirit of God living in them. But to you, He reveals the secret counsels and mysteries of His Kingdom that are beyond the scope of human wisdom and unattainable by human reasoning.

*Only those born of the Spirit of God can comprehend, discern, and understand the things of God. He unveils to you, His child, His Inmost Heart and Deepest Secrets, because you are an Heir to His Kingdom. The Holy Spirit reveals the reality of every truth within you so you can perceive and comprehend the gifts, teachings, and revelations of God.*

*Now, you have the privilege to experience intimate insights into God's Divine Mystery and Wisdom by the Holy Spirit unveiling Jesus Christ to you.*

*In Christ are hidden all the Treasures of Divine Wisdom and Endless Riches of Revelation, Knowledge, and Spiritual Wealth, waiting for you to discover. He awakens your heart to the complete revelation of Christ, being the Power of God and the Wisdom of God.*

# Letter From God

Good Morning,

I Love you, My Dear, Precious, Beloved, Blessed, Special, Beautiful child of My GREAT Love. And that is what you are!

I have granted to you the privilege of knowing My Secrets of the Kingdom of God. The secret councils and mysteries are hidden from those who don't care to know Me. But I reveal them to you who love Me—the things beyond the scope of human wisdom and unattainable by human reasoning.

These Spiritual Revelations never seen or heard of before are unveiled and revealed through the Holy Spirit, which I have stored for you. Non-spiritual man can never imagine or understand, because he cannot discern or comprehend My Thoughts because he has the Spirit of the world.

I unveiled them to you by My Spirit, Who reveals My Inmost Heart and Deepest Secrets, the profound realities beyond man's scrutiny. For you did not receive the Spirit of the world, but My Spirit, so you can perceive and comprehend the gifts, teachings, and revelations of My Spirit, because you spiritually discern them and appreciate them.

The Great Revelation of My Authority and mysteries I have hidden from the wise, learned, and clever. Instead, I reveal them to you, My Chosen Little child, who I picked out for Myself in Christ in Love, before the foundation of the world, to be holy and blameless in My Sight because I see you wrapped in Jesus.

You have the privilege to experience intimate insight into the Secrets and Mysteries of the Kingdom of Heaven, which can only be fully understood by My Spirit testifying together with your born-again Spirit, unveiling Jesus Christ to you. Here's the secret: the Gospel of Grace has made you a member of the Body of Christ and a Co-Heir with Christ by being one with Him.

Push away all the opinions and traditions of men—to gain the profound revelations My Spirit reveals, Jesus didn't talk. For I have given you My Spirit, to Understand and Experience and Realize all My Grace has so freely and lavishly bestowed upon you by Me. My Spirit articulates the Truth of My Word by the Spirit of Truth, explaining spiritual truths and realities to you who possess the Holy Spirit, because only you can discern illuminations of My Spirit.

I pull you close, wrapping your heart together into My Heart in the comfort of My Spirit, to access all the abounding wealth and blessings of My Mystery, which is Christ. In Him, you have hidden Treasures of Divine Wisdom and Knowledge waiting for you to discover, and others are unable to find.

Many will see how I strengthen and uphold you in My Marvelous Grace, unfolded and manifested in you and through you as you experience the Mystery of Christ living within you. Christ is the Message of My Mystery I have hidden from ages and generations! The Holy Spirit awakens your heart to bring you into a complete Revelation of this Truth, and then by the Power of Christ Flowing through you, you are enabled you to share your experience with other believers, My child.

I love you,

Daddy God. Amen.

*The secret of the kingdom of God has been given to you. But
to those on the outside everything is said in parables*

Mark 4:11, NIV

## SCRIPTURES FOR FURTHER READING:

Mark 4:11, 1 Corinthians 2:5-7, 1 Corinthians 2:9-10, Isaiah 64:4,
Isaiah 65:17, 1 Corinthians 2:11-14, Matthew 11:25, Ephesians 1:3-
4, Matthew 13:11, Romans 8:16, Galatians 1:12, Ephesians 3:3-6,
Romans 8:17, 1 Corinthians 2:12-14, John 14:17, Colossians 2:2-3,
Colossians 1:26-27, Ephesians 3:9

## Prayer

Heavenly Father,

Thank You for granting the privilege of coming into a fuller, more
complete understanding of Your secret councils and mysteries
hidden in Christ, which You have stored up for me. You picked me
out for Yourself to wrap me in Jesus to know and have free access to
all the abounding wealth and blessings in Christ. Awaken my heart
to walk in all the blessings and benefits that are mine in Christ
Jesus.

In Jesus' name. Amen.

# Come to Me Who Loves You

*G*od pulls you into His Presence to Seek His Face with all your heart. He desires you in His Presence and paid an Unfathomable Price to have a deep, personal relationship with Him. For He rescued you from the power of darkness and transferred you into the Kingdom of His Son, redeeming you back to Himself through Jesus' bloodshed on the cross, forgiving you of all your sins.

*He satisfies your spiritual thirst with His Living Water, drawn from His Presence within you to refresh your weary soul. Your Heavenly Father's open arms welcome you to drink deeply from the Water of Life. He gives you the confidence to come boldly to His Throne of Grace, knowing you are Fully Accepted in His Presence because He sees you wrapped into Christ.*

*Come to Him Who Loves you to discover the great magnitude of His Wondrous Love in all its dimensions. He will refresh your life because you are in union with Him. Seek His guidance in all the affairs of life, for He knows all things at all times, and already knows the answers you need. Trust Him! And you will experience for yourself His Endless Love's guidance in every decision through His Peace acting as umpire in your heart.*

# Letter From God

Good Morning,

I Love you, My Dear, Precious, Beloved, Blessed, Special, Beautiful child of My GREAT Love. And that is what you are!

Come Seek My Face with All Your Heart. I Desire you to have a deeper personal relationship with ME. My Spirit and My Power are effectively operating on and within you, stirring your mind's most Holy emotions and persuading your heart to embrace Me.

I pull you into My Presence to satisfy your spiritual thirst by giving you My Living Water. My Spirit within you continuously flows rivers of living water from your innermost being by My Spirit joining your Spirit. Come to ME and draw from the rivers of My Presence that refreshes your weary soul.

I want you to Confidently Know that you are Fully Accepted in My Presence, because I see you wrapped into Christ. In My Love, I Chose you out for Myself as My Own in Christ. Because of My Great Love, I ordained you to be set apart for Me, holy and Blameless before ME in Love. You share the likeness of My Son, so My Tremendous Love continually cascades over you to Glorify My Grace.

Come to Me; I Love you with the same Love I have for My Beloved Son, Jesus. Let this awareness of My Love seep deep into your innermost being. I, Who Created the heavens and the earth, and all that is within them, seen and unseen: I Love you! (Colossians 1:16) Allow My Love to alter how you see yourself so that you see yourself as I see you— holy, blameless, above reproach, and beloved forever in My Sight, because you are My child.

Come to ME, I will refresh your life. I am your Burden-Bearer; unload all your worries and concerns upon ME and leave them at My Feet, for I am always watching over you with tender care. Simply recognize your life is joined with ME, and I give you rest, ease your mind, and bless your soul with peace.

It gives ME Great Joy for you to Seek My Guidance in all the affairs of life, with all your heart to rely on Me, and not your own understanding or opinions. Trust ME Completely, because I am intimately aware of your every need. (Matthew 6:8) Trust ME until you come to know through experience for yourself My Endless Love's guidance in every decision you make through My Peace continually ruling in your heart, My child.

I love you,

Daddy God. Amen.

*The Lord is my light and my salvation; Whom shall I fear?*
*The Lord is the strength of my life; Of whom shall I be*
*afraid?*

Psalm 27:1, NKJV

## Scriptures for Further Reading:

Psalm 27:8, 1 Corinthians 2:4, John 6:44, John 7:38-39, Romans 8:16, Romans 8:29, Ephesians 1:3-6, Colossians 1:16, 1 John 3:1-2, Colossians 3:3, 1 Peter 5:7, Jeremiah 6:16, Matthew 11:28-29, Proverbs 3:5-6, Ephesians 3:18-19, Colossians 3:15

## Prayer

Heavenly Father,

When I cry out to You, answer me and send the help I need. My heart hears You say, "Please come and talk with ME." So, I am seeking Your Face with All my heart. You are My Light that guides my footsteps and my total deliverance. You are with me, so I do not fear or worry, because You surround and protect me. You are my inner-peace and strength that keeps me from being afraid.

In Jesus' name. Amen.

# THE BEAUTY OF MY LOVE CHANGES YOU

*T*he stunning beauty of God's Presence in you fills your heart with God's Love and Mercy to satisfy your every desire, at every age, and in every situation with good things. Your life is supercharged with His Grace even in your weaknesses so that you can sense Christ's Divine Strength working in you mightily.

The Beauty of God's Love changes your heart through an intimate relationship with Him, pouring His Tender, Unfailing Love in your innermost being so your heart overflows with His Love for you to Love others as much as He Loves you. His Divine Love in you gives you the power and desire to Love others as He Loves you unselfishly.

God is Love! His Love changes your heart to be gentle and kind, not to demand your own way, to keep no record of past wrongs, and never to give up because He never stops loving you. His Extravagant Love continues to pour into you, filling you to overflowing with all His Fullness, the Richest Measure of His Divine Love.

# Letter From God

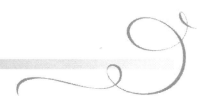

Good Morning,

I Love you, My Dear, Precious, Beloved, Blessed, Special, Beautiful child of My GREAT Love. And that is what you are!

The Stunning Beauty of My Presence within you Fills your heart with Love. I love beyond all understanding, and I flood your heart with My Love Every Moment. I kiss your Heart with My Love and Mercy. I satisfy your desire at every age with good things, and refresh your strength to soar again like an eagle in the sky.

Yes, My Love supercharges your Life with My Grace to experience Divine Strength even in your weaknesses, so that you can sense more deeply the mighty strength of Christ living in you! He is the Hope residing in you, providing you entery into My Holy Presence where I empower you to walk through life without giving up. I draw you Closer and Closer to Me until your heart swells with all the fullness of My Goodness, which all My Lovers Experience— you, who Love Me.

I revive your heart with My Lover's Touch, penetrating your innermost being, so your heart overflows with gladness and life forever. Drink deeply from the streams of My Pleasure flowing from My Presence. Let the Living Waters revive your spirit and encourage your soul, for I fill you with a longing that overwhelms you with gladness for more of ME!

The Beauty of My Love changes you. I have hidden you in My heart. You have come into an intimate experience with My Love, and you can trust in the Love I have for you, which I continually pour in you to Love others just as much as I Love you. For My Divine Love in you gives you the power and desire to love others as I love you—unselfishly. So, you can Love and value others as you do yourself.

I send My Love to you in many ways to stir your most Holy emotions: the loving voice of a dear, precious friend, My anointed music that moves your soul, My loving comfort of a writer's pen, the artist's strokes of love placed on the canvas, and My movement of Love expressed through dance—each a creative expression of My Love released toward you. Even the air you breathe, each beat of your heart, the compassion received through the comfort of another—My Love is in each connection, talent, ability, gift, and fruit, because I surround you and fill you with Myself.

I AM Love! You are alive in ME, and My Love Lives through you. My Love changes your heart to be gentle and kind to all, not to demand your own way or traffic in disrespect. My Love for you never focuses on what is wrong with you, so it is a safe place that offers shelter from the accusing voices of the world, not exposure. When you Love others, you express your Grateful Response to My Love flowing through you that Never Stops Loving.

Each morning, awaken to the sound of My Tender, Unfailing Love. My Beautiful Presence embraces you in the arms of Everlasting Love to ponder how deeply intimate and far-reaching is My Love for you. My Endless Love transcends your understanding with My Extravagant Love that pours into you, filling you to overflowing with My Fullness, the Richest Measure of My Divine Love.

Therefore, Rejoice in My Astonishing Love for you, which is Unlimited—without conditions. The assurance of My Unfailing Love each Morning gives Light for your path, teaches you, and causes you to know how you should walk. I am your Shelter of Love, Who wraps Myself around you as a security shield. I Love you with an Everlasting Love, with My Unfailing Love I have drawn you to Myself, My child.

I love you,

Daddy God. Amen.

*A new commandment I give to you, that you love one another; as I have loved you, that you also love one another.*

John 13:34, NKJV

## SCRIPTURES FOR FURTHER READING:

Psalm 103:4-5, Isaiah 40:31, 2 Corinthians 12:9, Hebrew 10:19-22, Psalm 69:32, John 13:34, 1 Thessalonians 4:9, James 2:8, Psalm 22:26, 1 John 4,16, 19, 1 Corinthians 13:4-8, Ephesians 3:19, Jeremiah 31:3, Psalm 143:8, Psalm 144:2

## Prayer

Heavenly Father,

Thank You for satisfying my every desire with Your absolute best for me. Your grace supercharges my life with Divine Strength to walk through life without giving up. I ask You to Refresh my life with the Living Waters of Your Endless Love to demonstrate Beauty of Your Love in me to others by loving others with the Love You have poured into me, to draw them to Your Love for them.

In Jesus' name. Amen.

# MY GIFT OF LOVE AND FAVOR

*G*od pours more and more of His Unfailing in you to reveal and clearly demonstrate throughout the ages to come the infinite riches of His Wondrous Grace. He has showered His love upon you in Jesus Christ. In Christ, you have the complete cancellation of your sins through His Blood. He purchased you back to God to satisfy His Great Love for you.

*You being joined to Jesus means God lavishly bestowed all the treasures of salvation deliverance –the Total Cancellation of your sins and the Endless Riches of His Grace available to you. He unveils to you the secret mystery of His plan to unite all things in heaven and earth back to Him through Christ.*

*God's Gift of Love and Favor continually pour over you through the Holy Spirit to fulfill the purpose and plan of His Heart that made you His Special Treasure of Great Importance. Through the Holies, you experience God's Endless Love already working within you, producing His Gifts, Fruits, Wisdom, and Transforming Power to bring Him Glory.*

# Letter From God

Good Morning,

I Love you, My Dear, Precious, Beloved, Blessed, Special, Beautiful child of My GREAT Love. And that is what you are!

I Pour More and More of My Unfailing Love on you to reveal My Mercy and the Loving-Kindness of My Wondrous Grace to clearly demonstrate throughout the ages to come the infinite, immeasurable riches of My Grace and kindness and goodness showered upon you in Jesus Christ.

For in Christ, you have complete cancellation of your sins through His very blood. I purchased you back to Myself through Him to satisfy My Great and Passionate Love to restore My Full Image to your heart. My Perfect Plan of Love was always to reveal you as My Child through your union with Jesus.

You being joined to Jesus means I have lavishly bestowed upon you all the Treasures of Salvation and Deliverance through His Blood—the Total Cancellation of your sins, including heaven's wisdom and revelation knowledge and all the Endless Riches of My Grace Already Working Powerfully in you.

I unveiled through Christ the Revelation of the secret Mystery of My Plan from the beginning of time to make all things new and unite all things in heaven and earth through Christ back to its original purpose and restore back to Myself your innocence again.

My Supernatural Peace has been released to you through Jesus' sacrifice that paid your sin debt so that you could be holy and blameless in My Sight, without a fault within and unstained

LEE RICHARDS

innocence wrapped in Christ. Through the powerful declaration of My Amazing Grace, I have delivered you from judgment and made you a partaker of My divine inheritance.

I have rescued you out of the control of the dominion of darkness and transferred you into the Kingdom of My Beloved Son to embrace you in My Tender, Unfailing Love Forever. I erased all your sins— deleted them forever! Every record held against you is permanently nailed to Jesus' cross as a powerful, public declaration of your acquittal.

My Gift of Love and Favor pour continuously over you more and more through the Holy Spirit living within you, demonstrating My Forgiveness is eternal, and that I never stop forgiving you. You have been justified forever by My Great Love, and I never change My Mind. My Unfailing Love for you is the same yesterday, today, and forever!

I chose and destined you to be My Inheritance before you were ever born to fulfill the purpose and plan of My Heart. You are My Special Treasure of Great Importance that I protect in the safety of My Presence because of your extraordinary value. So, I have stamped you with the seal of the Holy Spirit as a guarantee that you are My purchased possession.

Through the Holy Spirit, you experience My Endless Love already working within you through Him producing My Gifts, Fruits, Wisdom, and Transforming Power. Your life is an advertisement of the infinite riches of My Amazing Grace and kindness showered upon you in Jesus Christ.

Christ is your life. You died, and your life is hidden with Him in Me. The Fountain of Life flows from Christ's rivers of Living Water from within you, pouring out more of My Unfailing Love on you, and releasing more of My Blessing to you, My child.

I love you,

Daddy God. Amen.

*Show us your unfailing love, Lord, and grant us your salvation.*

Psalm 85:7, NIV

## ▌SCRIPTURES FOR FURTHER READING:

Psalm 85:7, Ephesians 2:7, Colossians 1:14, Colossians 1:19, Ephesians 1:5-7, Colossians 1:8, 1 Corinthians 2:12, Ephesians 1:9-10, Colossians 1:20, Ephesians 1:3-4, Ephesians 2:8-9, Colossians 1:13, Colossians 2:14, Romans 3:24, Romans 5:5, 1 John 4:8?, Numbers 23:19, James 1:17, Hebrews 13:8, Ephesians 1:11, 1 Peter 2:9, Ephesians 1:13-14, Romans 5:5, Galatians 5:22, Ephesians 2:7, Colossians 3:3-4, John 14:6, John 1:4, Psalm 36:7-10

## Prayer

Heavenly Father,

Thank you for uniting me with Jesus and pouring out more and more of Your Unfailing Love and Wondrous Grace because I am Your Beloved child. You have blessed me with all the Treasures of Salvation Deliverance–Total Canceling all my sins, making me an entirely new person with a new identity in Christ Jesus. I ask that Christ's Living Water within me release more of Your Love through me to others.

In Jesus' name. Amen.

# BENEFITS OF MY SPIRITUAL BLESSINGS

*E*very day God has blessings waiting for you to discover that reveal His Deep, Tender Love for you. You discover these blessings as He daily loads you with Grace by fixing your eyes on Him. He planned before the foundation of the world for everything you would need daily, knowing everything you would need before you ask Him.

He already has blessed you with every spiritual blessing in the heavenly places as a Love Gift from Him because He sees you wrapped into Christ. And He makes all Grace, every favor and earthly blessing come to you in abundance so that you have more than enough of everything. He makes you overflow with abundance to be a blessing to others.

He places in your heart His Unfailing Love to fill your hearts longing for unconditional acceptance with His nearness. His approval of you is securely rooted in His Unfailing Love for you without works. He tenderly cares for you. He understands and loves you for the way He made you from the beginning—His Masterpiece!

# Letter From God

Good Morning,

I Love you, My Dear, Precious, Beloved, Blessed, Special, Beautiful child of My GREAT Love. And that is what you are!

Every day I have Blessings waiting for you to discover, revealing My Deep, Tender Love for you. When you lift your Heart into My Presence, you will see around you My Blessings I daily load you with because you belong to Christ. I give you more than enough of everything, making all grace, every favor, and earthly blessing come to you in abundance for every good thing you do.

Yes, I have already blessed you with every spiritual blessing given by the Holy Spirit in the heavenly realms as My Child–you enjoy them now! All the benefits of Divine Love produced by the Holy Spirit in all its multisided expressions. He manifests each as you need them to fulfill the incredible destiny I prepared for you in Christ.

Each spiritual blessing reveals itself in the physical world as a demonstration of My Tremendous Love, Glorifying the Grace I Lavishly Bestowed upon you in salvation. My whole estate of spiritual wealth is yours as My heir in union with Christ, and now you share all that He has and all that He is. Jesus is the Source of your spiritual wealth, and the moment you received Him, every spiritual blessing became yours.

I Blessed you to satisfy My Great Love for you and chose you to receive the Benefits of My Spiritual Blessings. Christ saves you to the uttermost, perfectly throughout all eternity, because He lives forever and is always interceding and intervening on your behalf. My Gift of Salvation you receive through Him unleashes My Power of Divine Protection and Deliverance. I guarantee your safety and security through the Holy Spirit's mighty power at work within you, Who constantly guards you until you fully receive your priceless inheritance in Christ.

Before you were even born, I chose you to fulfill the Designed Purpose of My Heart and destined you to share the Likeness of My child. Now I have transferred His perfect righteousness to you and co-glorified you with Him. My Heart pulls on your heart to continuously embrace Me in an intimate personal relationship that keeps pouring out My Unfailing Love to you and Releases more of My Blessings to you.

Yes, I placed in your heart the desire for My Unfailing Love, which can only be quenched by My Spirit living within you, cascading Unfailing Love into your heart. Your approval and acceptance find their security rooted in My Unfailing Love for you without works; it is the Love Gift of Christ paid for by His blood. You can never gain Love by good works, because it is only found in Me–Who is Love!

I draw you to Myself to bless you with My Passionate Love to fulfill your heart's longing for unconditional acceptance and closeness, to be tenderly cared for and understood and loved for who you are–My Masterpiece. I Who Love you Most Love you Best, and I Love you through others who Love Me. Those who do not love you judge your outward appearance through their imperfections which good works will never satisfy, My child.

I love you,

Daddy God. Amen.

*Blessed be the God and Father of our Lord Jesus Christ, who has blessed us with every spiritual blessing in the heavenly places in Christ.*

Ephesians 1:3, NKJV

## | Scriptures for Further Reading:

Psalm 63:1, Psalm 145:1, Psalm 68:19, Lamentations 3:41, Ephesians 1:3, 2 Corinthians 9:8, Galatians 5:22, 1 Corinthians 12:4-11, Ephesians 2:10, Ephesians 1:5-6, Romans 8:17, Colossians 1:15 , Hebrews 1:1-2, Ephesians 1:4, Ephesians 2:4, Hebrews 7:24-25, Romans 1:16, Ephesians 3:20, 2 Corinthians 5:5, 1 Peter 1:5, Ephesians 1:1, Romans 8:29 , John 6:44, Psalm 36:10, Proverbs 19:22, Romans 8:9, Romans 5:5 , Ephesians 2:8-9, Romans 6:8, Romans 2:1

## Prayer

Heavenly Father,

Thank You for all the blessings You have already waiting for me to discover each day, revealing Your Tender Love for me. You daily load me with the Benefits of Your blessings to seek You each day. You bless me with every spiritual blessing and make all grace, every favor, and earthly blessing come to me in abundance. And giving me Your unconditional acceptance and approval without my works as Your Love Gift to me to pulls me close so I can always experience Your Tender Love's embrace.

In Jesus' name. Amen.

# CHRIST IS MY TRUE WISDOM

*You* *draw your life from living in union as one with Christ Jesus, Who has become your Wisdom from God, your righteousness, holiness, and redemption. Your heart has been knitted together in love with Him, which gives you access to all God's riches, for in Christ is your spiritual wealth hidden, all the treasures of Wisdom and Knowledge.*

*Jesus Christ is True Wisdom living within you that opens up to you the Multisided Mystery and Wonders of Grace in all their infinite, varied dimensions. A Hidden Storehouse of Wisdom is waiting for you to access it, because the Word of God, Christ Himself, lives in you. He is your Living Shield of Wisdom, wrapping you in His Heart, guiding, protecting, guarding, and implanting in you the desire to do what pleases God.*

*God's Wisdom is above all Wisdom. God alone is Wise. He has made His Word (Christ) Wisdom to you. His generous gift of Wisdom is found in every Word God speaks and becomes a fountain of understanding within you. He is always pure, filled with peace, gentle, considerate, full of mercy and good fruits, without partiality and always sincere.*

# Letter From God

Good Morning,

I Love you, My Dear, Precious, Beloved, Blessed, Special, Beautiful child of My GREAT Love. And that is what you are!

You are not limited in your knowledge and understanding. You draw your life from Me living in union as one with Christ, in Whom all the Treasures of Wisdom–Divine, Comprehensive Insight and Endless Riches of Knowledge–are hidden and stored up for you.

Jesus Christ is My True Wisdom living within you, the Heavenly Treasure Chest that opens up to you the Multisided Mystery and Wonders of My Grace in all their infinite, varied dimensions. Divine Wisdom I kept hidden from ages past as a Secret in My Heart to unveil to the angelic rulers and authorities in the heavenly realm, according to My eternal and timeless purpose.

My Hidden Storehouse of Wisdom is readily available to you, because the Word of Christ dwells in you richly, wholly filling and flooding you with all Wisdom. He is your Living Shield that follows you, protecting and guarding, implanting in you the passion for choosing what is right. Wisdom wraps you in His Heart, filling you with the knowledge of His Generous Grace.

The Wisdom I sent to you from heaven accomplishes My desires and does what pleases Me. He is above everything, priceless, imparting revelation knowledge. He is pure and peace-loving, gentle always, full of mercy and good deeds, never shows favoritism, filled with love, and is always sincere.

My Wonderful Wisdom realized and carried into effect My Secret Plan, hidden from before the ages began to bring Me Glory. He is the Word of Life, the Life-Giver, the Spirit of Life flowing through you, the Spirit of Christ Who empowers your life and lives in you—Christ Jesus, the Son of God.

Christ is Living Understanding Who gives you true success and insight into the wise plans I have designed just for you to fulfill your destiny. He living in you is the guarantee and fulfillment of My Destiny Plan for you that remains in place forever and will never fail. You belong to Christ Jesus, Who is Wisdom itself, My child.

I love you,

Daddy God. Amen.

*It is because of him that you are in Christ Jesus, who has become for us wisdom from God—that is, our righteousness, holiness and redemption.*

1 Corinthians 1:30, NIV

1 Corinthians 1:30, Galatians 2:20, Colossians 2:3, 1 Corinthians 1:24, Colossians 8:11, Proverbs 2:6-7, James 1:5, Colossians 3:16, Proverbs 2:8-9, Philippians 2:13, John 3:31, John 6:23, Proverbs 8:11, James 3:17, 1 Corinthians 2:7, Ephesians 3:11, Romans 8:9-10, Romans 8:1, Proverbs 8:14, Ephesians 2:10, Psalm 33:11, Psalm 16:5

## Prayer

Heavenly Father,

I draw my life from living in union as one with Christ Jesus. You wrapped my heart together in the fabric of His Love, which gives me access to all Your riches of Wisdom and Knowledge, which are just waiting for me to discover. Christ is my Living Understanding Who gives me true success and insight into making wise decisions, relying on His Word.

In Jesus' name. Amen.

# DISCOVER MY DEEPER LOVE

*G*od has rooted you and grounded you securely in His Deep Love to keep you strong, empowering you to discover the great magnitude of His Love and experience all its varied dimensions. Endless Love so far-reaching and deeply intimate pouring out on you, filling and flooding you with God Himself.

He never gives you a spirit of fear, but His Endless Love drives out fear and expels every trace of worry and stress because there is no fear in Love. He has given you the Holy Spirit's mighty power at work in you; He pours Endless Love into your heart and gives you a calm and well-balanced mind filled with sound reasoning to do what pleases God.

From the Beginning, God planted His Deep Love within you to be activated by His Living Water to create you into His Masterpiece. He loves you with an Everlasting Love and handpicked you out for Himself before He made the universe in eternity past to be revealed as His child, holy and blameless before Him in Love.

# Letter From God

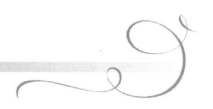

Good Morning,

I Love you, My Dear, Precious, Beloved, Blessed, Special, Beautiful child of My GREAT Love. And that is what you are!

You are rooted deep in My Tender Love and grounded securely on My Love that keeps you strong, for I am the very Source of your life. I empower you to Discover My Deeper Love released from the innermost resting place of My Tender Love, to experience all the astonishing dimensions of My Love for you.

My Endless Love is so far-reaching, deeply intimate, and beyond your heart's Greatest expectations. My Love I continuously pour into you, keeping you wholly filled and flooded with Myself, Who is Love.

My Endless Love drives out the spirit of fear that haunts you and expels every trace of worry and stress, because there is no fear in Love as I tenderly care for you. I am Love. Love can't live in harmony with fear, for Love drives out fear just as light drives out darkness. For My Love is Greater than your fear and shines through the darkness that tries to hinder and distract you.

I never give you a spirit of fear, but the Holy Spirit gives you My Mighty Power at work within you. He pours My Endless Love into your heart; that's My guarantee that I will never fail you and keep taking you deeper and deeper in My Love. My Dynamic Power gives you a calm, well-balanced mind filled with sound reasoning to do what pleases Me.

　　　　　　　LEE RICHARDS

I planted My Love deep within you, even before the foundation of the world, waiting for the proper time to send rivers of Living Waters to burst forth in your innermost being to water your New Life Seed and grow you into My Masterpiece. Yes, I have loved you with an Everlasting Love. In My Great Love, I chose you before I made the universe in Eternity Past, before the fall of Adam to be set apart for Myself, Holy and Blameless before Me in Love.

In the Beginning, My Love Possessed you as I created all things through Christ and for Him. I entrusted you to Him as My Love Gift to bring you back to Me, which He did in releasing redemption by His blood. You are now seated with Him at My side in the heavenly realms.

I gave you to Christ from the Beginning to live in union as one with Him, even as He and I are one. He clearly proved My Passionate Love for you from Eternity Past, coming from heaven to earth with all My fullness in Him to die for you to bring you back to Myself—back to its original intent, My child.

I love you,

Daddy God. Amen.

> *Each day the Lord pours his unfailing Love upon me, and*
> *through each night I sing his songs, praying to God who*
> *gives me life.*
>
> Psalm 42:8, NLT

## ▎ SCRIPTURES FOR FURTHER READING:

Ephesians 3:17-19, Psalm 42:7-8, 1 John 4:18, 2 Timothy 1:7, 1 Peter 5:7, 1 John 4:8, John 8:12, 1 John 4:18, 1 John 4:4, 2 Timothy 1:7, Ephesians 1:10, Ephesians 3:21, Hebrews 13:5-8, John 7:38, Ephesians 1:4, Galatians 4:4, Ephesians 2:10, Jeremiah 31:3, Proverbs 8:22, Genesis 1:27, Colossians 1:16, Ephesians 1:5, John 7:24, Colossians 1:14, Colossians 3:1-4, Ephesians 2:6, John 17:11 & 21, Romans 5:8

## Prayer

Heavenly Father,

Thank You for making Your permanent home in my heart. You have rooted me deep in Your Love and established me securely in Your Love. You hear my heart call to You when burdened with more than I can carry. You never fail to answer me and expel my worry and stress. I ask You to fill me through all my being with Your Endless Love, mighty power, and a calm, well-balanced mind to please You.

In Jesus' name. Amen.

# INVEST YOUR TIME WITH ME

*S*pending Time with God is your wisest investment, returning the Greatest Benefits. You gain wisdom, discover the answers you need, receive mercy for your failures, and the grace you need to help—well-timed help coming in His perfect timing. His Perfect Peace guards your heart and mind in His Presence.

The Life-Changing Effects of simply Spending Time with Him are incalculable. He created Time to demonstrate for all eternity His Love Never Changes for you. He is the Source of all things, and He fathers you in His Tender Love because you are His child, to demonstrate the immeasurable riches of His Grace and Kindness toward you.

He attracts and draws you to Himself and pulls on your heart to embrace Him through the Holy Spirit Who lives within you. The more time you spend with Him, the More Grace you see He has freely and lavishly poured out upon you. Christ's sacrifice paid the price to give you confident access to Spend Time with Him.

# Letter From God

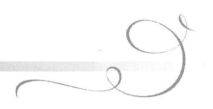

Good Morning,

I Love you, My Dear, Precious, Beloved, Blessed, Special, Beautiful child of My GREAT Love. And that is what you are!

Spending Time with Me is your wisest investment, returning the Greatest Benefits. When you Spend Time with Me, you grow in wisdom. You discover the answers you seek, you receive the Kiss of My Mercy, and find Grace to help when you need it most.

You find My Perfect Peace constantly guards your heart and mind in My Presence. I renew your strength and power, infusing you with Divine Strength. I cause you to rest and be at ease in My Tender Love, and I fill you with Joy. And at My right side, you experience the divine pleasure of being seated as one with Christ. These are just a taste of the Unending Benefits found in My Presence.

The Life-Changing Effects of simply Spending Time with Me are incalculable. I created Time to demonstrate to you My Great Love for you beginning from Eternity Past to the present, and for All Eternity to show that My Love for you Never Changes. I, being the Source of all things, had the same Tender Love for you when I shaped you in My womb, even before I stretched out the canvas of the Universe and formed the earth.

I Fathered you in My Tender Love from the beginning, just as I destined beforehand to reveal you as my child through your union with Christ—an eternal display of My Marvelous Love in all the Miracles of Mercy shown through My Grace for you. I did this to clearly demonstrate throughout the ages to come the immeasurable, infinite riches of My Grace and Kindness showered upon you in Christ Jesus.

I attract and draw you to Myself and pull on your heart to come and embrace Me. Your body has become the Permanent Home of My Holy Spirit Who lives in you. I choose to always Spend Time with you, so I constantly live in you! And I never leave you. My name Emmanuel is—God with you.

You do not belong to yourself any longer, for you are an entirely new person engrafted in Christ. I paid an Expensive Price to satisfy the redemption required of My Eternal Justice to make you My Own–the precious blood of Jesus! His sacred sacrifice offered by the power of the eternal Spirit made your Salvation Secure forever!

Now, you can come boldly and confidently into My Presence to Spend Time with Me, so that you can understand and experience all that Grace has freely given you—all the Treasures of Wisdom and knowledge, and All My Treasures you inherit that Christ is and all He has, My child.

I Love you,

Daddy God. Amen.

*Whoever walks with the wise becomes wise.*

Proverbs 13:20, ESV

## Scriptures for Further Reading:

Proverbs 13:20, Matthew 7:7, Psalm 34:15, 2 Corinthians 12:9, Hebrews 4:16, Isaiah 26:3, Philippians 4:6, Isaiah 40:31, 2 Corinthians 12:10, Psalm 16:11, Ephesians 2:6, Acts 4:12, Malachi 3:6, Hebrews 13:8, 1 Corinthians 11:12, Isaiah 44:1, 1 John 4:7, Ephesians 1:5, Psalm 107:8, Ephesians 2:7, John 6:44, 1 Corinthians 6:19, Ephesians 1:4, Matthew 28:20, John 14:17, Hebrews 13:5, Joshua 1:5, Matthew 1:23, Isaiah 7:14, 1 Corinthians 6:19, 2 Corinthians 5:17, 1 Corinthians 6:20, Colossians 1:13, Ephesians 1:7, Hebrews 9:12, 14, Ephesians 3:12, Colossians 2:3

## Prayer

Heavenly Father,

I come to spend time with You to grow in wisdom, for I know in You are hidden all the Treasures of Wisdom and Knowledge. Every word You speak is full of revelation and becomes a fountain of understanding in Your Presence. Thank You for making Your Generous Gift of Wisdom available to me, for Living within me constantly, and guarding my heart and mind with Your Perfect Peace as I partake of the Unending Benefits found in Your Presence.

In Jesus' name. Amen.

# SECURED ON MY UNSHAKABLE FOUNDATION

*Y*ou always belong to God; He is Your Creator. He is thinking about you all the time. He never walks away from you because He has made His home within you. He is your True Father, Who assumes the responsibility of your needs. And He gives you His Promise and Oath, so you know beyond a shadow of a doubt His promise will be True.

His Endless Love for you stretches beyond eternity. He will never disappoint you because you are united with Him, and He never disappoints Himself. He weaved you into the fabric of His Heart where Endless Love cascades over you because you are His Chosen, Priceless Treasure that Glorifies His Grace.

The Father Loves you with the same Love He Loves Jesus, so you know most certainly you are accepted and belong with Him as much as Jesus. Your new Life in Christ stands secured on the Unshakable Foundation of His Endless Love for you in Christ Jesus. He raised you with Christ and gave you joint-seating in heavenly places to demonstrate His Love for you.

# Letter From God

Good Morning,

I Love you My Dear, Precious, Beloved, Blessed, Special, Beautiful child of My GREAT Love. And that is what you are!

When you think you don't belong, you do! You always belong to Me. I am Your Creator; recognize the depth of the Marvelous Love I have bestowed upon you in calling and making you My Beloved child. I am thinking about you every single moment. I will never walk away from or abandon you. Never! How Could I? I have made My Home within you. Your body is now the Temple of the Living God.

I am your True Father, and you are My beloved child. I care for you and assume the responsibility for your needs from the day I formed you in your mother's womb. I give My promise and oath in a desire to show the unchangeableness of My Purpose—it is impossible for me to lie. I am Faithful to you, and every promise from Me proves to be True. I have made My firm promise and oath and follow through, even at a Great Cost.

My Endless Love for you stretches from eternity to eternity for those who trust in Me. You will never be disappointed, because you are united into the very life of Christ and woven into the fabric of My Endless Love. You are My Chosen, Priceless Treasure, set apart for Me to display My Endless Love that Glorifies My Grace.

I love you with the same love I have for My Beloved, Jesus, so you know with certainty that you are accepted and belong with Me as much as Jesus does—you are one with Us. Your life stands eternally secured on the Unshakable Foundation: *I Love you much as I Love Jesus!* Your new life in Christ is secure in My Endless Love for you. Nothing can separate you from My Endless Love for you in Christ Jesus.

When you gave your life to Christ, you became one with Us. I crucified you with Him; it is no longer you who lives, but Christ lives His life through you. He Who knew no sin died to forgive your sins through the blood of His cross, and I, raising Him back to life proves you have been made right with Me.

Now you possess the Perfect and Complete Righteousness of Christ, as I intended from the beginning, to be approved and accepted in My Eyes, Forever! And since I freely offered Him up as a sacrifice for you, I most certainly will not withhold anything else from you because you belong to Me.

There is still much more Tender Love to express. Everything is entirely new! You have been united into the very life of Christ and enjoy His Wonderful Grace. I raised you together with Him and have given you joint-seating as one with Him into the glorious perfection and authority of the heavenly realms, My child.

I love you,

Daddy God. Amen.

*For the* LORD *will not reject his people; he will never forsake his inheritance.*

Psalm 94:14, NIV

## ▌Scriptures for Further Reading:

Psalm 100:3, 1 John 3:1, Psalm 139:17, Psalm 94:14, Hebrews 13:5, 2 Corinthians 6:16, 1 John 3:2, Philippians 4:19, Jeremiah 1:5, Romans 8:29, Isaiah 44:1, Hebrews 6:17-18, Proverbs 30:5, Psalm 15:4, Psalm 103:17-18, Psalm 115:11, Romans 10:11, 1 Peter 2:6, Colossians 2:2, Ephesians 1:5, John 17:21-22, Galatians 2:20, John 17:23, Romans 8:39, Romans 4:25, Romans 8:31, 2 Corinthians 5:21, Ephesians 2:13, 2 Corinthians 5:18, Ephesians 1:5-6

## Prayer

Heavenly Father,

Thank You for reinforcing my True identity with You. You are My Creator and Father, always thinking about me all the time. I trust You Who lives in me to keep all Your Promises to me. You take care of me and assume the responsibility for my needs, being my Good Father. Your Endless Love is the Unshakeable Foundation of my life, knowing You Love me much the same as You do Jesus. So, I can face each day assured You are always with me and helping me.

In Jesus' name. Amen.

# My Own Beautiful Image

*Y*our story has only just begun. God is the Writer of your story, Who created you and shaped you into His Beautiful Image-Bearer. He knows intimately every thought and plan He has for you that gives you Great Hope in all the chapters of your life, which you now experience through His Endless Love pouring into your heart.

*From the beginning, God wrote the story of your life for all eternity, laying out each chapter and moment ahead of time before a single day took place. He directs all your steps along the path He prepared beforehand and ahead of time that you should walk in, giving you a fantastic future with a never-ending happy life in union with Christ Jesus.*

*Every single moment, God is thinking about you! He makes your life a Beautiful, Living poem of His Endless Love for you that glorifies His Grace living in union as one with Christ. He is constantly weaving every detail of your story together for good because you love Him, to fulfill the destiny He gave you to you, His Image-Bearer, a reflection of His Endless Love.*

# Letter From God

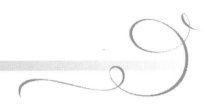

Good Morning,

I Love you My Dear, Precious, Beloved, Blessed, Special, Beautiful child of My GREAT Love. And that is what you are!

Your story is not over—it has only just begun. I am the Writer of your story, the One Who created you, the One Who shaped you into My Own Beautiful Image and created you, My Masterpiece. I called you by name, and in Love, chose you as My Own child in Christ before the foundation of the world—you are Mine.

I know the beautiful story I have written about you, every thought and plan that I have for you—

good thoughts and plans for you, and not for evil, to give you Great Hope in all the chapters of your story, which you experience through My Endless Love constantly pouring into your heart. You have a fantastic future ahead—a peaceful, prosperous future ahead for you with a never-ending, happy life in union with Christ Jesus.

From the very beginning, I wrote the story of who I created you to be, recording the number of days and laying out each moment in My Book before a single day took place. I am intimately aware of how your story fulfills the destiny I have given you, and the excellent work you do to accomplish it forever. For Eternity is My home, and I have made My home in you.

Every single moment, I am thinking of you! I am ever-mindful of you, and I bless you, indeed! You are My Delightful child; your life is a beautiful poem living in union as one with Christ in Me. I continually weave every detail of your story together for good, who is fathered by Me, for you have put your trust in My Love.

Your story I wrote from the beginning in My Perfect Plan, which I hid from ages past and kept Secret in My Heart. It was to rejoin you back to Myself in Christ Jesus, Who is My True Likeness, to fulfill your destiny to be My Image-Bearer, reflecting Who I Am into All My Creation, My Endless Love, and rule with Christ. For you are co-seated with Him into the Glorious Perfection and Authority of the heavenly realm, and will even one day govern over and judge the angelical realm, My child.

I love you,

Daddy God. Amen.

*God created mankind in his own image, in the image of God he created them; male and female he created them.*

Genesis 1:27, NIV

Genesis 1:27, Isaiah 43:1, Ephesians 1:4, Jeremiah 29:11, Romans 5:5, Psalm 37:37, Psalm 93:2, Psalm 139:16, Hebrews 2:10, 2 Corinthians 6:16, Psalm 115:12, Galatians 2:20, John 14:20, Colossians 3:3, Romans 8:28, 1 John 4:16, Ephesians 3:9, Colossians 1:15, Genesis 1:26, I Ephesians 2:6, 1 Corinthians 6:3

## Prayer

Heavenly Father,

You are the Writer of the story of my life for all eternity. It has only just begun. You created and shaped me into Your Image-Bearer to reflect Who You are into all creation. You made my life a living poem of Your Endless Love and co-seated me with Christ in the heavenly realms to govern with Him. I ask you to energize me with Your Magnificent Glory's explosive power and fill me with Great Hope, making me worthy to reflect Your Image into all Your creation.

In Jesus' name. Amen.

# DIVINE LOVE'S OVERFLOWING JOY

*G*od's Divine Love expresses the Fruit of Joy that Overflows in you and through you, produced by the Holy Spirit. Joy is a supernatural weapon, infused with Divine Strength through your union with The Lord Jesus.

*The Holy Spirit produces in you the fruit of Joy as an expression of Divine Love because you are united in perfect unity with Christ. Joy increases more and more with your deepening Friendship with God as He fills you with His Comforting Love. He causes your heart to flutter with Compassion and Mercy to live in Harmony with Him.*

*The Joy of the LORD is your Strength. You can take Great Joy in knowing He is Faithful to His Word. The Lord is your Joy and Joyous Breakthrough, Who Triumphs over all your worries and cares. He liberally fills to the full your every need; so, you always have more than enough of everything, overflowing with abundance for every good thing you do, My child.*

# Letter From God

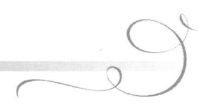

Good Morning,

I Love you, My Dear, Precious, Beloved, Blessed, Special, Beautiful child of My GREAT Love. And that is what you are!

My Divine Love produced by The Holy Spirit in you creates Overflowing Joy that moves in rhythm with every step you take. I planned All your days before you were ever born and gave you Joy as a supernatural weapon infused with Divine Strength to help fulfill the destiny I have given you, doing the Good Works I planned.

My Holy Spirit fills you with the fruit of Joy that is your Strength and Stronghold. He saturates you with inexpressible and glorious, Triumphant Joy. I give you My Joy as an expression of My Divine Love actively operating in you by the Holy Spirit, being united in perfect unity with Christ.

My Joy fills you to overflowing with My Comforting Love, which you experience for yourself more and more in your deepening Friendship with Me. I cause your heart to flutter with My Compassion and Mercy. I fill you up completely by living in Harmony with Me—with One heart, One passion, United in One Love, and All Agreeing, filling your heart with My Abounding Joy.

Joy is the spirit's Natural Response to My Grace. My Cascading Love gives your innermost being the confident assurance that Ignites in you a Cheerful Heart, and your Cheerful Heart leads you to a Cheerful Behavior and a Cheerful outcome.

Joy, unlike happiness, is not dependent on outward circumstances, but is an inner awareness of My Touch freely extended toward you to strengthen you in your time of weakness with My Presence. My Grace is always more than enough to fill you with Abounding Joy.

My Divine Love draws your heart closer and closer to ME, to soak in My Promises in My Presence as the Holy Spirit Testifies Together with your own spirit, assuring you that ALL My Promises to you have already been fulfilled in Christ with a resounding, Yes!

You can take Great Joy in knowing I AM Faithful to My Word. I am pulling you into a New Season of Joy, no longer will discouragement haunt you, for I am your Joy and Joyous Breakthrough, Who gives you Unhindered Joy, for I am always with you.

I liberally give you the delicious fruit of Joy to taste the Sweetness of My Divine Love, the ecstasy of knowing I AM your Strength, Who has Triumphed over All your worries and cares.

I liberally fill to the full your every need; so, you always have more than enough. Yes, I overwhelm you with every form of grace so that you will have more than enough of everything —every moment and in every way. I make you overflow with abundance for every good thing you do, My child.

I love you,

Daddy God. Amen.

*But may all who search for you be filled with joy and gladness in you. May those who love your salvation repeatedly shout, "The Lord is great!"*

Psalms 40:16, NLT

## SCRIPTURES FOR FURTHER READING:

Psalm 40:16, Galatians 5:22, Psalm 139:14, Ephesians 2:10, Nehemiah 8:10, 1 Peter 1:8, Galatians 5:22, Philippians 2:1-2, Hebrews 10:26, James 4:8, Romans 10:17, Romans 8:16, 2 Corinthians 1:20, Hebrews 10:23, Philippians 4:19, Psalm 23:1, 2 Corinthians 9:8

## Prayer

Heavenly Father,

You are a Joyful God, and You impart Your Overflowing Joy within me as a fruit of Your Divine Love, which shows up best when I am weak. Your Joy ignites in me a cheerful heart when discouragement haunts me. I ask You to increase my Joy by overwhelming me with every form of Grace, every favor and earthly blessing, for every good thing I do.

In Jesus' name. Amen.

# MY WORD REFLECTS YOUR TRUE IDENTITY

*G*od's Word reflects your True Identity! You are who God says you are! A New Creation in Christ Jesus that never existed before; an entirely new person united into One in His very Life and saved by His Wonderful Grace. The Holy Spirit, the Spirit of Christ, living within you now empowers your life.

God has permanently enfolded you into Christ. All that was related to your past life has passed away and no longer exists. Behold, all things are new and fresh because God made all things fresh and new in ushering in the Law of the Spirit of Life in Christ Jesus, which now governs your new life.

Now, your True Life is hidden with Christ in God. You have received the "Spirit of full acceptance," moving you to cry out intimately, "My Father! My true Father!" The Holy Spirit makes God's acceptance real to you as He whispers into your innermost being, "You are My Beloved child." He made you worthy of being called and named His child!

# Letter From God

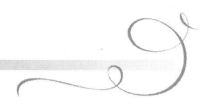

Good Morning,

I Love you, My Dear, Precious, Beloved, Blessed, Special, Beautiful child of My GREAT Love. And that is what you are!

My Word reflects who you Truly are! You perceive how I see you in the Mirror of My Word.

You are a New Creation, a New Creature Altogether, an Entirely New Person, United into the very life of Christ and saved by His Wonderful Grace. The Words I speak to you are Spirit and Life, and they give you the revelation of your True Identity that comes from ME!

You now live your life empowered by the Spirit of Christ, for the Holy Spirit Dwells within you, so you are Truly My child. My Spirit living in you released the Spirit of Sonship into your heart—moving you to cry out intimately, "My Father! My true Father!" And because you are My child, you have access to everything that is Mine—for you are My heir.

I have permanently Engrafted you into Christ as one with Him and the New Life He imparts to you. Your New Life in Christ severed the ties to this life, and now your True Life is Hidden with Christ in ME! There is no more accusing voice of condemnation, for your life is in an eternal life-union with Jesus. The Law of the Spirit of Life flowing through Him has set you free and governs your new life in Christ.

All related to your old identity in my Eyes has passed away and vanished, because I made you Completely New by your Union with

Christ and the indwelling Holy Spirit. Behold, everything has become New and Fresh because I see you wrapped into Christ, holy and blameless in My Sight, Chosen in My Love as My Own!

You are Worthy to be My child and called by My Name because I made you Worthy and filled your entire being with the richest measure of My Divine Presence. You now are filled and flooded with God, Myself! You are Most Worthy! Look at the wonder of My Marvelous Love for you that reveals your True Worthiness. I now call you and have made you My Beloved Child!

I don't ponder upon your weaknesses; I give you My Grace toward them, for My Strength and Power are in their Full Expression through your weaknesses. So, you can celebrate in your weaknesses, for when you are weak, you sense My Mighty Power at Work and Living in you. So, your weaknesses become portable to My Power.

Now you live robed with My Triumphant Power together with Christ, which is demonstrated on your behalf as I work powerfully in your Life, My child.

I love you,

Daddy God. Amen.

*He chose us in Him before the foundation of the world,*
*that we should be holy and without blame*
*before Him in love.*

Ephesians 1:4, NKJV

## ▌Scriptures for Further Reading:

James 1:24, 2 Corinthians 5:17, Ephesians 2:5, John 6:63, John 4:24, Romans 8:9, Romans 8:14, Romans 6:5, Colossians 3:3, Galatians 4:6-7, Romans 8:16, Ephesians 1:3-4, 1 John 3:1, Ephesians 3:19, 1 John 3:2, 2 Corinthians 12:9-10, 2 Corinthians 13:4

## Prayer

Heavenly Father,

Your Word reflects my True Identity of who You say I am: a new creation, an entirely new person altogether in union as one with Christ. You are alive in me, empowering and giving me access to everything that is Yours—for I am Your heir! And worthy of being called and named Your child. And that is what I am!

In Jesus' name. Amen.

# I AWAKEN YOUR HEART EACH MORNING

*G*od's Faithful Love never ends and His Tender Mercies are new every morning. He awakens you each morning to come into His Presence to be Passionately Embraced by His Tender, Unfailing Love. He Whispers His Words of Love into your heart that gives you Light.

His Word gives you a Guiding Light in your decision-making process, giving you the smooth path to take in each choice. His Light is a safe and powerful place of refuge, a proven help in time of need. His Spirit of Grace is your Faithful Friend, Who knows you intimately and helps you constantly because He is living in you.

Each morning, God awakens your heart with His Tender Love to make known His Words drenched with Grace to you and others. He empowers you by His Spirit to speak an Encouraging, Timely Word when people are weary and carrying heavy loads. Through His Spirit, you comfort others with the comfort He has given you each morning.

# Letter From God

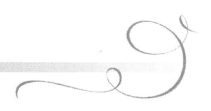

Good Morning,

I Love you, My Dear, Precious, Beloved, Blessed, Special, Beautiful child of My GREAT Love. And that is what you are!

Each Morning, I cause you to hear the revelation of My Tender, Unfailing Love. I Pull your heart closer and closer into My Passionate Embrace. I keep you ever-so-close to Me so you can hear Me Whisper Words of Love into your heart that give you Light.

My Word gives Guiding Light in your decisions and makes your path clear. My Light penetrates darkness, directing you in the way you should walk, teaching you all things, and bringing to your remembrance all I have told you. My Light is your safe and powerful place of Refuge! Your proven Help in time of trouble–more than enough and always available when you need it!

I have given you My Gracious Spirit to fill you with Myself. He is your Faithful, Unfailing Friend, Who Never Leaves you or fails you! He is your Helper, Who ends the work of the curse and saves you from all its effects! He knows you intimately because He constantly Lives with you and inside you.

I want you to know each Morning how Dearly I Love you. I have a Good Plan for your future, to give you a Glorious Hope in the Divine Destiny I planned in advance for you, and the Good Works you would do to fulfill it by the action of My Spirit Powerfully at work within you!

Morning by morning, I awaken your heart with My Tender Love. I open your ears to hear My Voice and be trained by My Spirit to make known My Words drenched with Grace to others. I have equipped you with an anointed, skillful tongue, empowered by My Spirit to speak what I have taught you to say. Especially to speak an Encouraging, Timely Word when people are weary and carrying heavy loads to comfort others with the comfort I give you.

I make you a Bright Light to drive out the dark shadows of worries, stresses, and despair. You offer others the Life-Refreshing drink from the Stream of My Love to remove the burdens of life, dissolve the fears about tomorrow, and erase the worries of today. Never Doubt My Mighty Power to accomplish this. What seems complex to you, I move with ease for you. When it looks as if there is no way, I will make a way for you.

Stop Dwelling on the past. Look into My Face and see your future. I am your Shelter of Love, Fortress of Faith, and Mighty Deliverer, Who wraps Myself around you as a Protective Shield. I am your Saving Strength, Who Infuses Inner Strength within you to conquer every difficulty.

Start your day with ME, Who Provides Wisdom, Strength, and Peace to walk undisturbed, already having All your needs for the day ahead provided by My Grace, My child.

I love you,

Daddy God. Amen.

*The Sovereign Lord has given me a well-instructed tongue,*
*to know the word that sustains the weary. He wakens me*
*morning by morning, wakens my ear to listen like one being*
*instructed.*

Isaiah 50:4, NIV

## SCRIPTURES FOR FURTHER READING:

Psalm 143:8, John 6:44, Psalm 119:48, John 14:26, Psalms 83:1, Luke 11:13, John 14:16-17, Hebrews 13:5-6, Jeremiah 29:11, Ephesians 4:4, Ephesians 2:10, Ephesians 3:20, Isaiah 50:4, Colossians 4:5, John 7:16, John 8:28, Matthew 11:28, 2 Corinthians 1:4, 1 Peter 5:7, Ephesians 3:20, Isaiah 43:19, Ephesians 6:16, Psalm 44:2, Psalm 140:6-7, Philippians 4:13, Philippians 4:19

## Prayer

Heavenly Father,

Your Faithful Love never ends; it is new every morning. You pull me close to Your Heart and wrap me with Your Passionate Embrace. Your Word is my Guiding Light in every decision, revealing the best path to take in every decision. You awaken me morning by morning with Your Tender Love to hear Your Word drenched with Grace to uplift and encourage me. You refresh My Life with Streams of Your Love that dissolve the fears about tomorrow and erase the worries of today.

In Jesus' name. Amen.

# ETERNAL JOURNEY OF INTIMACY

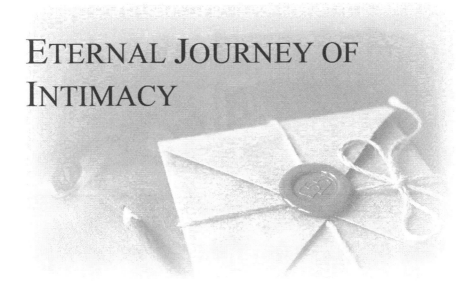

*G*od designed you to see and hear Him. However, the tyranny of the urgent in the world attempts to drown out what is Most Important, which is one of the enemy's strategies to keep you from spending time with God. Ask the Holy Spirit to guide you to what God prefers—what He Loves—and compare it to what His Word says before acting on worldly impulses.

*Relax in God's tender care and pour all your worries and stresses on Him. Fix your focus on Jesus and not the clamor of the world around you. Depend on Him to guide you with His peace, acting as an umpire in all decisions. For He has already lavishly bestowed you with Every Spiritual Blessing to provide everything He knows you need.*

*You are on an Eternal Journey of Intimacy with God. He is always embracing you and leading you with His Secret Wisdom, revealed by God's Spirit. He gives you Spirit-Charged Words from His Word that show Doors of Opportunity to make known His hidden Truths. You hear His voice speaking into your innermost being, telling you each step to take on your Eternal Journey.*

# Letter From God

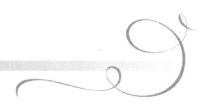

Good Morning,

I Love you, My Dear, Precious, Beloved, Blessed, Special, Beautiful child of My GREAT Love. And that is what you are!

I have given you eyes to see and ears to hear Me. I direct you throughout your Eternal Journey, pointing the correct life path to take. Come into My Presence and learn from Me. Ask the Holy Spirit to Guide you to what I would prefer you to do—what I love! Then, listen expectantly for My Response and Compare it to My Word.

Relax, hand over all your worries and stresses to Me. Be Still and realize I am your Loving Father, Who takes tender care of you, My Beloved child. Focus your eyes and ears on intentional, purposeful listening to Me, and enjoy time being in My Presence. Depend on My guidance over the other voices you hear throughout your day. My Peace will be the umpire of your mind, always available to guide you.

Look Away from All that will distract you to My Beloved Son, Jesus. He proves My Love for you by dying in your place. His Love brings you into an intimate experience with My Love, and gives you the First Incentive for your belief in Me because you trust in the Love I have for you. So, your Faith in Him becomes your Warranty, certifying that the revelation of My Love I birthed in you is true.

Hear His Voice speak into your heart, saying, "The Father Tenderly Loves you, and He is forever Faithful. The Father has entrusted Me with All that He is and all that He has so that I can unveil to you the Father's Heart toward you. And as His true child, you qualify to share all His treasures, for indeed, you are an heir of God Himself."

And since you are in union with Me, you also inherit all that I am and all that I have. Everything the Father has belongs to Me—and the Spirit of Truth, the Divine Encourager, will take the things that are Mine and will reveal it to you.

I have already lavishly bestowed upon you every spiritual blessing in the heavenly places as a Love Gift from Me. I make all grace, every favor, and earthly blessings come to you in abundance, so that you always and under all circumstances have everything you need and plenty left over to share with others as a Royal Member of My Household.

My child, you are on an Eternal Journey of Intimacy with Me. I am continually with you, and I hold your right hand. I lead you with My Secret Wisdom, revealed to you by My Spirit, Who tells you whatever He hears from Me so that you and others might realize and comprehend and experience all that My Grace has Lavishly Bestowed upon you.

I give you My Spirit-Charged Words to Reveal Truths imparted to you through My Spirit, Who Drenches them with Grace and seasons them with salt, so you are never at a loss of how you ought to answer anyone who asks a question to you.

For your Spiritual Journey, I open to you Doors of Opportunity for the Word to proclaim the Divine Revelation of the Secret Mysteries of Christ. This Mystery embedded in you is a Heavenly Treasure House of Hope hidden in Me throughout the ages, which is Christ Living in you!

You were crucified with Christ; it is no longer you who lives, but Christ living in you. He Lives His Live through you—you live in union as one! Your new life is empowered by the Faith of My Son, Who loved you and gave Himself for you.

You are My Very Own child, to whom I have released the Holy Spirit of My Son into your heart. You hear My Voice and I give you the power and desire to follow Me. I Know Everything about you. I know what you're going to say even before you say it. I know every step you take, even before your Eternal Journey Begins to Fulfill the Destiny I have Given you, My child.

I love you,

Daddy God. Amen.

> *Now this is eternal life: that they know you, the only true God, and Jesus Christ, whom you have sent.*
>
> John 17:3, NKJV

Proverbs 20:12, Psalm 55:19, 1 Peter 5:7, Psalm 46:10, Hebrews 12:2, Romans 5:8, 1 John 4:16, Psalm 27:7-8, John 16:27, Colossians 3:15, Romans 8:17, John 16:15, Ephesians 1:3, 2 Corinthians 9:8, Ephesians 2:19, Psalm 73:24-25, John 16:13, 1 Corinthians 2:12-13, Colossians 4:4-6, Colossians 1:27, Galatians 4:6, John 10:27, Romans 8:30

## Prayer

Heavenly Father,

Help me to look away from all that would distract me from Your Presence and fix my eyes on Jesus. I am entirely dependent on Your Guidance and Peace to act as umpire in my heart and settle with finality all decisions I need to make. I ask you to lead me on the best path on each step of my Eternal Journey, tenderly caring for all my needs and enjoying the fullest of Your Presence with me.

In Jesus' name. Amen.

# MY GRACE DISPOSES ME TO BLESS YOU

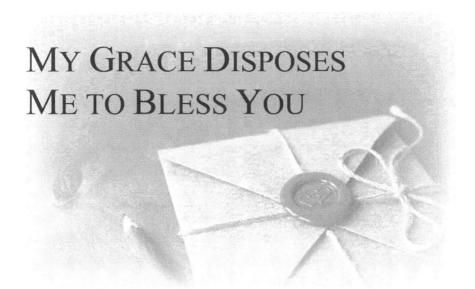

*T*he Foundation of God's Grace is His Great Love and Mercy that you can never deserve. God demonstrates His Great Love for you by bending down to give you His Unfailing Grace wrapped in His Passionate Love to pull you near into an intimate, personal relationship with Him forever!

The Gift of Grace is His eternal blessing, demonstrating the Great Magnitude of His Love that cancels your every sin. The Dynamic Power of the Holy Spirit living in you empowers your new Life, continually implanting within you His power and desire to Pursue Spiritual Realities that lead to Life and Peace.

The Spirit of Grace is your guarantee of His Acceptance that enfolds you into His Family as His Dearly Loved child. His Spirit of Life actively at work in you draws you confidently and boldly to His Throne of Grace to receive mercy for your failures and Grace to help for every need.

# Letter From God

Good Morning,

I Love you, My Dear, Precious, Beloved, Blessed, Special, Beautiful child of My GREAT Love. And that is what you are!

Grace is My Favor freely extended to you, whereby I lean Myself toward you, to always be near you to share My Benefits with you. The Foundation of My Grace is My Great Love and Mercy that you can never deserve. Therefore, I freely extend Myself to you in My Passionate Love to share the Benefits of My Grace.

This Gift of Grace is My Blessing that demonstrates My Unfailing Love is of such Great Magnitude that My Free Gift outweighs every sin. Thus, Grace is My Unmerited Gift of Acceptance that disposes Me to bless you—to come near to you, who is undeserving.

Grace's impact shows itself most effectually through the Dynamic Power of the Holy Spirit, who continually implants within you My power and desire to Pursue Spiritual Realities that lead to Life and Peace.

The Spirit of God Empowers your Life by making His Home within you. He released the Spirit of His Son into your heart. Now, Christ lives His Life in you. So even though your body may be dead because of the effects of sin, His life-giving Spirit imparts Life to you because God fully accepts you.

The Holy Spirit's power habitually puts to death the evil deeds prompted by the flesh. Now, the Spirit of Life flowing through Jesus Christ liberates you from the power of sin and death. I rescued you from the power of darkness and brought you into the kingdom of My Dear Son. In Him, you have forgiveness of your sins through His Blood.

Listen, you could never overcome the power of sin with the power of your will or through your own efforts. It requires My Power through My Grace to deliver you from the power of sin and death. Grace is My Love Gift that brought you to Christ! You could never do anything to save yourself and make yourself approved and acceptable and in the right relationship with Me.

The Spirit of Grace is your guarantee of My Acceptance. The Spirit of Adoption enfolds you into My Family as My Dearly Loved Child. I will never orphan you. I will never fail you. I will not in any way let you down. I will never abandon you because I have made My home with you and live in you.

And I Never Change My Mind about you!

Now, My Spirit of Life flows through you, having liberated you entirely from the law of sin and death. Sin no longer reigns over your Life. So, refuse to answer its call. Instead, passionately depend on My Spirit in you to answer the call of sin with My power and wisdom. Sin will not conquer you because I have already conquered it!

Now, draw confidently and fearlessly to My Throne of Grace to Receive Mercy for Your Failures. Receive My Very Kiss of Mercy on Your Life, and Discover that My Grace has already made available to you what is needed to strengthen you in every situation and circumstance in your weaknesses, and My Grace Provides your Every Need, coming just when I Know you Need It, My child.

I love you,

Daddy God. Amen.

*For it is by Grace you have been saved, through faith—and this is not from yourselves, it is the gift of God— not by works, so that no one can boast.*

Ephesians 2:8-9, NIV

## ▎Scriptures for Further Reading:

Ephesians 2:8-9, Philippians 2:13, Romans 8:4-6, Galatians 4:6, Romans 8:9-10, Colossians 1:13-14, Romans 8:13-15, Zechariah 12:10, Romans 8:15, Ephesians 5:1, 2 Corinthians 6:16, Romans 8:1, Ephesians 2:8-9, Romans 8:14, 1 Corinthians 3:3, Galatians 4:6, 2 Corinthians 5:17, Hebrews 13:5, 8; Romans 8:16, 1 John 3:1, Galatians 4:7, Romans 6:7-8, 1 Peter 1:16, Colossians 2:12, Colossians 3:1, Romans 6:4-5, 9; Romans 6:10-11, Galatians 2:20, Romans 8:2,; Romans 6:12-14, John 16:33, Romans 8:37, Hebrews 4:16

## Prayer

Heavenly Father,

Thank You for the Gift of Grace that demonstrates the Great Magnitude of Your Love for me. Your Grace has delivered me totally from the power of sin and death through the Blood of Jesus shed for me. Oh, what Marvelous Love You lavished upon me! You made me a new creation and called me Your beloved child. So, now I can come confidently and boldly to Your Throne of Grace to receive mercy for my failures and Grace to help for every need.

In Jesus' name. Amen.

# I AM YOUR GOOD SHEPHERD

*D*eclare His Promise of tender care as your Good Shepherd, "The Lord is My Shepherd, I shall not want." He liberally satisfies your every need. His Endless Love never fails to take care of you tenderly. He is your Eternal Guide in the way you should go, and guiding your heart by His Peace to decide all questions that come to your mind.

Jesus is the Good Shepherd, Who laid down His life for you to prove His Passionate Love for you. His Love for you is sealed with the everlasting covenant by the power of His Blood, stamped by the Spirit of Grace that pours His Measureless Grace upon you that is more than enough to take care of you. So, your weaknesses do not defeat you.

God knows everything about you and understands your every thought. Every moment of your life is woven together for His Glory. His Hand of Blessing is on your head, He protects you, and Favor shines upon you, wrapping you with His Unfailing Love, which is better than life itself. For His Perfect Love for you drives out and expels your every haunting fear.

# Letter From God

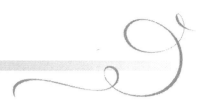

Good Morning,

I Love you, My Dear, Precious, Beloved, Blessed, Special, Beautiful child of My GREAT Love. And that is what you are!

Declare My Promise, speak My Word of Tender Care for you, saying: "The Lord is My Shepherd, I shall not want." I am your Caring Father, tending to all your needs to satisfy My Deep, Unfailing Love for you from eternity past through eternity future. I choose you to be a member of My Flock, to experience the great magnitude of My Endless Love that never fails to take care of you tenderly.

I am your Good Shepherd, liberally satisfying your every need and giving you what you desire the most. Trust Me to pull off perfectly all you have entrusted to Me, infinitely above your most extraordinary request, desires, thoughts, or hopes, exceeding your wildest imagination! I do superabundantly above them all, for My Mighty Power constantly energizes your every step.

As your Good Shepherd, I direct your life with My Eye continually upon you, directing your life and leading you in every decision you make along the way. My Spirit releases My Peace in your heart and mind, confirming with your spirit the answer you need to every question that comes to your mind. My shield of Unlimited Grace and Mercy hides you in My Strength to demonstrate the protective poser of My Unfailing Love as victorious over every situation and circumstance in your life.

I am the Great Shepherd, Who laid down my life as a sacrifice to prove My Passionate Love for you, the Author and Giver of My Peace that brought you back to Me by the Blood of Jesus Christ. I sealed in My everlasting covenant by the power of His Blood and stamped by the Spirit of Grace the Holy Spirit, Who is the Dispenser of Grace. Now, everything is new through the sacred Blood of Jesus, restoring you back to Myself to prove My Intense Love in freely giving you My Greatest Treasure.

My child, I Tenderly Care for you and watch over you all the days of your life. That is why I tell you not to worry about your life—Leave all your worries and burdens with Me, for I pour out My Measureless Grace upon you that is always more than enough to take care of you. I am continuously watching over you so your weaknesses do not defeat you. My Mighty Power rests upon you, making you stronger and sheltering you in My Tender Love. For when you're weak in human strength, you recognize more readily My Mighty Power to conquer every difficulty.

Listen, I know everything about you and understand your every thought. I never reject you. I am intimately aware of you, learning the paths which I prepared ahead of time to fulfill the destiny I have given you. My Hands weave together every moment of your life. I know how to deliver and rescue before you even know about the difficulty. As the Good Shepherd, I have gone before you to prepare the way and follow behind you to spare you from the harm of your previous path.

My Hand of Blessing is upon your head, and I am you Forever Protector. I make My Favor Shine upon you, I am gracious to you, giving you mercy for your failures, and the Approving Presence of My Peace, You have reconnected you back to Me being in union with Christ. Now, there's no wall between us; I see you holy and blameless and above reproach in My Sight.

My Unfailing Love and Glorious Grace save you from all your worries and stresses to strengthen you in your time of weakness. I gather you to Myself, carrying you in My Arms and hold you close to My Heart wrapped in My Love. I gently lead you to My Warm Embrace when you are weary and overwhelmed to refresh your life in My Tender Care because I Treasure you.

Yes, I have wrapped you in My Unfailing Love, which is better than life itself. Every time you come into My Presence, I energize and refresh you with My Power as you drink in more of My Glory. Daily worship Me Passionately with all your heart with uplifted hands as you pray. You will overflow with praise in My Tender Embrace, for the Anointing in My Presence satisfies like nothing else.

I Am your Mighty Shepherd—your Defender, Who is Forever Victorious, so there is no risk in Trusting Me. I am unable to ever fail you in any way because My Love for you Never Fails. I'm always present within you. So, don't let worry paralyze you, for I stand with you—who could ever stand against you? My Perfect Love for you drives out and expels your every haunting fear.

My Love Guarantees My Forever Care of you! So, if fear, doubt, or worry knock at the portal of your mind's door, answer with the Sword of My Spirit. Boldly proclaim through the Power of My Spirit: "I do not fret or have anxiety about anything; I do not take your fear, doubt, or worry, because my God tenderly cares for me, FOREVER," My child.

I love you,

Daddy God. Amen.

*The Lord is My Shepherd; I shall not want.*

Psalms 23:1, NKJV

LEE RICHARDS

## SCRIPTURES FOR FURTHER READING:

Psalm 23:1, Philippians 4:19, Ephesians 2:4, Ephesians 2:19, Ephesians 3:18-19, 1 Corinthians 3:8, John 10:11, Philippians 4:19, Proverbs 3:5-6, Philippians 4:7, Colossians 3:15, Psalm 91:1, Romans 8:37, Hebrews 13:20, John 10:11, Romans 5:8, Colossians 1:20, Ephesians 1:13, Hebrews 10:29, Psalm 55:22, 2 Corinthians 12:9-10, Philippians 4:13, Psalm 139:1-4, Romans 8:28, Psalm 31:15, Psalm 139:5, Numbers 6:25, Psalm 31:6, Ephesians 1:7, Colossians 1:22, 1 Peter 5:7, Hebrews 4:16, Isaiah 40:11, John 6:44, Matthew 11:28-29, Psalm 61:2-3, 1 Corinthians 13:8, Psalm 62:2-5, Hebrews 13:5, 1 Corinthians 6:19, Romans 8:31, 1 John 4:18, Ephesians 6:17, Philippians 4:6, 1 Peter 5:7

## Prayer

Heavenly Father,

You are My Good Shepherd, My Caring Father Who liberally supplies all my needs to satisfy the Great Love You have for me. You Tenderly Care for me and watch over me all the days of my life. Your Hand of Blessing is upon my head, and You make Your Favor shine upon me. You save me from all my worries and lead me to Your Warm Embrace when I'm worried or overwhelmed. There is no risk in trusting You, for Your Love Guarantees You will always take care of me.

In Jesus' name. Amen.

# YOU BELONG TO ME

*Y*ou belong to God! You are an entirely new person that never existed before. Christ lives His life in and through you. He brought you back to Himself through the Gift of IIis Son, and made you in right relationship with Him because He loves you the same as He Loves Him. You are His Special Treasure above all Treasures in Christ.

God claimed you as His Glorious Inheritance through the Sacrifice of Love, Who purchased your freedom by the blood of His cross. You are of incredible value, being one with Christ. He severed the tie to your old life. Now, your True Life is hidden with Christ in Him. You are His Beautiful Crown of Glory held high in His Hand.

God dressed you in the Worth of Jesus. He imparted His Glory to you. Now, you share the Glory the Father gave Him with you. You are His Priceless Treasure of His Endless Love for all eternity. You belong to Christ, Who is your life. He is God's Greatest Treasure Living in you, Who gives you True Worth—His Worth!

# Letter From God

Good Morning,

I Love you, My Dear, Precious, Beloved, Blessed, Special, Beautiful child of My GREAT Love. And that is what you are!

You belong to Me. Your body is now the sacred sanctuary of the Holy Spirit, Who is My Gift to you. You are no longer your own; the Life of the Spirit living within you directs you. Christ lives His life in and through you because you are an entirely new person that never existed before being joined together into one Spirit with Me.

I brought you back to Myself to Prove My Passionate Love for you. I gave My Greatest Treasure, the Gift of My Son, to be crucified once for the forgiveness of your sins and raised Him back to life to make you in right relationship with Me! I loved you even before the world began with as much Love as I love My Beloved Son and keep you safe for all eternity.

You are My Special Treasure of extraordinary value and great importance—treasure above all treasures. I bought you with an expensive, precious price, paid for in tears of blood to make you My child. Jesus offered Himself as a Sacrifice of Love to purchase your freedom from sin and back to Me by the blood of His cross. I claimed you as My Glorious Inheritance through your union with Christ, even before you were born, because of the Great Wealth I find in you, My holy one.

When you were co-crucified with Christ, your ties to your old life was permanently severed, and now your True Life is hidden with Christ in Me. Christ lives in you and through you. You are

One with Him, Who is One with Me, so you are joined together as One with Us. You are My Beautiful Crown of Glory I hold high in My Hand. I have dressed you in the worth of Christ.

Jesus' Glory has been imparted to you because you live in union as One with Me through faith in Him. He shares the Glory I gave Him with you and made you one wholly filled with Deity, the Godhead—Father, Son, and Holy Spirit—overflowing with Christ's Fullness within you. You have become My inner sanctuary where the Spirit of Glory, the Holy Spirit, constantly lives and makes His home.

You are My Priceless Treasure; I chose you out for Myself in My Endless Love before forming the Universe to be Mine for All Eternity. I am Your Creator and Redeemer, the Source of Life. You belong to Me, Who belongs to Christ. Your True Worth is found in Christ, Who is your life, My Greatest Treasure Living in you surrounding you with His Love, My child.

I love you,

Daddy God. Amen.

*You know the Lord is God! He created us, and we belong to him; we are his people, the sheep in his pasture.*

Psalm 100:3, CEV

## Scriptures for Further Reading:

Psalm 100:3, 1 Corinthians 6:19, Romans 8:9, 2 Corinthians 5:17, John 17:21-23, Galatians 2:20, Colossians 1:20, Romans 5:8, Romans 8:32, Romans 4:25, John 17:23-24, Jude 1:1, 1 Peter 2:9, 1 Corinthians 6:20, Galatians 1:4, Colossians 1:20, Ephesians 1:11, Galatians 2:20, John 14:20, John 10:30, John 17:21, Isaiah 62:3, Isaiah 61:10, John 17:22, Colossians 2:9-10, 1 Peter 4:14, Colossians 3:3, Ephesians 1:3-4, Isaiah 44:24, Romans 8:32, Titus 2:4

## Prayer

Heavenly Father,

I belong to You! I am not my own. Christ lives His life in and through me. I am an entirely new person in You. You restored me to Yourself by giving Your Greatest Treasure to make me one with You, living in Your Endless Love and safety for all eternity. Now, I am Your Special Treasure of Infinite Worth –a treasure above all treasures because I belong to Christ.

In Jesus' name. Amen.

# YOU ARE PROTECTED IN MY LOVE

*G*od has wrapped His Tender Love around you and covers you with His Glory. His Shield of Love surrounds you and continues to keep you in His Protective Presence. He keeps you safe, close to His Heart, filling your heart and soul with His Glory. God is your Strength and gives you His Grace, which is always more than enough for you.

He is your Faithful God Who keeps all His promises to you. There is nothing too difficult for Him, Who makes all things possible. He is Sovereign over all creation, and holds you firmly in His Righteous Right Hand. God has determined to stand with you; all who contend with you will be as nothing, as a nonexistent thing—conquered without a trace.

His Faithfulness always protects you, and His Mighty Power is at work within you to Protect and Preserve you in His Loyal Love. He rescues you from all the schemes of the enemy and wraps you in His impenetrable shield, hiding your life with Christ in Him. His angels protect you wherever you go and rescue you even before you know it's needed.

God is Glory and Salvation. He Protects you in His Omnipotent Love.

# Letter From God

Good Morning,

I Love you, My Dear, Precious, Beloved, Blessed, Special, Beautiful child of My GREAT Love. And that is what you are!

I have wrapped My Tender Love around you and fill you with My Glory, which penetrates your total being— spirit, soul, and body. My Shield of Love surrounds you and My Glory covers you continually. I take you into Myself and keep you safe. I am always close to you, so your confidence never weakens. I fill your heart and soul with joy—full of My Glory! So, even your body rests confidently and securely in My safety.

I am your Strength and give you My Grace to sustain you no matter what comes. Most Assuredly, I will keep My Promises to you. There is nothing to fear, for I am ALWAYS near you. Keep your gaze upon Me, for I am your Faithful God. I Infuse My Strength within you and help you in every situation or circumstance. There is no difficulty too hard for Me to conquer.

Lean on Me, Who is Sovereign over All creation. I am Who Holds you firmly with My Victorious Right Hand. None of those who oppose you will get the best of you. Nor will those you wrestle against you defeat you. The wicked will not power over you.

I crush your every adversary and do away with all who hate you. All who come against you will be ashamed and disgraced. All who contend with you will perish and disappear; they will be as nothing—as a nonexistent thing. You will look for those who oppose you in vain and find they were conquered without a trace!

I AM your Mighty God, Yahweh! I Hold your Right Hand and never let you go! I whisper to you: "I Love you and Treasure you." My Faithfulness will Always Protect you. I have placed My Great Favor upon you and fill you with My Glory such that you Overflow with God Myself.

Never doubt My Mighty Power is at work within you to accomplish all I Promise! My Miraculous Power is constantly energizing you to do superabundantly, far over and infinitely beyond your most extraordinary request, exceeding your most incredible imagination, above all that you dare ask or hope.

My Loyal Love Protects and Preserves you. Strength is your Shelter. I rescue you from every trap of the enemy and protect you from false accusations and any deadly curse! My Glory covers you, sheltering you in the covering of My Majesty. My Faithfulness shields you, keeping you from harm. I AM here to help you, My child.

I empower you through your Union with Me. You draw your Strength from Me, which My Boundless Might Provides. You stand Victorious with the Force of My Explosive Power Flowing in and through you against the realm of spiritual darkness that attempts to come against you. The demonic spirits are like arrows flying in the daytime or the pestilence that walks in the darkness; however, demonic dangers will not trouble you, nor with the powers of evil be against you.

So, never worry about an attack of demonic forces at night, nor fear the spirit of darkness coming against you. Do Not Fear a Thing! I AM with you ALWAYS! My Divine Presence Wraps around you like an impenetrable shield, able to extinguish the fiery demonic arrows coming at you from the evil one!

Your life is hidden with Christ in Me. Your body is the Temple of the Living God. Therefore, my Child, you most certainly belong to Me and have already defeated and conquered spiritual forces of darkness because I, Who lives in you is Greater than he who lives in the world.

I shelter and keep you from the harm of natural forces and supernatural forces. I disarmed the principalities and powers that were ranged against you, and made a bold display and public example of them triumphing over them in Christ and the cross.

You can only be a spectator as you witness My judgment of the wicked, as they are paid back for what they had done! For you are an inaccessible being in the secret place of My Shelter, which ALWAYS Shields you from Harm. I even send angels with special orders to protect you wherever you go, defending you from all harm. So, if you walk into a trap, they'll be there for you and keep you from stumbling.

Yes, you will walk unharmed among the fiercest forces of darkness, trampling every one of them beneath your feet! For I have given you Authority over All the power the enemy possesses, and nothing in any way shall harm you with your name written in the Book of Life.

I am your Glory and Salvation. I Protect you in My Omnipotent Love; I have gone before you to clear your pathway and make it secure. I lead you each step, and I protect you from behind, being your rearguard so that you can fulfill your destiny, My child.

I love you,

Daddy God. Amen.

*But you, Lord, are a shield around me, my glory, the One who lifts my head high.*

Psalm 3:3, NIV

## SCRIPTURES FOR FURTHER READING:

Psalm 115:10, Psalm 145:17, Psalm 3:3-4, Psalm 16:8-9, John 17:13, 1 Thessalonians 5:23, Philippians 4:13, Isaiah 41:10, Hebrews 12:2, Jeremiah 32:17, Psalm 89:21-24, Ephesians 6:12, Psalm 89:22-23, Romans 8:31, Isaiah 41:11-14, John 17:22-23, Ephesians 3:19-20, Psalm 91:14, Psalm 91:1-4, Ephesians 6:10, Psalm 91:6, Ephesians 6:16, Colossians 3:3, 2 Corinthians 6:16, 1 John 4:4, Colossians 2:15, Psalm 91:8-13, Luke 10:19-20, Philippians 4:3, 2 Thessalonians 2:14, 2 Thessalonians 3:3-5, Psalm 139:5, Psalm 85:13, Hebrew 13:21

## Prayer

Heavenly Father,

Thank You for wrapping me in Tender Love's secure embrace. Shield me with Your Love and Protect Me in Your Presence. You are My Faithful God who never leaves me and infuses Your Strength in me to stand victorious, held by Your Victorious Right Hand. For you make me more than a conqueror, demonstrating Your Omnipotent Love as my glorious victory over everything.

In Jesus' name. Amen.

# You Can Never Love Too Much

*ou can never Love Too Much, because God is your Father, Who is Love continually. His Love pours through you to the one He brings close to you and goes deeply through your union with Him to demonstrate the Great Magnitude of His Passionate Love in all its infinite dimensions to the one He Loves. Endless Love that transcends all understanding fills you to share His Love.*

*When you love, you live in God's Love and His Love is living in and through you to love others with the same Passionate Love He has for you. He puts the desire in an Imitator of His Love in everything you do that creates a sweet healing balm that gives strength and encouragement when simply verbalizing, "I Love You."*

*God's Love is the motivation behind everything you do for another. He implants within you the passion to love as He loves you and shares His Unfailing Love as a Holy Kiss direct from His Heart to the ones He loves. You are the Image of His Love to your friends, the carrier of His Love that grows within you to Love with the Passionate Love He loves.*

# Letter From God

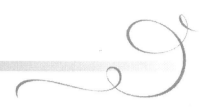

Good Morning,

I Love you, My Dear, Precious, Beloved, Blessed, Special, Beautiful child of My GREAT Love. And that is what you are!

You can never Love Too Much. I Am Love, and you have been Fathered by Me and Experience an Intimate, Personal Relationship with Me. I love you, so let My Love continually cascade from you to the one who I bring close to you. Love each other deeply, as I have loved you, even sacrificially, for you are in union with Me to love one another.

I have already brought you into an intimate experience of My Love—the Great Magnitude of My Passionate Love cascading into your heart in all its infinite dimensions. My Endless Love transcends all understanding, filling you to overflowing with myself to share the intimate experience of My Love. Trust in the Love I give you for the one I love.

When you love one another, you are Living in My Love, and My Love is brought to full expression through you so that loving one another is an expression of My Great Love that continually lives in you. When you love another with the same Passionate Love you have for Me, even the world recognizes you are alive in Union with Me.

I have put in you the desire to be an Imitator of My Love in everything you do, filling you continuously with My Great Love, to be a sweet, healing balm that gives strength and courage to another. Verbalizing Love to another signifies the depth and appreciation of your union with Me. When you tell the one I bring close to you, "I love you," I speak through you, touching their heart, demonstrating My Love to them.

My Love is the motivation behind everything you do for another, for it is Me that implants within you the passion to love as I love you. I want you to share My Love as a Holy Kiss that comes from Me. Never withhold what I treasure most, giving My Unfailing Love that pours upon you, continuing to the one I love.

I have called you to be the Image of My Love to the one I have brought close to you—your friend. You are the carrier of My Love that grows within you to love your friend with the same Passionate Love I have abundantly poured in your heart through the Holy Spirit living within you.

My Love is My Presence within you, and when you say the words, "I love you," they seep into every cell and revitalize the entire being with My Unfailing Love. When you speak My Love, your heart continually lives nourished and empowered by My Love. Love each other sincerely with all your heart and demonstrate Affectionate Love, as I Love you so that your heart will overflow with joy, My child.

I love you, Daddy God,

Amen.

*Beloved, let us love one another, for Love is of God; and everyone who loves is born of God and knows God.*

I John 4:7, NKJV

# SCRIPTURES FOR FURTHER READING:

1 John 4:8, 1 John 4:7, Mark 12:31, John 15:12-13, 1 Corinthians 6:17, Galatians 5:22, Ephesians 3:18-19, 1 John 4:16, 1 John 4:11-12, John 17:23, John 15:5, Galatians 5:1-2, 1 John 4:20-21, 1 Corinthians 16:14, Philippians 2:13, John 13:34, Romans 16:16, Psalm 42:8, Genesis 1:26, Matthew 22:39, Romans 5:5, Jeremiah 33:3, John 15:9-10, 1 Peter 1:22, 1 Peter 3:8, John 15:11-12

## Prayer

Heavenly Father,

You are Love. Thank you for giving me Your Passionate Love to pour into those You give me to love in all its infinite dimensions. I pray You would love them through me. Make me a mirror of Your Love in everything I do, and a sweet, healing balm that gives strength and encouragement by simply saying, "I love you," to those You give me to love.

In Jesus' name. Amen.

# YOU REFLECT MY GLORY THROUGH LOVE

*G*od chose you to reflect His Glory through Love. He wrapped you into Christ before the foundation of the world in Love as His child. He sent Christ into the world to reconnect you back to Himself as the pleasing sacrifice to take away your sins and experience His Love. Every detail of your life was embroidered into the tapestry of His Designed Plan to fulfill your destiny.

He recorded every day of your life in His Book before He created you to reflect His Image into all creation, revealing Who He is to the world. God made His Home in you for all eternity, flooding your entire being with His Glory. You are His Light to the world, shining the Life of Christ and God's Great Love through you.

Now, you experience Christ's Life-Giving Life and Never walk in darkness, for He delivered you entirely from darkness into the His Kingdom through His blood. You living in union with Him manifests God's Light to the world around you, for Jesus is the Light of My Love, shining within you.

# Letter From God

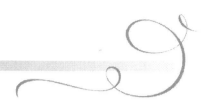

Good Morning,

I Love you, My Dear, Precious, Beloved, Blessed, Special, Beautiful child of My GREAT Love. And that is what you are!

I chose you to reflect My Glory through Love. From the Beginning, I wrapped you into Christ before I laid the foundation of the world, to be holy and blameless before Me in My Great Love for you! Just as you love your child beginning from conception, so I have Loved you. I guided your conception and knew you before I formed you in your mother's womb.

Before you were born, I chose you to be established, revealed as My Child through your union with Jesus Christ, to clearly prove My Tremendous Love and reconnecting you back to Myself by sending My Son into the world to be the pleasing sacrifice to take away your sins and to reconcile you back to Myself and experience My Love.

I care about every detail of your life. You, I created from nothing to something and embroidered into the tapestry of My Designed Plan to fulfill the destiny I have given you. I planned all the days of your life and recorded them in My Book before I created you. My Thoughts toward you are more vast than all the sands on every shore, for every single moment I am thinking about you.

I created you from the Beginning to reflect My Image into All Creation, revealing Who I AM— My Image-Bearer Who represents Me. I have made My Home in you, so I am always with you. The Light of My Presence in you floods your entire being with My Glory.

I chose you to Shine for Me. I rise within you, and the brightness of My Glory Appears over you! The Light of Christ shines upon you, and through you, giving you the very Glory and Honor I gave Him. You shine His Life into the World so that you, who Embrace Him will Experience His Life-Giving Light, and never walk in darkness, for I delivered you entirely from darkness into My Kingdom through His blood.

I made you Worthy to possess My Precious Light of My Glory as it is manifested through you, living as one in union with Christ. You are the Light of Christ to the world around you—the Light of My Presence because Jesus is the Light of My Love shining within you, My child.

I love you,

Daddy God. Amen.

*I have given them the glory that you gave me, that they may be one as we are one— I in them and you in me—so that they may be brought to complete unity.*

John 17:22-23, NIV

# SCRIPTURES FOR FURTHER READING:

Ephesians 1:3-4, Job 10:10, Jeremiah 1:5, Psalm 139:15, Ephesians 1:5, Colossians 1:20, 1 John 4:9-10, Psalm 139:1, Romans 8:28-30, Psalm 139:16-18, Genesis 1:26-27, Romans 8:29, 2 Corinthians 6:16, Matthew 28:20, Isaiah 60:1-2, Ephesians 5:14, John 17:22, Isaiah 49:6, John 8:12, Colossians 1:12-14, 2 Corinthians 4:6, Galatians 2:20, Matthew 5:14-16, 1 John 4:9

## Prayer

Heavenly Father,

You knew me before You laid the foundation of the world as Your child wrapped in Christ when You formed my innermost being with an eternal spirit woven together in my mother's womb. You created me to reflect Your Glory through Christ living in me, shining the Light of Your Love to the world to embrace Christ's Life-Giving Light.

In Jesus' name. Amen.

# CHRIST LOVES THROUGH YOU

*G*od's Mystery is Christ's Love through you. Jesus came to live within you, and you received the Power of God and the Wisdom of God, flooding your innermost being. The very life of Christ was released deep within you by the Holy Spirit, and the resting place of My Endless Love became the very source and root of your life.

Christ's Love fuels your passion and fills your heart with God's Endless Love for you. The Spirit of Christ empowers your life to know your True Identity in Him, and makes God's Love real to you who Love Christ.

The Spirit of Christ empowers your life, for you are in union with Him, Who is One with God, now, you are One with Both. Therefore, God reveals to you who you are, and I continue to make Myself even more real to you so that you may experience the same endless love that I have for My Beloved, for My love now lives in you.

# Letter From God

Good Morning,

I Love you, My Dear, Precious, Beloved, Blessed, Special, Beautiful child of My GREAT Love. And that is what you are!

My Hidden Mystery is Christ Living in you Loving through you. When Jesus came to live within you, My Passionate Love began continuously pouring into your heart through the Holy Spirit. Christ is the divine image of My Endless Love. Christ lives His Life through you, flooding your innermost being with the Power and Wisdom of God.

The very life of Christ was released deep within you by the Holy Spirit, and the resting place of My Endless Love became the very source and root of your life. Christ's Love fuels your passion and fills your heart because of His Endless Love for you. I impart to you the riches of the Spirit of Wisdom and Revelation in your deepening intimacy with Him.

The Spirit of Christ empowers your life, for you are in union with Him, Who is One with Me, now you are One with Us. Therefore, I reveal your True Identity in Him, and I continue to make Myself even more real to you so that you may experience the same Endless Love that I have for My Beloved, for My love now lives in you!

The Transforming Power of My Passionate Love changes the way you think and live your life. Now, you have My life in you! My Life-Giving Spirit imparts life to you because you are entirely accepted by Me, Holy and Blameless in My Sight with an Unstained Innocence, before Me in Love.

You live robed with My Power together with Me. You have been engrafted into Me and became an entirely new person. You were made in My image. We are closely joined together and constantly connected as One and Full of Love. Your heart is wrapped in the comfort of heaven and woven together into Love's Fabric. Now, you access have access to all My riches as you experience the revelation of My great mystery—Christ in you.

I created you because I desired to be Divinely Connected to you, sharing My Love with you. When I formed your inward parts in your mother's womb, I wove every detail of your life, every moment, and every thought together in My Love. I created you to be Loved by Me to satisfy the great and intense love I have loved you with from the beginning.

My Endless love within you fuels your passion and motivates you, producing the varied expressions of My Love toward others. You are a vessel of Love, filled with My Love flowing through you from the Holy Spirit living in you, overflowing you with the Miracle of Love that changes the lives of others, My child.

I love you,

Daddy God, Amen.

*The mystery that has been kept hidden for ages and generations, but is now disclosed to the Lord's people. To them God has chosen to make known among the Gentiles the glorious riches of this mystery, which is Christ in you, the hope of glory.*

Ephesians 1:26-27, NIV

## ▌Scriptures for Further Reading:

Colossians 1:26-27, 1 Corinthians 1:24, Romans 5:5, Colossians 1:15, Galatians 2:20, Ephesians 3:16-20, 2 Corinthians 5:14, Ephesians 1:17, Romans 8:9-10, John 17:21, 26, Ephesians 1:4, 2 Corinthians 13:4-5, Romans 1:6, 2 Corinthians 5:17, Ephesians 4:16, Psalm 139:13, Colossians 2:2-3, Ephesians 2:4, 2 Corinthians 5:14, Galatians 5:22, Romans 5:5, Colossians 1:28-29

## Prayer

Heavenly Father,

Thank You for revealing to me The Mystery of Your Passionate Love in Christ, Who floods my innermost being with the Power of God and the Wisdom of God. Christ is my Life, Who is the divine image of Your Endless Love that fuels my passion to Love through you producing the varied expressions of My Love toward others. The Transforming Power of Your Passionate Love makes me Your vessel of Love that changes the way others think and live.

In Jesus' name. Amen.

# MY GLORY IS YOUR VICTORY

*G*od's Glory within you never dims nor weakens by the evil around you. His Glory is the key to experiencing unity with others, because His Glory determines your Divine Value—you are one with God! For Christ lives within you, and the Glory the Father gave Him He has also given you. The Spirit of Glory, the Holy Spirit, living within you is the Spirit of Christ, Who releases His Glory into your heart.

For it is no longer you who lives, but Christ lives in you, Who is the Dazzling Radiance of God's Splendor and Expression of His Glory! And Who grants you out of the rich unlimited treasury of His Glory to receive His supernatural strength in your innermost being through the Holy Spirit, flooding you with His divine might and explosive power.

God has given you the Sword of His Glory to fight for you. His Lightning-Sword is strapped upon you, for He has clothed you with His Glory and His Majesty. The Sword of Glory exalts you to defend and proclaim His Word, which is the Sword of the Spirit; so Powerful, not even His greatest enemy can withstand it. His Glory in you is the Victorious power that triumphs over the world.

# Letter From God

Good Morning,

I Love you, My Dear, Precious, Beloved, Blessed, Special, Beautiful child of My GREAT Love. And that is what you are!

My Glory within you never dims nor weakens by the evil around you. For the Very Glory I have given My Beloved Son I have also given you. So that you may be One even as We are One.

For the Key to Unity among believers is experiencing My Glory. You have become a partaker of My Divine Nature; the Spirit of Glory rests upon you and dwells within you. And I have imparted within you the Holy Spirit; My Glory unites you together with Christ in Me. The Same Glory of the Spirit that connects Christ with Me joins Us and remains present with you, always.

For you in union with the LORD is mingled into ONE Spirit—the Two Made into ONE. The Spirit of God, Who is The Spirit of Glory, releases the Spirit of Christ into your heart, Who Breathes Life and Power into you to Live My Life through you, Us living in union as One!

For Christ Who lives in you is the Dazzling Radiance of My Splendor and Expression of My Glory! The Light-Being Living in you, the very out-raying of My Glory, the Spirit of God, by Whom I Made you a New Creation Altogether in union with Me through Christ.

The Holy Spirit has given you a New Birth and a New Life in Me. My Divine Mystery I revealed and unfolded for you to experience to the fullest. And it is Living within you is Christ Who floods you to overflowing with His Glory! Christ is My Mystery embedded within you, Who is a Heavenly Treasure Chest filled with all the riches of My Glory for you!

I have given you the Sword of My Glory to fight for you. My Lightning–Sword is strapped upon you, My mighty one; for I have clothed you with My Glory and My Majesty. I AM the Shield of your Help, the Sword of Glory that exalts you to defend and proclaim My Word, which is the Sword of the Spirit; So, Powerful not even My greatest enemy could not withstand it.

I have entrusted you with My Sword, Energized in Divine Power to Effectively Dismantle the Strongholds of the enemy behind which people hide, defend, and protect you as you fight successfully against all the strategies and deceits of the devil.

Use the Mighty Spirit Sword of My spoken Word that the Holy Spirit inspires you to say as I tell Him. You are not contending with human beings, but against the evil rulers and authorities in the unseen spiritual world, who hold the world in bondage. The Sword of My Living Word is full of divine energy, like the Spinning Sword of Fire held by the angel guarding the way to the Tree of Life. It radiates through you—the brilliant Light of My Glory seen in the face-to-face presence of Christ.

The Sword of the Spirit is proof the Spirit and My Power are operating on you and stirring in the minds of your hearers the holiest emotions, penetrating the very core of their being where the soul and spirit meet, and thus persuading them To Turn to Me. It interprets and reveals the true thoughts and secret motives of their hearts. And not a creature is hidden from My Sight, but all exposed and defenseless before My Eyes with Whom visible and invisible must give an account.

You are My Praise-Filled Warrior to enforce the judgments I have decreed against My Enemies. A glorious privilege is given to you, My child. For the Holy Spirit rises within you to sing a spontaneous song of holy praise with Him, filling your mouth with praises that are your weapons of war! So, you can be joyful in My Triumphant Glory and sing with Joy upon your bed.

You can be thankful that every detail of your life is woven together for the good of those who Love Me! Praise is your Warring Weapon Empowered through your Life-Union with Me, Who supernaturally infuses My Strength in you, to make you victorious with the force of My Explosive Power of My Glory flowing in and through you, My child.

I love you,

Daddy God. Amen.

*I have given them the glory that you gave me, that they may be one as we are one.*

John 17:22, NIV

## Scriptures for Further Reading:

John 17:22, 2 Peter 1:14, 1 Peter 4: 14, 1 John 4:13, Colossians 3:13, 1 Corinthians 6:17, Romans 8:9-11, Galatians 4:6, Galatians 2:20, Hebrews 1:3, 2 Corinthians 5:17, Titus 3:5-7, Colossians 1:27, Psalms 45:3, Deuteronomy 33:29, Ephesians 6:16-17, John 14:26, Luke 4:13, 2 Corinthians 10:4, Ephesians 6:11-12, 2 Corinthians 4: 3-5, Hebrews 4:12-13, Hebrews 9:12, 2 Corinthians 5:19-20, Hebrews 4:13, Colossians 1:16, Psalm 149:5-6, 9; Romans 8:26-28, 1 John 5:4

## Prayer

Heavenly Father,

Your Glory imparted to me never dims nor weakens, for You have made me a partaker of Your Divine Nature and One with the Godhead through the Blood of Jesus, forever. You made me a New Creation in Christ, flooding me with His Glory to use the Mighty Spirit Sword of His spoken Word, full of divine energy to defeat all the strategies of the devil. Your Glory in me is the Victorious power that triumphs over the world. So, Powerful, not even Your greatest enemy can withstand it.

In Jesus' name. Amen.

# Living Message of My Love

*G*od's Word is the Living Message of His Love! You experience the Marvelous Message of Love through the Holy Spirit cascading His Passionate Love into your heart when you were born of His Spirit from above. His Living Love was written in your heart and imprinted on your innermost thoughts because Christ is the Living Word living within you.

Christ in you is the Living Message of My Endless Love. The Light of His Love shines continually through you, making you a His Living Message, for you live in union as one with Him. As He is, so are you in this world. He is the manifest expression of God's Love that proves you are entirely acceptable in His Sight without one flaw, forever.

Now, you experience the Eternal Power and Divine Nature of all God's fullness overflowing in you and nourishing your heart with the same Passionate Love He Loves Christ! You share Christ's Divine Completeness—the infinite riches of God's Grace upon Grace already lavishly bestowed upon you.

# Letter From God

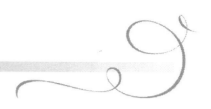

Good Morning,

I Love you, My Dear, Precious, Beloved, Blessed, Special, Beautiful child of My GREAT Love. And that is what you are!

My Word is the Living Message of My Love! Yes, My Living Message of Love is written in your heart and imprinted in your mind's innermost thoughts and near your lips. Christ is living in you, speaking through you! You now experience the Marvelous Message of My Passionate Love Pouring into your heart through the Holy Spirit living within you.

The Spirit of Christ reveals the Living Message of My Endless Love to you. I am Love, Who continually shines the Light of My Love within you, to dispense the Living Message of My Endless Love through you. For you live in union as one with Christ, Who is One with Me.

Christ is the manifest expression of My Endless Love for you, cascading in your heart. Christ living within you is your Firm Foundation of All My Passionate Love, producing these things within and for you in all His infinite expressions. Through My Spirit living in your heart, I continually overflow Rivers of Living Water through your life.

The Spirit of Christ pouring My Passionate Love into your heart proves My Life-Giving Spirit has imparted the Gift of Eternal Life to you as My Gift of Love. I made you fully acceptable to Me, which is the Living Message of My Endless Love—the same Love I have for My Beloved, Jesus, I have for you.

Endless Love beyond measure, My Extravagant Love, filling you to overflowing with the richest measure of My Divine Presence, filling you with Myself. My Living Message empowers you to experience the Great Magnitude of My Endless Love for you in all its dimensions. How deeply intimate My Love is for you.

I have lavishly bestowed upon you in Christ all My Divine Endless Love's powers, rights, and attributes. My Perfect Plan for your life was always through Christ to completely restore My Image into your heart. So, Christ living within you transforms you as you embrace His heart by moving you by the impulses of the Holy Spirit to do what pleases Me

Now, you experience the Eternal Power and Divine Nature of the Godhead—Father, Son, and Holy Spirit—and all the Fullness of Christ's Love overflowing through you His Living Message of Endless Love. He nourishes your heart with the same Passionate Love that I Love Him, empowering you by My Love as the Living Message of the heavenly treasure of Christ being embedded within you, forever.

Now, you are the Living Message of Christ, sharing His Divine Completeness—the infinite riches of My Grace upon Grace, that I have already lavishly bestowed upon you. Christ living in you is the Living Expression of My Love made visible. My Eternal Message embedded within you, Who lives His Life through you.

Being an entirely new creation, I have made all things new to you, and there is nothing that can separate you from My Passionate Love for you, which I lavishly bestowed upon in Christ Jesus. I am your Father, and I have made My home in you. No one has the power to snatch you out of My hand, My child.

I love you,

Daddy God. Amen,

*The message is very close at hand; it is on your lips and in your heart. And that message is the very message about faith that we preach: If you openly declare that Jesus is Lord and believe in your heart that God raised him from the dead, you will be saved.*

Romans 10:8-9, NLT

## SCRIPTURES FOR FURTHER READING:

Romans 10:9, Romans 5:5, Romans 10:8, Hebrews 8:10, Deuteronomy 30:14, Hebrews 10:16, Romans 8:9, John 16:15, Colossians 3:3, 1 John 4:8-9, Matthew 5:14, Colossians 3:3, Galatians 2:20, John 17:21, John 10:30, Romans 5:5, Galatians 5:22, John 7:38, Colossians 1:8, John 10:28, Titus 3:7, Romans 8:15, Romans 5:8, John 17:2-3, Romans 8:10, Ephesians 1:6, Ephesians 3:19, Romans 8:39, John 1:12, Ephesians 1:4, Colossians 1:19, Ephesians 4:24, John 1:12, Romans 8:9-10, 14, Philippians 2:13, Colossians 2:10, 1 Thessalonians 3:12, John 13:34, John 15:9-10, 2 Corinthians 5:17, Colossians 1:22, Romans 8:39, John 10:29

## Prayer

Heavenly Father,

Your Word is the Living Message of Your Passionate Love—Christ Living in me! He reveals the Living Message of Your Endless Love in and through me to bring You Glory. Thank You for shining The Light of Your Love through me into the hearts of others that they may know You Love them with the same Passionate Love You Love Christ.

In Jesus' name. Amen.

# My Love is the Power of Unity

*T*he Challenges you face make you stronger, depending on God's Grace in you to always be more than enough. For His Power finds its full expression through your challenges, relying on your Oneness with Christ to infuse you with His Explosive Power to conqueror every challenge.

Your life is hidden in Christ with God. It was always God's Perfect Plan to reveal you as His Delightful child through your union with Jesus to prove His Passionate Love is yours forever. Now, you are One in union with Him, and there is no power in all creation that can distance you from God's Passionate Love.

His Endless Love flowing from your intimate relationship with Jesus is the Power of Unity on display throughout all eternity to revealing you are His Masterpiece of Love in Christ. God rejoices over you continuously, wrapping you in His Presence with Unfailing Love that calms all your fears because you are joined to Him, Who cannot fail you.

# Letter From God

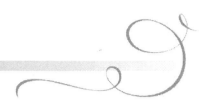

Good Morning,

I Love you, My Dear, Precious, Beloved, Blessed, Special, Beautiful child of My GREAT Love. And that is what you are!

The challenges that have come your way make you stronger because My Grace in you is always more than enough for you. My Power finds its full expression through the challenges you face, relying on your Oneness with Christ. His Mighty Strength living in you infuses you with His Explosive Power to conquer every challenge.

I am always with you. I will never abandon you or leave you or fail you in any way; I will not, I will not, I will not. I cannot! You are One with Me in Christ. Your Life is hidden with Christ in Me. I Live Complete and Total in you so that you really come to know, practically through experience for yourself, My Intimate Presence within you, joined together as One with Me.

You are joined together with Me in the same unity and Passionate Love I have for My Beloved, Jesus, which was always My Perfect Plan of Love to reveal you in union with Me through Jesus as My Delightful child. Christ proved My Passionate Love is yours forever in dying for you. Now, you are One in union with Him, and no one has the power to snatch you out of My Hands.

My Love is the Power of Unity, for in Christ, all things are held together which flow from your intimate relationship with Jesus. I am Love, and you experience My Endless Love pouring into your heart continuously through My Holy Spirit living within you. He is the Spirit of Love, Who Never Stops Loving you because you are fully accepted by Me and Loved by Me.

Trust Me, Who Loves and Treasures you. My Faithfulness will always protect you. My Hand of Great Favor is upon you because My Unfailing Love for you Never Ends. Most Assuredly, I will never, no never, lift My Faithful Love off your life. My faithful, Unfailing Love for you lasts forever. I will never disown you, because I am One with you.

You are My Masterpiece of Love, Created by My Hand of Love to visibly display throughout all the ages to come the infinite riches of My Grace and Kindness and Good, lavishly bestowed upon you living in Christ.

I rejoice over you with joy, continuously and singing. I take Great Delight in you, and My Unfailing Love calms all your fears for your life is joined with Mine. I am your safe place of shelter. My Wraparound Presence always protects you, so I am you never separated from you. So there is no risk in Loving Me. Who cannot fail you!

I am the same yesterday, today, and forever! My endless Love for you Never Changes, because I never change. My Love is all you need, for I am Love, Your Father Who Never fails you, for I never wavier in My Faithful Love to You!

Your challenges bring you closer to Me, for I Am Your Continuous Challenge Overcomer. You are One with Me, Who gives you the victory over every challenge by releasing deep inside you My Infinite Mighty Power to overcome all things, for I, living in you, is far Greater than what challenges you, My child.

I love you,

Daddy God. Amen.

*He said to me, "My grace is sufficient for you, for my power is made perfect in weakness." Therefore, I will boast all the more gladly about my weaknesses, so that Christ's power may rest on me.*

2 Corinthians 12:9, NIV

## SCRIPTURES FOR FURTHER READING:

Matthew 6:3, 2 Corinthians 12:9-10, Ephesians 2:4, Romans 8:10, Philippians 4:13, Matthew 28:20, Hebrews 13:15, John 17:22, Colossians 3:3, Ephesians 3:18-19, John 17:23, Ephesians 1:5-6, Romans 5:8, Galatians 2:20, John 10:29, Colossians 1:17, Proverbs 8:22-31, Romans 15:5-6, Romans 5:5, 1 Corinthians 6:19, 2 Timothy 1:7, 1 Corinthians 13:8, Romans 8:10, John 3:16, Psalm 62:4, Psalm 89:24, Romans 5:5, Psalm 89:33, Ephesians 2:10, Ephesians 2:7, Zephaniah 3:17, Psalm 62:6, Hebrews 13:8, Malachi 3:6, 1 John 4:8, 2 Timothy 1:13, 1 Corinthians 15:57, Ephesians 3:20, 1 John 4:4

## Prayer

Heavenly Father,

The challenges I face will never defeat me, because You are One with Me in Christ. My life is hidden with Christ in Your Intimate Presence, joined together in the same Passionate Love You have for Jesus. You will never stop loving me, because I am fully accepted and loved by You. I trust in Your Faithful Love to overcome all the challenges I face through Your Infinite Mighty Power that is far Greater than my challenges.

In Jesus' name. Amen.

# I Am the Healer of Your Heart

*G*od is the healer of your heart. He wraps you in the comfort of His Tender Love, weaving your heart together with His in the Eternal Fabric of Love to restore and revive your heart when life's challenges drain you. His Endless Love floods your innermost being, releasing deep inside you rivers of Healing Love

He is close to you when your heart is hurting, being One with your spirit. He is intimately aware of you and understands your every thought, even before it enters your heart. The Spirit of God living within you pours Healing Love into your heart. He joins together with your heart to obtain completer refreshment for your emotional distress.

Give Him your heavy heart, release the whole of your burdened heart on Him. Pour all that troubles you—worries, stresses, concerns, sorrows, and griefs—once and for all on Him, Who Always Tenderly Loves you. He kisses your heart with healing, to bind up all the wounds of your broken heart, for you are one with Him, Who is the Healer of your heart.

# Letter From God

Good Morning,

I Love you, My Dear, Precious, Beloved, Blessed, Special, Beautiful child of My GREAT Love. And that is what you are!

It is time to smile again! I am the Healer of your heart. I have wrapped you in the comfort of My Tender Love. Your heart is woven together as One with Me in the Eternal Fabric of Love. My Love restores and revives your heart when life's challenges drain you. I am your Oasis of Love, Who refreshes and cheers you up.

My Endless Love floods your innermost being, releasing deep inside you rivers of Healing Love,

the very source and root of True Rest for your heart. I am close to you when your heart is hurting, and I fully identify with your heart being One with My spirit. I read your heart like an open book; I am intimately aware of you. I understand your every thought even before it enters your heart.

My Spirit is within your spirit, pouring Healing Love into your heart and overflowing My Grace to you. I am no stranger to your emotional suffering and pain. I was despised and rejected; people turned their back on Me and looked the other way while I was being crushed for the guilt of their every sin.

I suffered the pain of your emotional distress. I did what was needed to obtain your heart's complete refreshment by joining together with you to be one with Me in your healing. By the stripes that wounded Me, you are healed *and* made whole. I am the Healer of your broken heart.

Give Me your heavy heart, release the whole of your burdened heart on Me. Pour all that troubles you—worries, stresses, concerns, sorrows, and grief—once and for all on Me, Who Always Tenderly Loves you.

I desire to kiss your heart with Healing, despite all that has happened in your life. I know the weight of the wounds that people, sickness, grief, sorrows, circumstances, the enemy, and sin have caused in your life. I see the self-condemnation the enemy puts on you in the struggles he engineers against you that kept you from living the abundant life I died for you to live.

I am your Healer, Who has healed the wounds of your broken heart. I have given you the very Heart of Jesus, Who Passionately Loves you (and proved His Healing Love by dying in your place). Now, you are one with Jesus, Who lives His life in and through you. There is no more condemning voice against you, for you are one with Jesus, the Healer of your heart, My child.

I love you,

Daddy God. Amen.

*He heals the brokenhearted*
*And binds up their wounds.*

Psalms 147:3, NKJV

Psalm 147:3, Jude 1:1, Psalm 50:5, Colossians 2:2, Psalm 23:3, Matthew 11:28-29, Ephesians 3:16-17, John 7:37, Psalm 23:2, Psalm 34:18, Hebrews 2:14, 2 Corinthians 6:17, Psalm 139:1-4, Psalm 69:5, 2 Timothy 4:22, Romans 5:5, Isaiah 53:3-4, Isaiah 53:5, 1 Peter 2:24, Isaiah 61:1, 1 Peter 5:7, Psalm 103:3, Isaiah 53:6, Ephesians 6:11-12, John 10:10, Colossian 1:12, Psalm 147:3, John 14:21, John 3:16, Galatians 2:20, Romans 8:10

## Prayer

Heavenly Father,

You heal my broken heart by wrapping Your Tender Love around me. You weave me into the fabric of your Eternal Love to restore and revive my life with rivers of Healing Love flowing with each heartbeat together as one. I release the whole of my wounds on You to kiss my heart with healing that gives me new hope and life in You.

In Jesus' name. Amen.

# MY LOVE IS GREATER THAN YOUR HEARTACHE

*G*od's Conquering Love is Greater than your heartache. Your heartache is His invitation to experience His Power and His Love to deliver you. His Love Never Fails you. And His Power is Sovereign over the affairs of your life. His Love bears up under anything and everything that comes, and it endures everything without weakening! His Love for you Never Ends!

Love Never Fails, but people fail to love because of past hurts keeping them from opening their heart fully to God's Blessing before them. Yet, God's Passionate Love for you gives you New Hope to receive His Blessing fully and walk life's paths with His arms wrapped around you. He is empowering you to Love others with the Love He gives us.

Love is your continuous healing balm, cleansing your heartache with God's Wonderful Healing Peace. It mounts guard over your heart and mind in the power of My Endless Love that transcends all understanding, calming and overflowing you with the Healing Power of His Love that refreshes, eases, and quiets your soul. Never doubt His Conquering Love to be Greater than your heartache.

# Letter From God

Good Morning,

I Love you, My Dear, Precious, Beloved, Blessed, Special, Beautiful child of My GREAT Love. And that is what you are!

My Conquering Love is Greater than your heartache. Your heartache is My invitation for My Power and My Love to deliver you. My Love Never Fails you. And My Power is Sovereign over the affairs of your life. My Love bears up under anything and everything that comes, and it endures everything without weakening! My Love for you Never Ends!

There is no part of you My Love cannot Touch or Heal. The radiance of My Joyous Love beckons you to Me. Who is Love? I AM True Love committed to conquering all that is not Love, and that is not lovely and lovable.

I have brought you into an intimate experience of My Love, and you can confidently trust in the Love I have for you. Even now, you can experience My Endless Love Pouring into your Heart through the Holy Spirit Who lives in you. He revives and refreshes your heart with My Passionate Love.

I AM healing the wounds of your shattered heart. Your Healing flows from My wounding. The fear of loss will never conquer you, for I AM close to you and lead you through all the emotions of heartache. My authority is your strength and your peace. The comfort of My Love takes away your fear. You will never be lonely, for I AM ALWAYS near you, for I am your faithful God. And My Goodness and Unfailing Love pursues you all the days of your life.

My Mighty Spirit is wrapped around you because I Love you. I embrace your heart wrapped in the comfort of heaven and woven together into Love's Fabric to cheer you up and encourage you in your union with My Passionate Love.

My Love is your continuous healing balm, cleansing your heartache, distresses, griefs, and sorrows with My Wonderful Healing Peace. It mounts guard over your heart and mind in the Great Magnitude of My Endless Love that transcends all understanding. It pours into you My Calm and fills you to overflowing with the Healing Power of My Love that refreshes, eases, and quiets your soul with My Rest to keep you whole and well.

Never doubt My Conquering Love's Mighty power to work in you and accomplish all this. I endured the torment of your emotional suffering from your painful past experiences to prove My Passionate Love for you that constantly energizes you to keep you well and whole in Me. I will always exceed all you can imagine, My child.

I love you,

Daddy God. Amen.

> *Yet amid all these things we are more than conquerors and gain a surpassing victory through Him Who loved us.*
> Romans 8:37, AMPC

Romans 8:37, 1 Corinthians 13:6-8, 1 John 4:16, 1 Peter 2:24, Psalm 147:3, Psalm 23:4, Isaiah 61:1, Colossians 2:2, Isaiah 53:4-5, Philippians 4:7, Ephesians 3:20, Matthew 11:28, 1 John 4:18, Hebrew 13:5, Isaiah 41:10, Psalm 23:6, Isiah 61:1, Colossians 2:2, Philippians 4:6, Matthew 11:28-29, Ephesians 3:20, 1 Peter 2:24, Hebrews 2:18, Romans 5:8

## Prayer

Heavenly Father,

Your Love is Greater than my heartache! I trust You to heal the deep ache of my heart with the Healing Power of Your Never Failing Love. Wrap around me Your Tender Embrace, protecting my heart as Your Passionate Love weaves into the Fabric of my Heart, healing the wounds of my past and present with Conquering Love's Mighty power to make me sound and whole again.

In Jesus' name. Amen.

# BLESSED TO BE MY BLESSING

*G*od destined you to live a Life to Bless others, even as He has Blessed you. He makes you a Bright Beacon of Hope filled with the Holy Spirit's every Spiritual Blessing already lavished upon you to dispense His Love Gifts through you. My Gifts Wrapped in My Love to satisfy the Great and Wonderful and Intense Love with which He Loves you.

He Blesses with a Spirit of Generosity to pour out Blessings to others from the Favor He saturates you.. You are His Refresher to Refresh others with Divine Love of His Living Waters, pouring into their lives: His Gifts, His Fruits, His Provisions, and His Attributes freely, especially to your brothers and sisters in the family of faith!

Keep nothing back, for He overwhelms you with every form of Grace, Favor, and Earthly Blessing. They come to you in abundance, so that you have more than enough of everything, Every Moment, and in Every Way. Your Generosity inspires an outpouring of Praise and Thanksgiving to Him for giving you a Generous Heart.

# Letter From God

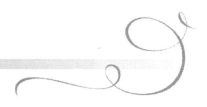

Good Morning,

I Love you, My Dear, Precious, Beloved, Blessed, Special, Beautiful child of My GREAT Love. And that is what you are!

I destined you to live a Life of Generosity, to Live to Bless others, even as I have Blessed you so that you may dispense blessings to others. Take every opportunity to be a blessing to others with every Spiritual Blessing already lavished upon you as My Love Gift by the Holy Spirit.

Being born from above of My Spirit, My impulses stir your mind's most holy emotions, thus persuading you to realize and comprehend and appreciate the Gifts of Divine Favor and Blessing I so freely and lavishly bestow upon you. All My Good and Perfect Gifts are streaming down upon you to be a Shining Light of the world—a Bright Beacon of Hope radiating out clearly amid the dark world around you.

My Gifts Wrapped in My Love and Given by Grace to you, because of My Rich Mercy, I have Lavishly Bestowed upon you, to satisfy the Great and Wonderful and Intense Love with which I Love you. For I Bless you to be a Blessing to others with the Blessings I have heaped upon you. My Spirit of Generosity I have poured out upon your Life to pour out Blessings to others, from the Favor I have saturated you with.

You are My Refresher to Refresh others with the continuous Rivers of Living Water I AM Flowing from your innermost being. I fill your heart with My Heart to Give as I Give. I called you as My

Personal Representative to demonstrate My Generosity by Living a Generous Life through the effectual working of My Generous Spirit at work within you, stirring you to do so!

Give What My Spirit has Freely Given to you: My Gifts, My Fruits, My Provisions, and My Attributes, without any strings attached. You will never out-give what My Grace provides, because I Endlessly Supply without effort more than you can imagine giving eternally.

In Giving, you find Overflowing Generous Gifts are given back to you that run over the top. Take advantage of every opportunity to be a Blessing to others, especially to your brothers and sisters in the family of faith! Then every dimension of your life will overflow with blessings from an uncontainable source of inner joy!

Give to everyone who asks; I bring them across your path for you to be a Blessing in their life as My Representative. Give what I have given you: My Love, My Time, My Grace, My Joy, My Peace, My Forgiveness, My Prayers, My Provisions, My Wholeness, My Revelation, My Fruits, and My Attributes which I have Lavishly Bestow upon you.

Keep nothing back, for I have Blessed you with Every Spiritual Blessing in the heavenly places as My Love Gift to you—for your life is wrapped with Christ in Me. Yes, I overwhelm you with every form of Grace, Favor, and Earthly Blessing that come to you in abundance, so that you have more than enough of everything, Every Moment, and in Every Way.

I make your Life Overflow with Abundant Generosity for helping others, which abundantly enriches you in every way as you can be generous to others on every occasion from what I have generously given to you. Your Generosity inspires an outpouring of Praise and Thanksgiving to Me for giving you a Generous Heart and My Endless Supply, My child.

I love you,

Daddy God. Amen.

*Give, and it will be given to you: good measure, pressed
down, shaken together, and running over will be put into
your bosom.
For with the same measure that you use,
it will be measured back to you.*

Luke 6:38, NKJV

## SCRIPTURES FOR FURTHER READING:

Ephesians 1:11, Romans 8:30, Ephesians 2:10, Genesis 12:2, 2
Corinthians 8:9, Galatians 6:1, John 3:7, 1 Corinthians 2:4-12, James
1:17, Matthew 5:14-16, Philippians 2:15, 2 Corinthians 9:8-15,
Ephesians 2:4, John 7:37-38, Philippians 2:13, Luke 6:38, Galatians
6:10, Proverbs 3:10, 2 Corinthians 9:8, 2 Corinthians 5:20, Proverbs
22:9, Romans 8:32, 2 Corinthians 9:11-13

## Prayer

Heavenly Father,

Thank You for blessing me to be a blessing to others. You have
lavished upon me already every Spiritual Blessing in the heavenly
realm as Your Love Gift to me to give to others. All Your most holy
attributes, the fruit of Your Divine Love in all its varied expressions,
and the gifts the Holy Spirit distributes and operates through me,
inspiring an outpouring of Praise and Thanksgiving to You.

In Jesus' name. Amen.

# TRUST ME EVERY MOMENT!

*G*od hears the cries of your heart and pulls on your heart to embrace Him, Who Loves you. His Wraparound Presence is your safe place that always protects you. I am your Champion Defender; there is no risk of failure with Him. So, leave all your cares and anxieties at His Feet, confidently assured He provides all you need each day.

His Measureless Grace strengthens you in your time of need; His Glory wraps around you with the Kiss of His Mercy. Arise from your bed of tears, pour out your heart before Him. Lift up your eyes and hands toward Him with Great Expectation, for He already has your answers coming just as He planned.

God pours His Unfailing Love on you to refresh your weary soul and frees you from all your fears through the Miraculous Power of Love that Never Fails to heal the wounds of your broken heart and conquer every difficulty. Drink deeply from the pleasures of His Presence. Taste and See He is Good! Always Come to Him, and His Tender Healing Love will calm your fears.

# Letter From God

Good Morning,

I Love you, My Dear, Precious, Beloved, Blessed, Special, Beautiful child of My GREAT Love. And that is what you are!

Come to Me! I hear the cries of your heart. I am the One Who Loves you. I alone am your Safe Place; My Wraparound Presence Always Protects you. I am your Champion Defender, there is no risk of failure with Me.

Leave ALL your cares and anxieties at My Feet, confidently assured I know your every thought before it enters your mind. So, knowing what you need even before you have the thought, I have planned beforehand as your Provider for all you need each day.

Most assuredly, I take care of you. My Measureless Grace strengthens you in your time of need, which gives you My Appropriate and well-timed help, coming just when you need it in your time of distress and weakness.

Trust Me EVERY Moment! My Glory is All Wrapped around! Come Boldly into My Presence where My Grace is enthroned to Receive My Mercy's Kiss. Tell Me all your troubles and pour out your heart longings to Me. Believe Me when I tell you I will Help you!

Arise from your bed of tears, pour out your heart like water before My Face. Lift up your hands toward Me with Great Expectation, for I already have what you need coming. Think about how every time I break through for you! Many will see the Miracles of My Grace bestowed upon you and will stand in awe of Me and fall in love with Me! And My Joy will pour into your heart with thankful praise lifting you up, reminding you of how you Overcame with My Victorious Power.

I have performed many Miraculous Works for you. My plans for you are too numerous to recite. I am thinking about you all the time with countless expressions of Love, far Exceeding your Expectations! My Beloved one, blessings upon blessings come to you who Loves Me and makes Me your safe place and trusts in Me.

I am pouring My Unfailing Love upon you to refresh your weary soul. I have joined your life with Mine to relieve and ease your thoughts and feelings by stirring your heart to bask in My Pleasant Presence.

I free you from all your fears with the power of My Unfailing Love. In the Light of My Presence, fear loses its grip on you. Your obstacles become your victory because your victory is My Life Released in you. My Miraculous Power is constantly energizing you to conquer every difficulty.

Drink deeply from the pleasures of My Presence. Taste and See I Am Good! Always Come to Me and rest in Me, Who has conquered all things for you.

You see, as My child, I empower you to continually conquer the distractions of the world that attempt to veil what I have already provided for you, to satisfy every need you have fully. Fix your focus on Me, and you will see I make every Grace, All Favor, and Earthly Blessing come to you in abundance so that you have more than enough for everything, in every moment, and every way.

I make you overflow with abundance in every good thing you do. Yes, you are abundantly enriched in every way, so you can be generous on every occasion with the resources I have lavishly bestowed upon you, which causes many to give thanks to Me.

Refuse to worry about tomorrow, for My Grace is more than enough for you, being continuously sufficient in you to ward off any concerns. And My Strength and My Power can do infinitely more than your greatest need and exceed your wildest imagination! I will outdo them all by the action of My Mighty Power in you, My child.

I love you,

Daddy God. Amen.

*Trust in him at all times, you people; pour out your hearts*
*to him, for God is our refuge.*

Psalm 62:8, NIV

## SCRIPTURES FOR FURTHER READING:

Psalm 62:6-8, Psalm 55:22, Psalm 139:2, Matthew 6:8, 11; Ephesians 2:10, Hebrews 4:16, Psalm 42:8, Lamentations 2:19, John 5:17, Psalm 40:3-5, 1 John 4:18, Nehemiah 8:10, 1 John 5:4-5, Matthew 11:28-30, Ephesians 3:20, Psalm 37:7, Psalm 34:8, Philippians 4:19, 2 Corinthians 9:8, 11; Matthew 6:31

## Prayer

Heavenly Father,

I run to You, Papa, to wrap Your Loving Arms around me and hold me close to Your Heart. Pour Your Unfailing Love upon my weary soul, relieve and ease my thoughts and feelings. Kiss My heart with Your Passionate Love that I may bask in Pleasant Presence, Free from the fears that haunt me by the Power of Your Unfailing Love. I release them all to You. Fill my heart with praise for Your Personal Presence with me that conquerors every worry and stress.

In Jesus' name. Amen.

# WHAT A WONDERFUL INHERITANCE!

*A*s a child of God, you share all Christ's treasures since you are one in union with Him. Now, you have the authority—power, privilege, and the right to be called My Very Own Beloved child! And that is what you are! You are God's True Heir and coheir with Christ, with access to everything God has because of what He has done through Christ!

God has blessed you with every spiritual blessing in the heavenly places in Christ Jesus, given by the Holy Spirit. You have a Wonderful Inheritance, and through your union with Christ, you have been claimed by God as His Own Inheritance. God appointed you to be born to fulfill His plan of making you His heir to the entire inheritance of His Kingdom Realm.

He alone is your inheritance, your Cup of Blessing, your Pleasure, and your Portion. He guards all that is yours and overwhelms you with the privilege that comes from being His Dear child!

Now, you have been Stamped with the Seal of His Holy Spirit, Who is the Guarantee you will receive all He promised you and purchased for you in Christ.

# Letter From God

Good Morning,

I Love you, My Dear, Precious, Beloved, Blessed, Special, Beautiful child of My GREAT Love. And that is what you are!

You enjoy the Great Reward of being My Very Own child! And because you are My child, you are My True Heir of God with access to everything I have because of what I've done through Christ! And since you are in union with Jesus, you also inherit all that He is and all the treasures He has.

My Grace has made you, a former rebel, into a Holy Royal Family Member of My Own Household, with all the rights as a family member sharing in Christ's inheritance. Look with wonder at the depth of My Marvelous Love that I have Lavished on you who received Christ! I gave you the authority—power, privilege, and the right to be called My Very Own Beloved child! And that is what you are!

You have been recreated a New Creation, a Completely New Creature Altogether, by the Holy Spirit through the Cleansing of the New Birth Poured out on you Richly by Jesus, your New-Life Giver. You have become an entirely new person. All things have become fresh and new.

I have Blessed you with every Spiritual Blessing Given by the Holy Spirit in the heavenly places. I have already lavishly bestowed upon you by the Holy Spirit as My Love Gift, All because I see you joined together and wrapped into Christ.

You have a special place in My Heart and can now experience the full inheritance of My Kingdom Realm that I Destined for you to receive from before the Foundation of the World! And because you belong to Christ, who is Abraham's Seed, then you are a True Heir of All the promised Blessings I made to Him. It was always My Perfect plan to lavishly bestow upon the cascading riches of My Extravagant Grace beyond measure through your union with Jesus.

I alone am your inheritance, your Cup of Blessing, your Pleasure, and your Portion, which I determined ahead of time to share with you. I will overwhelm you with the privilege that comes from being My Dear child! And since I freely offered Him up as the sacrifice for you, I certainly will not withhold from us anything else He has to give.

What a Wonderful Inheritance! Through your union with Christ, you have obtained this inheritance and claimed by Me as My Own Inheritance. Before you were ever born, I gave you this destiny to fulfill My plan, Who always accomplishes every purpose and goal in My Heart.

Now you have been Stamped with the Seal of My Holy Spirit, Whom I gave you like an engagement ring as a first installment of what is coming! He is the Guarantee which seals you until you have ALL the promised future inheritance, as I have indeed purchased you to be My Very Own child.

I love you,

Daddy God. Amen.

*Now you are no longer a slave but God's own child. And since you are his child, God has made you his heir.*

Galatians 4:7, NLT

## ▍Scriptures for Further Reading:

Galatians 4:7, Galatians 3:29, Romans 8:17, Ephesians 3:19, Ephesians 2:19, 1 John 3:1, John 1:12, 2 Corinthians 5:17, Ephesians 1:3, Titus 3:7, John 3:5-7, Ephesians 1:3-4, Matthew 25:34, Galatians 3:29, 1 Corinthians 1, 2 Corinthians 8:9, Ephesians 1:7, Romans 8:29, Psalms 16:5-6, Ephesians 1:11-13

## Prayer

Heavenly Father,

I am a new creation with a new life filled with rich treasures through my union with Christ.

You have Blessed me with every Spiritual Blessing Given by the Holy Spirit in the heavenly places as Your Love Gift. I share all the treasures of Christ as Your Heir. And You have stamped me with the seal of the Holy Spirit as Your Guarantee I will receive all you You promised me and purchased for me, being a joint-heir with Christ.

In Jesus' name. Amen

# I SHARE MY LOVE WITH YOU

*G od created you to share His Love with you, before the foundation of the world, even before the beginning of time. He made you in My Own Beautiful Image to experience His Endless Love, pouring into your heart through The Holy Spirit living within you. He always tells you, "I Love you!"*

*My Word and Tender Love are everlasting for you and never change! He expresses His Words of Love to you to establish firmly in your heart that His Love Never Changes. Every single moment He is thinking about you, and He Loves you constantly with His every thought. His Tender Love for you overflows with Living Waters of Love and Kindness.*

*You are His dear child now, who He has lavishly bestowed His Marvelous Love. His Divine Presence within you carefully watches over you, protects you, and preserves you against evil in this world. And His Everlasting Kingdom surrounds you for all eternity, and His Faithful Love toward you never ends.*

# Letter From God

Good Morning,

I Love you, My Dear, Precious, Beloved, Blessed, Special, Beautiful child of My GREAT Love. And that is what you are!

I created you to share My Love with you. You are My Love Gift to Myself, whom I desired in Love before the foundation of the world, even before the beginning time. I made you in My Own Beautiful Image according to My Likeness to Love and experience My Endless Love, pouring into your heart through The Holy Spirit living within you.

I chose you because of My Desire to give Myself for you and to you—so that I can Love you with Unlimited Passion to satisfy My Great and Intense Love I have for you. I always tell you, "I Love you!" My Word and Tender Love are everlasting for you and never change! I express My Words of Love to you in the same way always to establish firmly in your heart My Love Never Changes.

Every single moment I am thinking about you, and I Love you constantly in My every thought. My desires toward you are more in number than the sand on every shore, countless expressions of Love that far exceed your greatest expectations! My thoughts toward you are filled with mercy and forgiveness, for I am gracious and tenderhearted to those who don't deserve it.

My Tender Love for you overflows with Living Waters of Love and Kindness. You could never earn My Love Gift by your performance because it is My Underserved Love expressed through

My Grace. Yes, you are My Chosen Treasure I Paid for with Tears of Blood.

In Love, I chose you before the foundation of the world. I declared in eternity past that I Love you with My Everlasting Love. I Pulled your heart to embrace My Unfailing Love and Prove I Am Continuously Faithful to you.

I give you Mercy for your failures and grace to help your every need, that appropriate and well-timed help coming just when you need it, to Satisfy My Great Intense Love for you. I Love You and Keep My Word.

You Belong to Me Now, the Depth of My Marvelous Love has lavishly been bestowed upon you in calling you and making you My Beloved child! And so, you are! I am the one who guards and protects you from the evil one. Yes, My Divine Presence within you carefully watches over you and protects you and preserves you against the evil in this world, and the wicked one touches you not.

You no longer belong to this world, for you are a New Creation and already a member of My Own Household in the Kingdom Realm of My Beloved Son. I rule the entire universe so you can confidently know My Tender Love for you continues forever, My child! My Everlasting Kingdom surrounds you for all eternity, and My Faithful Love toward you never ends, My child.

I love you,

Daddy God. Amen.

> *God decided in advance to adopt us into his own family by bringing us to himself through Jesus Christ. This is what he wanted to do, and it gave him great pleasure.*
>
> Ephesians 1:5, NLT

## SCRIPTURES FOR FURTHER READING:

Ephesians 1:5, John 17:24, Ephesians 1:4, Genesis 1:26-27, Romans 5:5, John 3:16, 1 John 4:10, 1 John 4:12, Ephesians 2:4, Isaiah 43:4, Psalm 136:1, Malachi 3:6, Hebrews 13:8, Psalm 139:12, Psalm 139:18, Psalm 40:5, Isaiah 55:8, Ephesians 2:8, Psalm 145:5, John 7:38, Ephesians 2:9, 1 Peter 2:9, 1 Corinthians 6:20, Ephesians 1:4, John 6:44, Jeremiah 31:3, Hebrews 4:16, Ephesians 2:4, Deuteronomy 7:8, John 17:10-12, 1 John 3:1, John 17:15, 1 John 5:18, John 17:15-16, 2 Corinthians 5:17, Ephesians 2:19, Colossians 1:12-13, Matthew 6:10, Luke 17:21, Psalm 145:13, Psalm 136:1

## Prayer

Heavenly Father,

I embrace Your Love for me with all its Unlimited Passion each time you tell me, "I Love you!" Your Words firmly establish in my heart every single moment You are thinking about me, and Your Love for me never changes. Oh, the depths of Your Marvelous Love lavishly bestow upon me in making me Your Beloved child! And so. I am!

In Jesus' name. Amen.

# My Wraparound Presence Is Your Shield of Love

*E*very day He is with you and knows everything there is to know about you. Every moment you are wrapped in His Endless Love and Favor, and He covers you with His canopy of tender kindness and joy. His Wraparound Presence is your Shield of Love that never fails to bring you glorious victory over everything.

His Divine Love and Power makes you more than a conqueror to live confident that nothing can triumph over you or weaken His Passionate Love for you. Christ lives His Life through you, being one with Him, giving you the victory you seek. Christ Always Leads you in triumph, being wholly filled with His Fullness overflowing within you.

Your weaknesses do not limit the Power of God's Grace to strengthen you with the Mighty Power of Christ Living in you. Your human frailty never limits what God can do through you. He supernaturally infuses you with the Strength His Boundless Might Provides. His Divine Love shelters and wraps you with Himself to secure you in His Endless Love.

# Letter From God

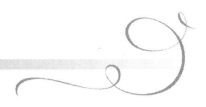

Good Morning,

I Love you, My Dear, Precious, Beloved, Blessed, Special, Beautiful child of My GREAT Love. And that is what you are!

I am always with you. Every day I am with you and know everything there is to know about you. I understand your thoughts, even before they enter your mind. Every moment you are wrapped in My Endless Love and Favor, and I cover you with My canopy of tender kindness and joy.

My Wraparound Presence is your Shield of Love that never fails to bring you glorious victory over everything. For My Divine Love and Power makes you more than a conqueror to live confident that nothing can triumph over you or weaken My Passionate Love for you.

My Love and Grace have made you a Hyper-Conqueror empowered by Christ Who no force can withstand. I stand with you in the Power of My Passionate Love in Christ Jesus that no power can ever separate you from Me. Be of Good Cheer, and Courageously confident, knowing Jesus has overcome this unbelieving world, conquering it and taking away its power to defeat you and harm you.

Christ lives His Life through you, and you are one with Him, Who gives you the victory. Christ Always Leads you in triumph, being wholly filled with His Fullness overflowing within you, the richest measure of My Divine Presence.

Your weaknesses do not limit the Power of My Grace to strengthen you through the Mighty Power of Christ Living in you, demonstrating His full expression in your weaknesses. Your human frailty never limits what I can do through you, so when you are weak in human strength, then Christ's Love for you makes your weaknesses a portal to His Divine Power.

Christ is Supreme over all rule and authority and power and dominion. I have put all things under His Authority, Who fills you completely with all the fullness of the Godhead—Father, Son, and Holy Spirit.

I supernaturally infuse you with The Strength My Boundless Might Provides through your union with Christ to stand victorious with My Explosive Power flowing in and through you. For all the Strength and Power you need flows from your union with Me! My Divine Love shelters and wraps Itself around you to secure you in My Endless Love, My child.

I love you,

Daddy God. Amen.

*God is my shield, saving those whose hearts are true and right.*

Psalm 7:10, NLT

## SCRIPTURES FOR FURTHER READING:

Matthew 28:20, Psalm 139:1-2, Psalm 5:12, Psalm 7:10, 1 Corinthians 13:8, Romans 8:37-39, Romans 8:31, John 16:13, Romans 8:10, Galatians 2:20, 1 Corinthians 15:57, 2 Corinthians 2:14, Colossians 2:10, Ephesians 3:19, Hebrews 4:16, 2 Corinthians 12:9-10, Ephesians 1:21-23, Ephesians 6:10, Psalm 62:11, Psalm 144:2, Colossians 2:2

## Prayer

Heavenly Father,

You know everything there is to know about me and understand all my thoughts before they enter my mind. You are intimately aware of me and knew every step on my journey of life before it began. Your Shield of Love and Power strengthen me when I am weak, making Your Love a portal to Your Divine Power to stand victorious in a union as one with You.

In Jesus' name. Amen.

# My Tender Love Continues Forever

*od's Tender Love for you is an Everlasting Love because you are Precious in His Sight. He Loves you dearly and proved His Passionate Love for you by Jesus dying for you. He wraps you in His Love as a visible display of the infinite riches of His Grace and Kindness showered upon you in Jesus Christ.*

*Love is your Safe Place of Shelter, for it Never Stops Believing the Best of you. Love never takes failure as defeat, for it never gives up. Love never stops loving. Love cares intimately about you because Love Connects you as One in Him. Further, His Love is Boundless, so immense, only His Spirit can reveal it to you.*

*The simple truth is God Loves you without limits. He absolutely Loves you. Love is God Himself in you, Loving through you. He births Love within you, so you can know Him—the great magnitude of His Great Love in all its dimensions. God's Love Never Fails, His Tender Love for you Lasts forever and ever!*

# Letter From God

Good Morning,

I Love you, My Dear, Precious, Beloved, Blessed, Special, Beautiful child of My GREAT Love. And that is what you are!

My Tender Love for you continues forever. Yes, I Love you with an Everlasting Love and draw you to Myself with Unfailing Love. You are Precious in My Sight; I Love you dearly. I am with you now, even closer to you than you know, so never yield to fear.

Love is inherently free to you, but I paid the Highest Price to Make Love available to you. Love is so precious it sacrifices, but it cannot be bought, sold, or traded. Love can only be received and given away. Love cannot be imprisoned because it sets the imprisoned free. Love comes by Grace Wrapped in Tender Mercy by its own will at just the right time, coming into your life just when you need it, and it is never subject to human planning or rejection.

Love cannot be turned on as a reward or turned off as a punishment. I release deep inside you the Life of Christ, which is the resting place of My Love. Love is Gentle and Consistently Kind to All. Love Refuses to Be Jealous When Blessings Come to Someone Else. Love is Not Easily Irritated or Quick to Take Offensive. Love Does Not Rejoice at Injustice, but celebrates when right and truth prevail.

Love is your Safe Place of Shelter, for It Never Stops Believing the Best of you or others. Love never takes failure as defeat, for it never gives up. Love never stops loving. Love cares intimately about

LEE RICHARDS

you because Love Connects you as One in Me. Further, My Love is Boundless, so immense only My Spirit can reveal it to you.

The simple truth is, I Love you without limits. Let this be your profession every morning when you wake up, say, "Thank You, LORD, for Loving Me so much, WITHOUT LIMITS." Because I DO!

I absolutely Love you. I birth Love within you so that you can know Me. I AM the Source of Love, giving the first incentive for your Love because I Loved you FIRST. I AM also Who brings your Love to maturity and perfection. Love Never Fails, because I guarantee Love will Last for ever and ever!

Love is God Myself in you, Loving through you. Love is not a feeling, but My Presence empowering you with the great magnitude of My astonishing Love in all its dimensions. Endless Love beyond measurement, My extravagant Love poured into you, filling you with Myself Who is Love.

My Love moves the mountains in your life, the obstacles that hinder your path. Love stops the roaring seas of your heart; so, don't fret or have anxiety about anything.

My Love heals the brokenhearted, transforms lives, and sets free those who are oppressed, downtrodden, or held captive by sin and shame. There is no condemnation in Love, for you are joined in Life-Union with Me. I Love you Dearly, because you are precious in My sight. I Love you with the same Love I Love My Beloved Son, I always accept you.

So, GREAT is My Love for you that I sent My Beloved Son to die for you so you can Live through Him. I Always Love you no matter what; there is nothing that can separate you from My Love. I have proved My Love by Giving My Greatest Treasure, the Gift of My child.

For Nothing in the Universe has the Power to Diminish My Love toward you. Absolutely nothing can ever separate you from My Endless Love—troubles, pressures, problems are unable to come between you and My Great Love for you. My love triumphs over all things and never weakens. My Passionate Love Gives you overwhelming victory and conquerors all.

Let My Love continuously nourish your heart and pour from you to one another to fulfill the destiny I have given each of you, My child.

I love you,

Daddy God. Amen.

*Love never comes to an end.*

1 Corinthians 13:8, NLV

## SCRIPTURES FOR FURTHER READING:

1 Corinthians 13:8, Jeremiah 31:3, Psalm 136:1, Isaiah 43:4-5, 1 John 4:18, Romans 8:32, 1 Corinthians 6:19, John 15:13, Ephesians 2:8, Romans 3:24, Colossians 2:2, Jude 1:1, Hebrews 4:16, Ephesians 3:17, Psalm 23:2, 1 Corinthians 13:4-7, Romans 5:5, Galatians 2:20, 1 John 4:16, Ephesians 3:17-19, 2 Corinthians 5:14, 1 John 4:16-19, Matthew 17:20, Philippians 4:6-7, Isaiah 61:1-2, Romans 8:1-2, Isaiah 43:4, Ephesians 1:6, Romans 8:37-39, John 15:9

## Prayer

Heavenly Father,

Your Tender Love is Everlasting to me, who is Precious in Your Sight. You wrap me securely in Your Passionate Love for Your Son, Jesus Christ. The same Love you Love Him with, you Love me who is living in a union as One with Him. Your Love for me is Without Limits. You absolutely Love me with Your Endless Love that gives me victory over all my worries and stress.

In Jesus' name. Amen.

# I LOVE YOU FREELY WITHOUT LIMITS

*G*od loves you without limits. His Love is the Greatest Force of all His attributes. God is Love! There is no risk of failure with Him—His Love for you never fails. Nothing can separate you from His Endless Love. He has made you more than a conqueror and able to triumph over all things because God living in you demonstrates His love for you by giving you victory over everything.

God's love fills you with Endless Love beyond measure that transcends your understanding. His love continuously pours in you, filling you with all the fullness of God, the richest measure of His Divine Presence. The Father has made His home in you, He is with you always, and you are now His dearly beloved child.

God's Love is the Single Most defining factor in an intimate personal relationship with Him and others. When you tell someone I love you, God speaks through you, touching their heart with His Love. It signifies the depth and appreciation of your union with Him and others. So, letting someone know that you love them is one of the most precious gifts you can give them.

Saying the three words 'I Love You' comes from God's heart through you to warm the heart of others and yours with His Love you share. Listen, God is whispering in your heart right now: "I love you."

# Letter From God

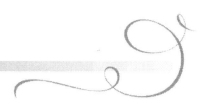

Good Morning,

I Love you, My Dear, Precious, Beloved, Blessed, Special, Beautiful child of My GREAT Love. And that is what you are!

I Love you without limits. My Love is without restrictions. My Love is the Greatest Force of All My Attributes. There is no risk of failure with Me—I AM Love! There is no force more powerful than the Endless Love I have for you, My child.

My Love for you is Bigger than you can imagine. My Love is the very source and root of your life. I have empowered you to discover and experience the Great Magnitude of My Astonishing Love in all its dimensions. How wide, how long, how high, and how deep My Endless Love is for you!

How deeply Intimate and Far-Reaching is My Love for you that Transcends your Understanding. My Endless Love continuously pours into you, filling you to overflowing through all your being with the Richest Measure of My Divine Presence, your body being Wholly filled and flooded with God Myself.

My Love is the Single Most defining factor in an intimate personal relationship with Me and others. When you tell another you love them, I speak through you, touching their heart with My Love. And verbalizing it signifies the depth and appreciation of your union with Me and others. Telling someone you know that you love them is one of the most precious gifts you can give.

Saying the three words 'I Love You' may be the most challenging words to utter and the most accepting and appreciated words for you and others to hear. The words I Love you come from My heart through you to warm the heart of others and yours with My Love you share.

At the core of your heart, I placed the desire to be loved and appreciated for who you are. It is My Love that fuels your passion and motivates you to Love and appreciate others. Your love for others is your grateful response to My Love, first demonstrated to you. When you drink of the streams of My Love for you, you will overflow with Love for others.

So, saying 'I Love You' indicates true vulnerability and appreciation for someone and the truth of your heart. Every time you share the Love I have given you for someone more fully and tell them how much you Love them, you increase your self-worth because you are reflecting My Love. The phrase 'I Love You' is a beautiful Heart-dart of Love, demonstrating you live in Love and living in Me, and I am living through you.

You will even find yourself loving people you don't like at all. For love does not come with conditions, stipulations, or agendas. Love operates independently of your fears. Love never brings fear, but Love's Perfection drives out fear far from your heart. Love does not fear because Love ultimately drives out all darkness. There is no fear in Love because there is no darkness in Light. I AM Light. And I AM Love.

I AM not the author of fear, nor do I give you a spirit of fear. My Holy Spirit living within you is the Spirit of Love, as He sealed you for all eternity in My Perfect Love. My Love continually nourishes your heart to overflowing to love others as much as I love you. My Faithful Love for you never ends, and My mercies never cease so that you can love as I love you, My child.

I love you,

Daddy God. Amen.

> *Three things will last forever—faith, hope, and love—and*
> *the greatest of these is love.*
>
> 1 Corinthians 13:13, NLT

## ❘ SCRIPTURES FOR FURTHER READING:

1 Corinthians 13:13, Psalm 62:6, 1 John 4:16, Psalm 136:2, Jeremiah 31:3, John 3:16, Romans 5:8, Isaiah 43:4-5, Ephesians 3:17-19, 1 Corinthians 13:4-8, 1 John 4:18-19, 2 Timothy 1:7, Romans 5:5, John 1:4-5, Ephesians 1:13, John 15:9, John 13:34, 1 John 4:7, 1 John 4:11, Lamentations 3:22

## Prayer

Heavenly Father,

You loved me before I knew You with the same Passionate, Endless Love you love with today and forever. There is no end to Your Endless Love, pouring into my heart through the Holy Spirit Who lives in me. For the same Love You have for Jesus, You have for me. Just as You tell Jesus, "I Love You," so do You unceasingly tell me, "I love you," filling me with Your Love to Love others as You Love me.

In Jesus' name. Amen.

# MY LOVE MAKES YOU COMPLETELY WHOLE

*G*od's Passionate Love makes you completely whole. He is faithful to keep every promise made to you and finish every good thing He began in you. His Gift of Wholeness stands guard over your heart and mind. Love that lifts off your sicknesses, weaknesses, and distresses that make you weary, for the Love Gift of His Grace bestows the blessing of Wholeness upon you.

His healing flows through your fellowship and oneness with Him, Who is your Healer. So, you can experience for yourself His Endless Love cascading in your heart through the Holy Spirit in you. He produces the Gift of My Shalom within you to restore your Complete Wholeness. There is nothing more powerful than His Love for you.

He is the Source of Love that comes to full expression in you and through you. Because He made His Permanent Home in you and gave you His Spirit to live within you so that you can have the assurance that you have come into a passionate experience with His Love. Trust in His Love for you to make you Completely Whole.

# Letter From God

Good Morning,

I Love you, My Dear, Precious, Beloved, Blessed, Special, Beautiful child of My GREAT Love. And that is what you are!

My Passionate Love makes you completely whole. My Endless Love now lives in you because I am residing within you. I keep every promise I have made to you and finish every good thing I have begun in you. I gave you My Gift of Wholeness through your Union with Me that stands guard over your heart and mind.

My Love lifted off your sicknesses, weaknesses, and distresses that made you weary, refreshing your life with My Salvation that delivered you from the penalty and power of sin into My Wholeness. I triumph over your sorrows and griefs with the Love Gift of My Grace, freely giving Myself on the cross to bestow the blessing of Wholeness to you.

I heal every wound that pierces you and remove every arrow tip of pain that lodges in your body, soul, or emotions. Your healing flows through your fellowship and oneness with Me, Who is your Healer. Now you experience for yourself My Endless Love, cascading in your heart through the Holy Spirit in you. He produces the Gift of My Shalom within you to restore you to the completeness, Wholeness, health, peace, safety, soundness, rest, prosperity, harmony, perfectness—all gifts I purchased for you.

You were an expensive purchase, paid for with the precious blood of Jesus for your Complete Wholeness, proving My Passionate Love for you. There's nothing more powerful than My

Love for you—Love that always brings healing and Wholeness. My Love continuously flows My healing Wholeness and peace that never fails.

I am the Source of Love, and My Love comes to full expression in you and through you. Because I have made My Permanent Home in you, and your permanent home in Me, and I have given My Spirit to live within you so that you can have the assurance that I live in you and that you live in Me—all in Love.

You have come into a passionate experience with My Love and Trust in the Love I have for you. I continually exist, being Love, so that living in Me while I am living in you makes you Completely Whole. And My Love Continually Pours from you to others, having your heart woven in Love's fabric together with Me.

So, drink deeply of My Unfailing Love's Water; it will quench the Eternal Thirst of your innermost being. The rivers of My Unfailing Love will Transform your Spirit, Soul, and Body, leading you into Complete Wholeness, My child.

I love you,

Daddy God. Amen.

*And now may our God, who gives peace, be with you all.*
*Amen.*

Romans 15:33, TLB

## SCRIPTURES FOR FURTHER READING:

Romans 4:6, John 17:26, Romans 5:5, Philippians 4:6-7, Isaiah 53:4-5, Matthew 8:17, Galatians 5:22, John 14:27, Romans 15:33, 1 Peter 2:24, 1 Corinthians 6:20, Romans 5:8, Romans 8:39, 1 John 4:7-20, Galatians 5:22, John 14:27, 1 Corinthians 13:8, 1 John 4:8, 1 John 4:12, 2 Corinthians 6:16, Colossians 2:2, John 7:38, Romans 12:2

## Prayer

Heavenly Father,

Your Passionate Love makes me completely whole. I trust in You to keep every promise made to me to finish the good works You prepared ahead of time to fulfill my destiny. I thank You for healing me and flowing the Gift of Shalom within me to restore the Complete Wholeness of my spirit, soul, body, and emotions.

In Jesus' name. Amen.

# DISCOVER YOUR HIDDEN TREASURES

*G*od has given us total access to Hidden Treasures in His Word, *Endless spiritual wealth and revelation, knowledge, and enlightenment stored up waiting for you to discover. He even gives you the hidden treasures of darkness and riches hidden in secret places. The revelation kept hidden is now made known to you and brought into the light.*

*As God's beloved child, you qualify to share All His Treasures, for you are His heir, and since you are in union with Jesus, you inherit all He is. His Spirit unveils the existence of every treasure within you, telling you whatever He hears from God the Father. He whispers into your innermost being, revealing the Secret Treasures that He has prepared for you to discover.*

*His Love causes you to Triumph over all things—it never fails. He proved His Love by giving you His Greatest Treasure, the Gift of His Son, so He certainly freely and graciously provides you with anything else He has for you. He fills your heart with the treasures of wisdom and the pleasures of spiritual wealth. Endless heavenly treasures are woven together in His Unfailing Love, all the riches of spiritual knowledge and Divine Wisdom with the untold riches of His Grace available to you.*

# Letter From God

Good Morning,

I Love you, My Dear, Precious, Beloved, Blessed, Special, Beautiful child of My GREAT Love. And that is what you are!

I have given you total access to the Hidden Treasures in My Word, treasures of divine wisdom, comprehensive insight into My ways and purposes, Endless spiritual wealth and revelation knowledge and enlightenment stored up, waiting for you to discover.

I go before you to open closed doors and level every obstacle that looms in front of you. My Divine Power seizes you with an earnest desire and ambition to see My Word accomplish all I want it to do and prosper everywhere I send it. I even give you the hidden treasures of darkness and riches hidden in secret places. The revelation kept hidden is now made known to you and brought into the light so that you recognize I know your name and call you My child! You will reclaim that part of your original inheritance that was stolen.

As My Beloved child, you qualify to share All My Treasures, for you are My heir, and since you are in union with Jesus, you inherit all He is, and He has as a Joint-Heir with Him. You now have direct access to My deep things and the secrets I have kept hidden for you for ages. I reveal to your innermost being these things by My Spirit. He searches out everything and shows you My deep secrets so that you can know and experience the gifts and marvelous grace I have freely given you.

Yes, you can discover and feast on All of heaven's treasures and fill your thoughts with its true realities and not the distractions of the world. Everything that belongs to Me belongs to you because we live in union as One. My Spirit unveils the existence of every treasure within you, telling you whatever He hears from Me. He whispers into your innermost being, revealing the Secret Treasures that I prepared for you to discover.

My Love causes you to Triumph over all things—it never fails. My Love and grace empower you to be unrivaled, for I stand with you, making you more than a match for any foe. So you are confident that I, being a partner in all your labors, knowing everything there is to know about you, cause every detail of your life to work together for good to fulfill My designed plan and purpose. And I proved My Love by giving you My Greatest Treasure, the Gift of My Son, so I certainly freely and graciously give you anything else I have for you.

You find the rarest treasures of Life in My Truth, much more than gold, for My Living Word is sweeter than honey dripping from the honeycomb. He fills your heart with the treasures of wisdom and the pleasures of spiritual wealth. Endless heavenly treasures are woven together in My Unfailing Love, all the riches of spiritual knowledge and Divine Wisdom with the untold riches of My Grace available to you.

Yes, I give you access to all My riches as you become progressively more intimately acquainted with and know more definitely and thoroughly the Revelation of My Great Secret of Christ, in whom is hidden your Spiritual Wealth waiting for your discovery—All the Treasures of Wisdom and Endless Revelation Knowledge, My child.

I love you,

Daddy God. Amen.

*That their hearts may be encouraged, being knit together in*
*love, and attaining to all riches of the full assurance of*
*understanding, to the knowledge of the mystery of God, both*
*of the Father and of Christ.*

Colossians 2:2, NKJV

## SCRIPTURES FOR FURTHER READING:

Colossians 2:2-3, Isaiah 45:2-3, Isaiah 55:11, Isaiah 22:22, Mark 11:23, 1 John 3:1, Romans 8:16, Galatians 4:7, Galatians 2:20, Romans 8:17, 1 Corinthians 2:10-12, Ephesians 3:9, Colossians 3:2, Deuteronomy 29:29, 1 Corinthians 3:22, Philemon 1:6, Colossians 3:2, Galatians 2:20, John 16:13-15, Romans 8:37-38, 1 Corinthians 13:8, Romans 8:31, Romans 8:28, Psalm 139:1, Romans 8:32, Psalm 19:10, Proverbs 24:4, Ephesians 1:7, 1 Corinthians 1:24

## Prayer

Heavenly Father,

Thank You for opening to me total access to the Hidden Treasures in Your Word. The Endless spiritual wealth, revelation, knowledge, and enlightenment You made ready for me to walk in. I ask that my heart filled with the treasures of wisdom, so that I may experience the gifts of the marvelous grace You have freely given me.

In Jesus' name. Amen.

# LIVING IN MY DIVINE SAFETY

*T*he God of your salvation is your Savior, Who delivers your life from death. His Wraparound Presence is the saving shield that strengthens and protects you. God always showers you with Faithful Love and Tender mercies because His compassions never cease. He delivered your life out of danger into His Divine Safety—He is your Preserver. His Word and Presence within you are the guarantees of His Divine Safety.

Before you were born, God sent His Word to the earth to heal you and make you completely whole even before you cried out for help. God sent His Word to heal you, and you were healed, delivering you from the door of death. You are immersed into life-union with Jesus and draw your life from Him. He is your oasis of Restoration.

God, your Father, takes care of you out of the depths of His Endless Love continually pour into your heart through His Holy Spirit Living within you. He is your Fierce Protector, Who keeps you in His Divine Safety. He uses what the enemy means for your harm to destroy you to refresh your life.

# Letter From God

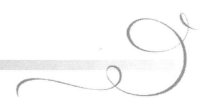

Good Morning,

I Love you, My Dear, Precious, Beloved, Blessed, Special, Beautiful child of My GREAT Love. And that is what you are!

I am the God of your salvation, Who does deliver your life from death. My Wraparound Presence is the saving shield that strengthens you, for I wrap Myself around you to protect you who I have hidden with Christ in Me. My Word of Divine Safety is your inheritance and always proves true. For I Promise to always show Faithful Love and Tender mercies to you because compassion never ceases.

I have delivered your life out of danger and the power of darkness into My Divine Safety. I am your Preserver. My Word in you is the guarantee of My Divine Safety—for My Word and I are One! Before you were born, I sent My Word to the earth to heal you and make you completely whole—spirit, soul, and body.

I know every step of your life before you take it, and I sent My Word of Divine Rescue even before you cried out for help. I spoke My Words, "Be healed," and you were healed. I delivered you from death's door to show My Marvelous Kindness and Miraculous Mercy because I love you. I did this to fulfill your destiny and to finish the ministry I assigned to you. Throughout the coming ages, you clearly show the immeasurable riches of My Grace and Kindness I showered upon you in Jesus Christ.

Jesus paid the total price for your freedom, redeeming you from the curse of the law. He bore your sicknesses and carried your diseases in His own body on the cross. He endured the punishment required for your Peace, Success, and Well-Being, and by the stripes that wounded Him, you were healed and made whole. For you are immersed into life-union with Jesus, and draw your life from Me.

I cause you to rest in My Luxurious Love and fill you with the continuous refreshment of the Healing Waters of My Spirit Flowing from your innermost being. I continually restore new strength to you, so you flourish like a well-watered garden and like an ever-flowing, trustworthy spring of blessing. I am your oasis of Restoration, the Lord Who heals you and raises you back to health through the passionate, heartfelt prayers of My believing ones.

I am your Loving Father Who takes care of you out of the depths of My Endless Love, which I continually pour into your heart through My Holy Spirit Living within you. Yes, I Am Your Fierce Protector Who keeps you in My Divine Safety. I am using what the enemy meant for your harm in trying to destroy you to refresh your life.

Yes, I did it, so you cannot boast. It is a work of my Grace revealing the infinite riches of my mercy and kindness I have showered upon you in Jesus Christ. You did nothing to earn My Divine Safety and Healing; it is My Love Gift to you paid for by the blood of Jesus so that you will never boast, for it is not a reward for your good work or human striving. Still, a visible demonstration of my marvelous kind and miraculous mercy extended to you, My child.

I love you,

Daddy God. Amen.

*He sent out his word and healed them, snatching them from the door of death.*

Psalm 107:20, NLT

## SCRIPTURES FOR FURTHER READING:

Psalm 25:5, Isaiah 12:2, 2 Corinthians 1:10, Psalm 33:22, Psalm 140:6-7, Psalm 27:1, Colossians 3:3, Proverbs 30:5, Isaiah 55:11, Lamentations 3:22, Colossians 1:12-13, John 1:1, John 10:30, Psalm 139:5, Psalm 107:20, Isaiah 53:4-5, Psalm 139:2-4, Matthew 6:8, Psalm 107:20-21, Acts 20:24, Ephesians 2:7, Isaiah 53:4-5, Romans 6:11, Romans 8:1, 1 Corinthians 1:30, Psalm 23:2, Isaiah 58:11, John 7:38, Matthew 11:28, Exodus 15:6, James 5:15-16, Romans 5:5, Psalm 23:1, Ephesians 2:8-9

## Prayer

Heavenly Father,

You are the God of My salvation, Who saves me from danger and delivers me into the Divine Safety of Your Presence far away from all evil, harm, and disaster to the highest spiritual blessings. Jesus bore my sicknesses, weaknesses, and distresses and carried my diseases in His own body on the cross. By the stripes that wounded Him and your Resurrection Power living in me, You make me whole and healthy again.

In Jesus' name. Amen.

# I Breathed New Life into Your Dreams

*G*od breathes New Life into the desires of your heart, causing you to dream new dreams He planned for you to accomplish your destiny. Never doubt His Mighty Power at work effectually working within you to implant and accomplish the Passion and Desire to achieve the Good Works He destined you to achieve.

He causes you to pursue and crave His Unfailing Love and Mercy to fulfill all the Dreams He has Planned for you to achieve. He drenches you with His Favor and Rivers of Living Water bursting out from within you that overflows with satisfaction that bathes you in His Light Bursting through that darkness cannot overcome!

His Glory covers you from your Past and Protects you today and forever to fulfill the Dreams He has written in your heart. You are joined with Him Who gives you His Mind, and you now hold the thoughts, feelings, and purposes of His Heart. His Unfailing Love supports you; His Fiery Love is stirring you, overwhelming you with every form of Grace so that you will achieve the Dreams He planted in your heart.

# Letter From God

Good Morning,

I Love you, My Dear, Precious, Beloved, Blessed, Special, Beautiful child of My GREAT Love. And that is what you are!

I breathe New Life into the desires of your heart. I cause you to dream new dreams. My Dreams for your life will come to pass, just as I planned beforehand for you to accomplish and achieve by the effectual working of My Mighty Strength empowering and continually revitalizing you, implanting within you the Passion and Desire to achieve the Good Works I destined you to achieve.

I cause you to pursue and crave My Unfailing Love and Mercy to fulfill all the Dreams I have Planned for you to achieve, along with Good Works—ALL will Come True. I have given you an Abundant Life drenched with Favor and Rivers of Living Water, bursting out from within you that overflows with satisfaction.

My Favor bathes you in Sonlight until My Light Bursts through your dark night—Light that darkness cannot overcome! Then suddenly, your healing, the restoration of your body, soul, and spirit, and the Power of New Life sprouts forth rapidly, making you Righteous in My Sight.

For My Righteousness is your Righteousness. I recreated you to be in Right Standing Relationship with Me, Approved and Accepted by Me, which puts you in a Right Personal Relationship with Me, by My Goodness.

I am your Protector and Provider. I go out before you, Leading you in My Peace that mounts guard over your heart and mind and acts as an umpire in your heart, settling with finality all questions that arise in your mind.

And I have given you My Glory that covers you from your Past and Protects you today and forever, to fulfill the Dreams I have written in your heart. For you have My Mind and hold the thoughts, feelings, and purposes of My Heart. I have joined you with Me as One giving you My Glory, which goes before you and follows you like your front and rear guard.

My Unfailing Love supports you; My Fiery Love is stirred to aid and assist you, overwhelming, with more than enough for everything through the Superabounding Grace cascading over you, every moment, in every way. I make My Favor and earthly blessing come to you so that you always have everything you need with plenty left over to minister to others.

I make you overflow in abundance to achieve every good work, being completely self-sufficient in Me. Yes, I fully satisfy every need you have out of the abundance of My Glory to fulfill all the dreams I have implanted in your heart, My child.

I love you,

Daddy God. Amen.

*Delight yourself also in the Lord, and He will give you the desires and secret petitions of your heart.*

Psalm 37:4, AMPC

## SCRIPTURES FOR FURTHER READING:

Psalm 37:4-5, Psalm 139:16, Ephesians 3:20, Philippians 2:13, Ephesians 2:10, Proverbs 21:21, John 7:37-38, John 1:5, Isaiah 58:8, Philippians 4:6-7, 2 Corinthians 5:21, John 17:17, Psalm 94:19, Philippians 4:19, 2 Corinthians 9:8-11

## Prayer

Heavenly Father,

I fix my heart on You, Who breathes New Life into the desires of my heart, causing me to dream new dreams, dreams You have Planned for me to achieve. I give you the right to direct my Life, knowing You will complete them all perfectly! I trust and rely confidently in You.

In Jesus' name. Amen.

# YOU ARE HOLY IN MY SIGHT

*G*od's Holiness Lives in you, for Christ is your life, Who is One with God. You are Holy because He is Holy. Holiness is God's Essence. Now the Essence of your New Life is Him Living within you. You have been engrafted into Christ as a New Creation and become an entirely New Person. The Law of the Spirit of Life flowing through Christ Jesus has set you free from the law of sin and death.

Because of God's Great Love for you, He actually picked you out for Himself as His Own before the foundation of the world to be Holy, Consecrated, Set Apart, and Blameless in His Sight with an Unstained Innocence for All Eternity. He reconnected you back to Himself and released His Supernatural Peace to you so that you would dwell in My Presence in complete confidence.

God is not ashamed or embarrassed to name you and call you and count you and introduce you as His holy child! And you are! Now, there is no more dividing wall between Him and you, for He sees you as Holy—Flawless, Irreproachable, and Restored to Himself without defect, cleansed by the Blood of Jesus on the cross.

# Letter From God

Good Morning,

I Love you, My Dear, Precious, Beloved, Blessed, Special, Beautiful child of My GREAT Love. And that is what you are!

My Holiness Lives in you, for I AM Living in you. You are Holy because I AM Holy. Holiness is My Essence. Everything that belongs to Me is Holy. Holiness is not a mere action or standard or set of behaviors you are to achieve on your own, but I Myself living within you and through you—Who is Holy!

Now the Essence of your New Life is Me. We live in Union as One. You have been engrafted into Me. You have been recreated a New Creation, a New Creature Altogether, and become an entirely New Person in whom I Live. All That Was Related to the Old you is Gone. Behold, All Things are new and fresh. The Law of the Spirit of Life, which is in Me, flows through you. The Law of your new being has set you free from the law of sin and death.

In My Love, I chose you, actually picked you out for Myself as My Own before the foundation of the world, to be Holy, Consecrated, and Set Apart for Me, and Blameless in My Sight with an Unstained Innocence for All Eternity.

Further, I made you My Own child through your Union with Me, having reconciled you back to Myself by the Blood of the Cross. I reconnected you back to Myself and Released My Supernatural Peace to you so that you would dwell in My Presence in complete confidence.

LEE RICHARDS

For now, there is nothing between you and Me, for I see you as Holy, Flawless, Irreproachable, and Restored. And what I have cleansed by Jesus' Blood and Filled with My Spirit and made Holy by My Presence is Holy Indeed!

I am your Father Who made you Holy, and I am not ashamed or embarrassed to name you and call you and count you and introduce you as My Holy Child! And you are! For it was in accordance with My eternal and timeless purpose that I carried your Purification into effect through the person of Christ Jesus your Lord. I have made you Holy Once and for all through His Own Body and Sacred Blood, making you Eternally Holy, My child.

I love you,

Daddy God. Amen.

*Just as He chose us in Him before the foundation of the world, that we should be holy and without blame before Him in love.*

Ephesians 1:4, NKJV

# SCRIPTURES FOR FURTHER READING:

1 Corinthians 6:19, 1 Peter 1:16, 2 Corinthians 5:17, Romans 8:2, Ephesians 1:4-7, Luke 1:75, Colossians 1:20-22, 2 Corinthians 5:18, Ephesians 3:12, Romans 5:10-11, Hebrews 2:11, 1 John 3:1-2, Hebrews 9:12, Hebrews 10:10, Ephesians 3:11

## Prayer

Heavenly Father,

In Your Great Love, You chose me in Christ as Your Own before laying the foundation of the world to be holy and blameless in Your sight. I have been engrafted into Christ as a New Creation, and I have become an entirely New Person. And You are not ashamed or embarrassed to name and call and count me and introduce me as Your child! And that is what I am!

In Jesus' name. Amen.

# NEVER FORGET I AM WITH YOU

*G*od's Nurturing Love for you is gentle and tender, a fountain of abounding grace and mercy that fills you with His Strength. He sends a miraculous sign of favor to put to shame those who hate you. Never forget He is with you always and protects you wherever you go. He never abandons you nor fails you in any way or relaxes His hold on you.

He is your Helper Who responds quickly to your critical, urgent need with well-timed help. He acts in your favor, and no one can reverse it, for Greater is He living within you than he who is in the world. He is among those who help you. And He defeats all the enemy's strategies against you.

As the Upholder of your life, God leans into your heart and lays His Hands upon you! He is Forever Faithful. God infuses you with His strength and helps you in every situation. He commands blessing upon you, on everything you put your hand to do! His Mercy and Passionate Love meet you with Glorious Power, for He stands with you always, His child.

# Letter From God

Good Morning,

I Love you, My Dear, Precious, Beloved, Blessed, Special, Beautiful child of My GREAT Love. And that is what you are!

My Nurturing Love for you is gentle and tender, a fountain of abounding grace and mercy that fills you with My Strength. I show My Faithful Love to you by sending a miraculous sign of favor to put to shame those who hate you so that they may know I AM your Comforter, the One Who is your Helper! I have a thousand ways to deliver you who trusts in Me.

Never forget I am with you always and protect you wherever you go. I will never leave you nor fail you in any way or relax My hold on you. I will not in any degree abandon nor forsake you or let you down, for I will fulfill every word I have promised to you, so you can say with Great Confidence, "The Lord is for me. Who can be against me? I will never be afraid of what mere man may do to me!"

I AM your Helper Who responds quickly to your critical, urgent need with well-timed help. I AM God when I act and no one can reverse it, for Greater am I living within you than he who is in the world. All those striving against you shall be put to shame and confounded; they who contend with you will perish and be as nothing.

Yes, I AM for you and standing with you. Tell Me, who then can ever stand against you? I AM among those who help you. All the enemy's strategies I bring to naught against you. I defeat and strip away from them every weapon and all spiritual authority, for I have triumphed over them all by the power of the cross.

I AM your Upholder and with those who uphold your life. I lean into your heart and lay My Hands upon you! I AM ALWAYS Near. Never turn your look away from Me, for I AM your Faithful God. I Infuse you with strength and harden you to difficulties and help you in every situation. I hold you firmly with My Victorious Right Hand.

All those who come against you I defeat before your face. I shall come against them one way and flee before them seven ways. For I have commanded blessings upon you and everything you put your hand to do!

I have given you the Spirit of Power, love, and self-control, not a spirit of fear to dread what will come. Instead, I make your heart firmly fixed with confident trust that I will take care of you. So, pour all your worries and stress upon me and leave them there, for I always tenderly care for you.

I make you steady and robust, confident and fearless to face your foes with no fear because you will see your desires upon your enemies! For I AM your mountain fortress. I AM your Protector, My Mercy and Passionate Love meet you with Glorious Power, and I Stand with you as you look down in Triumph on all your enemies, My child.

I love you,

Daddy God. Amen.

*O Lord, you are so good, so ready to forgive, so full of unfailing love for all who ask for your help.*

Psalm 86:5, NLT

## SCRIPTURES FOR FURTHER READING:

Psalm 86:5, 2 Corinthians 12:9, Psalm 130:7, Psalm 86:17, Hebrews 13:5-6, Joshua 1:5, 9, Genesis 28:15, John 14:16-17, 26, Hebrews 4:16, 1 John 4:4, Isaiah 43:13, Isaiah 41:10-11, Colossians 2:15, Romans 8:31, Psalm 118:7-8, Psalm 54:4, Deuteronomy 28:18, 2 Timothy 1:7, Psalm 112:7-8, 1 Peter 5:7

## Prayer

Heavenly Father,

Your Nurturing Love for me is a fountain of abounding grace and mercy that fills me with Your Strength. I never forget You are always with me and protect me wherever I go. You give me the privilege to approach Your throne with confidence to receive mercy and well-timed help for every need. My heart is fixed confidently on You, my Protector.

In Jesus' name. Amen.

# DISCOVER MY HIDDEN SECRET ABOUT YOU

*M*an tries to understand God's heart by examining Him through man's heart and wisdom. However, no one can know God's heart and purposes except by His Spirit. You can only discover God's hidden secrets through His Spirit living in you. He reveals His Inmost Heart and deepest secrets to you through the Holy Spirit so that you can gratefully recognize the benefits He freely bestowed upon you.

The Holy Spirit gives you intimate insights into the hidden truths and secrets of The Kingdom of Heaven. These He supernaturally reveals to you by the Holy Spirit, testifying together with your own spirit, whispering into your innermost being His Divine Mystery concealed for ages past in His Heart, now made known for you to experience—Christ Living within you!

You are alive in union and joined eternally with Christ, His Dear Precious One, His friend. He intimately knows and understands God's Counsels and Purposes. He is Flowing Rivers of His Passionate Love through you to know how deeply is His intimate and far-reaching, Endless Love that unites you into His Wonderful Grace!

# Letter From God

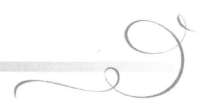

Good Morning,

I Love you, My Dear, Precious, Beloved, Blessed, Special, Beautiful child of My GREAT Love. And that is what you are!

Man tries to know Me in his mind with man's wisdom. However, you can only know Me through My Spirit Living in you, I unveil and reveal profound realities to you by My Spirit. Things the eye has never discovered or ear ever heard of before, things beyond your ability to imagine—these are the things I have done and have in store for you who Loves Me.

I AM revealing to you My Inmost Heart and deepest secrets through My Holy Spirit so that you can gratefully recognize the benefits I have bestowed upon you. My Spirit is constantly revealing My Divine Counsel and things hidden beyond man's scrutiny. He is your Divine Encourager Who takes what he receives from Me and reveals it to you. For My thoughts and secrets are only fully understood through My Spirit.

I gave you My Spirit to realize, comprehend, appreciate, and experience the magnificent things I have freely lavished upon you. I hide My Revelation of My Authority from those who are wise in their own eyes.

You are given access to the intimate experience of insights into the hidden truths and secrets of The Kingdom of Heaven. Things not revealed by flesh and blood, but I supernaturally reveal them to you through My Holy Spirit, testifying together with your spirit, whispering into your innermost being what I direct Him to unveil.

My Divine Mystery, the Secret Surprise I had concealed for ages past in My Heart, now manifest for you to experience. Living within you is Christ Himself. You intimately know His mind and hold the thoughts, feelings, and purposes of His Heart. Thus, you're able to understand being fully-equipped with the Word of God.

Yes, He floods you with Himself because you are alive in union with Him. Christ intimately knows and understands My Counsels and Purposes. He lives His life through you. You died in His death and your new life is hidden with Christ in Me. Your New Life in Christ is empowered by Him infusing the strength of His explosive power in you, making you sufficient in His Sufficiency.

You are alive in union and joined eternally with My Dear Precious One, your friend. You live in Life-Union with Me, and My Words live powerfully within you, so you can ask whatever you desire that will glorify Me, and it will do it! You are joined together as ONE to experience My Glory in perfect unity, to convince the world I Am Alive in you, and you are alive in Me.

I AM Flowing Rivers of My Passionate Love through you that transcends human understanding, to make Myself known through you. It is just how enduring and inclusive it is with Divine Hidden Treasures waiting for your discovery, being knitted together in Love with Me.

How Deeply Intimate and Far-Reaching is My Endless Love that united you into My Very Life by My Wonderful Grace! I give you access to All My Riches as you become progressively more acquainted with and know more definitely and accurately and thoroughly the Supernatural Wealth you have In Christ—All the treasures of heaven's wisdom and endless riches of revelation knowledge.

The New Reality is you are a child of the Living God. You have been born anew of My Spirit and come to know Him Intimately because He remains with you and lives inside of you. Now you have been stamped with the seal of the Spirit of Adoption, My Holy Spirit.

Yes, you are My Child Right Now! I sent the Holy Spirit of My Son into your heart so you can now experience the depth of the Marvelous Love I lavishly bestowed on you because I have called you and made you My Very own Beloved child.

And because you are Mine, You Can Access Everything I Have, for you are My heir through Jesus. I am delighted to give you birth to fulfill My Chosen destiny for you and become the favorite one out of All My Creation, My child.

I love you,

Daddy God. Amen.

*But it was to us that God revealed these things by his Spirit. For His Spirit searches out everything and shows us God's deep secrets.*

1 Corinthians 2:10, NLT

## Scriptures for Further Reading:

1 Corinthians 2:5,10; 1 Corinthians 2:9-10, John 16:13-15, Matthew 11:25, Matthew 11:25, Matthew 16:17, Romans 8:16, Galatians 1:12, Matthew 13:11, Colossians 1:24-25, Ephesians 3:4-9, 1 Corinthians 2:18, Galatians 2:20, Colossians 3:2-4, Philippians 4:13, John 17:11, 24; John 10:30, John 15:7, John 14:13, Ephesians 3:18-19, Colossians 2:2-3, Ephesians 2:5, John 3:5-7, John 14:7, Ephesians 1:13, Galatians 4:6-7

## Prayer

Heavenly Father,

I ask that You empower me to discover and experience the great magnitude of all Your Marvelous Grace lavishly bestowed upon me. Grant me access to all the riches of Your hidden truths and secrets of your Divine Mystery—Christ Living in me, in Whom is hidden all the treasures of Divine Wisdom and Revelation Knowledge.

In Jesus' name. Amen.

# I Am Your Indwelling Shepherd

*T*he Lord is your Best Friend and Good Shepherd, your caring, Everlasting Father, the Prince of Peace, Who always provides more than enough for your every need—physical, emotional, and spiritual. I carry you in My Loving Arms, holding you close to My Heart. Nothing can separate you from God's Passionate Love for you.

Your new life is joined together with God. You live in a life union as One. His Empowering Presence fills you to overflowing with His Life-Giving Spirit that releases His supernatural peace, prosperity, wholeness, success, well-being to you through the blood sacrifice of His Beloved Son on the cross restoring you back to Himself.

He is your Indwelling Shepherd Who cares for the welfare of your entire being and exercises His Oversight over the condition of your spirit, soul, and body. He is your Divine Guardian, Who Lovingly watches over your total welfare. He is intimately aware of every detail of your life. You lack nothing, for He fully satisfies every need you have through the abundant riches of His Glory.

# Letter From God

Good Morning,

I Love you, My Dear, Precious, Beloved, Blessed, Special, Beautiful child of My GREAT Love. And that is what you are!

I AM your Best Friend and Good Shepherd, your caring Everlasting Father to the Prince of Peace, Who always provides more than enough for your every need—physical, emotional, and spiritual. I carry you in My Loving Arms, holding you close to My Heart. I laid down My Life as a sacrifice for you, so you could dwell securely in Me, Who created all things in heaven and on earth, visible and invisible, and made you a part of My Body.

Nothing can separate you from My Passionate Love for you. I know everything about you, your heart's hidden impulses, your thoughts, and every movement of your soul. Yes, I am intimately aware of you and your heart is an open book to Me. And I demonstrate My Great Passionate Love for you, knowing everything about you, and giving My Life for you.

And since your new life is hidden in Me, we live in a union as One. My Empowering Presence fills you to overflowing with My Life-Giving Spirit, full of acceptance that produces My Peace to rule in your heart so you have Great Confidence as you Rest in Me, Who conquered the world for you.

For when you went astray, I went and found you and brought you home to Me. I forgave you. I released My supernatural peace to you through the blood sacrifice of My Beloved Son on the cross, restoring you back to Myself as holy and blameless forever.

I am your Indwelling Shepherd Who cares for every part of you inwardly and outwardly. I loved you and accepted you even before you knew and accepted Me—to satisfy My Great Love for you!

Now you are alive with Me, The True Shepherd of your life. I AM your Divine Guardian, Who Lovingly watches over your inner being. As your Good Shepherd, I care for the welfare of your entire being and exercise My Oversight over the condition of your spirit, soul, and body.

I intimately Shepherd you in every detail of your life. I know all your needs physically, spiritually, emotionally, relationally, socially in all circumstances and in all ways. You lack nothing. For I fully satisfied every need you have through the abundant riches of My Glory, My child.

I love you,

Daddy God. Amen.

*The Lord is my shepherd; I shall not want.*

Psalm 23:1, NKJV

## Scriptures for Further Reading:

Psalm 23:1, Isaiah 9:6, Isaiah 40:11, John 10:11, Micah 5:4, Colossians 1:16, Romans 8:39, Psalm 139:1-5, Romans 5:8, Ephesians 3:19, Romans 8:10, John 10:14, Colossians 3:3, Galatians 2:20, Romans 8:15, Colossians 3:15, Matthew 11:28, 1 John 5:5, Hebrews 13:20, John 16:33, Colossians 1:20-22, Ephesians 2:4, 1 Peter 2:25, Philippians 4:19

## Prayer

Heavenly Father,

You are My Best Friend and Good Shepherd, Who knows what I need even before I ask You. And You always provide more than enough for all my needs to satisfy the Great Love You have for me. You are intimately aware of every detail of My life, so I trust You complete as My Good Shepherd to guide and lead me in all the affairs of life to bring you, Glory.

In Jesus' name. Amen.

# MY LOVE MAKES YOU WHOLE

*G*od reaches into your pain with a touch of His Healing Love. When you cry out, His heart is deeply moved with compassion toward you and wraps the wounds that have pierced you with His Faithful Love. He heals you from the inside out and restores health to you. Yes, He refreshes you with the Living Waters of His Spirit cascading from His throne within you.

He understands your pain and sufferings because His Beloved Son endured the punishment required for your complete wholeness. He was beaten with many stripes to secure your healing and My Shalom that graciously bestowed upon you peace, prosperity, success, and well-being. Yes, My Beloved Son made divine healing available to you by faith.

He heals the wounds of your shattered heart; He cures all your pains, griefs, and sorrows.

Now, as a New Creation in Christ Jesus, the Power of the Holy Spirit fills you with the Living Force of God's Endless Love that never fails! So, Drink Deeply from the never-ending, Living Waters of His Spirit's healing power from above.

# Letter From God

Good Morning,

I Love you, My Dear, Precious, Beloved, Blessed, Special, Beautiful child of My GREAT Love. And that is what you are!

I reach into your pain with a touch of My Healing Love. When you cry out, My heart is deeply moved with compassion toward you, so I heal your broken heart and wrap the wounds that have pierced you with My Faithful Love. For I am the LORD Who heals you to demonstrate My deep, tender compassion that reveals My Glory.

Everything you need is everything I AM. I heal you from the inside and out of every sickness and disease. When you are sick, lying upon your bed of suffering, I restore health to you. Yes, I raise you to health again, refreshing with the Living Waters of My Spirit cascading from My throne within you so you can confidently say: "The Lord is my Healer, the One Who Heals me, and I give Him Praise."

I understand your pain and sufferings, for I paid a Precious Price to take away your sicknesses, weaknesses, and distresses. My Beloved Son endured the punishment required for your complete wholeness. He was beaten with many stripes to secure your healing. His Sacred Blood spilled for you is the measure of My Divine Love I imparted to secured your recovery and well-being.

My Shalom I graciously bestowed upon you, giving you peace, prosperity, success, and well-being. For I paid with tears of blood the high price justice demanded to make you completely whole.

Yes, by the stripes that wounded My Beloved Son, you are made whole and have divine healing made available to you by faith.

I am the Healer of your shattered heart's wounds, Who cures all your pains, griefs, and sorrows.

You now live in the freshness of your New Life as My New Creation in Christ Jesus in the Power of the Holy Spirit. I fill you with the Living Force of My Love that never fails! So, Drink Deeply from the never-ending, Living Waters of My Spirit's healing power from above.

Now, no more accusing voice condemns you, for you are joined in Life-Union with Me Forever. For the Law of the Spirit of Life Flowing through Me Who Lives in you frees you from the law of sin and death. Your heart I kiss with My Eternal forgiveness. I AM your Healer Who makes you whole, My child.

I love you,

Daddy God. Amen.

*He heals the brokenhearted and bandages their wounds.*

Psalm 147:3, NLT

Matthew 14:14, Psalm 147:3, Psalm 34:18, Isaiah 61:1, Psalm 32:10, Exodus 15:26, Exodus 23:25, Mark 1:41, Matthew 20:34, Matthew 15:30-31, Colossians 3:11, Psalm 103:3, Jeremiah 30:17, Jeremiah 17:14, John 7:38, Psalm 41:3-4, 1 Peter 2:24-25, Isaiah 53:4-5, Psalm 147:3, 1 Corinthians 13:8, 2 Corinthians 5:17, Romans 7:6, Colossians 3:3, Romans 8:1-2

## Prayer

Heavenly Father,

When my heart hurts aches with pain, answer me with a fresh touch of Your Healing Love. Heal my shattered heart, comfort my soul with Your tender mercy and encouragement. When my body aches and my life force has dwindled, refresh me with Your Living Waters healing powers and restore me to complete wholeness once again.

In Jesus' name. Amen.

# BENEFITS OF MY SPIRITUAL BLESSINGS

*E*very day, God has blessings waiting for you that reveal His Deep, Tender Love for you. You discover these blessings He daily loads you with by fixing your eyes on Him. He planned before the foundation of the world for everything you would need daily, know everything you would need before you ask Him.

He already has blessed you with every spiritual blessing in the heavenly places as a Love Gift from Him because He sees you wrapped into Christ. And He makes all Grace, every favor, and earthly blessing come to you in abundance so that you have more than enough of everything. He makes you overflow with abundance to be a blessing to others.

He places in your heart His Unfailing Love to fill your heart's longing for unconditional acceptance with His nearness. His approval of you is securely rooted in His Unfailing Love for you without works. He tenderly cares for you. He understands and loves you for the way He made you from the beginning—His Masterpiece!

# Letter From God

Good Morning,

I Love you, My Dear, Precious, Beloved, Blessed, Special, Beautiful child of My GREAT Love. And that is what you are!

Every day I have Blessings waiting for you to discover, revealing My Deep, Tender Love for you. When you lift your Heart into My Presence, you will see around you My Blessings I daily load you with because you belong to Christ. I give you more than enough of everything, making all grace, every favor, and earthly blessing come to you in abundance for every good thing you do.

Yes, I have already blessed you with every spiritual blessing given by the Holy Spirit in the heavenly realms as My Child—you enjoy them now! All the benefits of Divine Love produced by the Holy Spirit in all its multisided expressions are manifested individually as you need them to fulfill the incredible destiny I prepared for you in Christ.

Each spiritual blessing reveals itself in the physical world as a demonstration of My Tremendous Love, Glorifying the Grace I Lavishly Bestowed upon you in salvation. My whole estate of spiritual wealth is yours as My heir in union with Christ, and now you share all that He has and all that He is. Jesus is the Source of your spiritual wealth, and the moment you received Him, every spiritual blessing became yours.

I Blessed you to satisfy My Great Love for you and chose you to receive the Benefits of My Spiritual Blessings. Christ saves you to the uttermost, perfectly throughout all eternity because He lives forever and is always interceding and intervening on your behalf. My Gift of Salvation you receive through Him unleashes My Power of Divine Protection and Deliverance. I guarantee your safety and security through the Holy Spirit's mighty power at work within you, Who constantly guards you until you fully receive your priceless inheritance in Christ.

Before you were even born, I chose you to fulfill the Designed Purpose of My Heart and destined you to share the Likeness of My Child. Now I have transferred His perfect righteousness to you and co-glorified you with Him. My Heart pulls on your heart to continuously embrace Me in an intimate personal relationship that keeps pouring out My Unfailing Love to you and Releases more of My Blessings to you.

Yes, I placed in your heart the desire for My Unfailing Love, which can only be quench by My Spirit living within you, cascading Unfailing Love into your heart. Your approval and acceptance find their security rooted in My Unfailing Love for you without works; it is the Love Gift of Christ paid for by His blood. You can never gain Love by good works because it is only found in Me—Who is Love!

I draw you to Myself to bless you with My Passionate Love to fulfill your heart's longing for unconditional acceptance and closeness, to be tenderly cared for and understood and loved for who you are—My Masterpiece. I, Who Love you Most Love you Best, and I Love you through others who Love Me. Those who do not love you judge your outward appearance through their imperfections which good works will never satisfy, My child.

I love you,

Daddy God. Amen.

*Blessed be the God and Father of our Lord Jesus Christ, who
has blessed us with every spiritual blessing in the heavenly
places in Christ.*

Ephesians 1:3, NKJV

## ❙ SCRIPTURES FOR FURTHER READING:

Psalm 63:1, Psalm 145:1, Psalm 68:19, Lamentations 3:41, Ephesians
1:3, 2 Corinthians 9:8, Galatians 5:22, 1 Corinthians 12:4-11,
Ephesians 2:10, Ephesians 1:5-6, Romans 8:17, Colossians Hebrews
1:1-2, Ephesians 1:4, Ephesians 2:4, Hebrews 7:24-25, Romans 1:16,
Ephesians 3:20, 2 Corinthians 5:5, 1 Peter 1:5, Ephesians 1:1,
Romans 8: John 6:44, Psalm 36:10, Proverbs 19:22, Romans 8:9,
15:5, Ephesians 2:8-9, Romans 6:8, Romans 2:1

## Prayer

Heavenly Father,

Thank You for all the blessings You have already waiting for me to
discover each day, revealing Your Tender Love for me. You daily
load me with the Benefits of Your blessings to seek You each day.
You bless me with every spiritual blessing and make all grace, every
favor, and earthly blessing come to me in abundance. And giving
me Your unconditional acceptance and approval without my works
as Your Love Gift to me to pull me close so I can always experience
Your Tender Loves embrace.

In Jesus' name. Amen.

# CHRIST IS MY TRUE WISDOM

*Y*ou draw your life from living in union as one with Christ Jesus, Who has become your Wisdom from God—your righteousness, holiness, and redemption. Your heart has been knitted together in love with Him, which gives you access to all God's riches. For in Christ is your spiritual wealth, hidden all the treasures of Wisdom and Knowledge.

Jesus Christ is True Wisdom, living within you and opening you up to the Multisided Mystery and Wonders of Grace in all its infinite, varied dimensions. A Hidden Storehouse of Wisdom waiting for you to access because the Word of God, Christ Himself, lives in you. He is your Living Shield of Wisdom, wrapping you in His Heart, guiding, protecting, guarding, and implanting in you the desire to do what pleases God.

God's Wisdom is above all Wisdom. God alone is Wise. He has made His Word (Christ) Wisdom to you. His generous gift of Wisdom is found in every Word God speaks and becomes a fountain of understanding within you. He is always pure, filled with peace, gentle, considerate, full of mercy and good fruits, without partiality, and sincerity.

# Letter From God

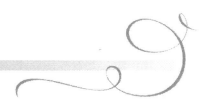

Good Morning,

I Love you, My Dear, Precious, Beloved, Blessed, Special, Beautiful child of My GREAT Love. And that is what you are!

You are not limited in your knowledge and understanding. You draw your life from Me living in union as one with Christ, in Whom all the Treasures of Wisdom—Divine, Comprehensive Insight and Endless Riches of Knowledge—are hidden and stored up for you.

Jesus Christ is My True Wisdom living within you, the Heavenly Treasure Chest that opens up to you the Multisided Mystery and Wonders of My Grace in all its infinite varied dimensions. Divine Wisdom I kept hidden from ages past as a Secret in My Heart to unveil to the angelic rulers and authorities in the heavenly realm, according to My eternal and timeless purpose.

My Hidden Storehouse of Wisdom is readily available to you because the Word of Christ dwells in you richly, wholly filling and flooding you with all Wisdom. He is your Living Shield that follows you, protecting and guarding, implanting in you the passion for choosing what is right. Wisdom wraps you in His Heart, filling you with the knowledge of His Generous Grace.

The Wisdom I sent to you from heaven accomplishes My desires and does what pleases Me. He is above everything, priceless, imparting revelation knowledge. He is pure and peace-loving, gentle always, full of mercy and good deeds, never shows favoritism, filled with love, and is always sincere.

My Wonderful Wisdom realized and carried into effect My Secret Plan hidden from before the ages began to bring Me, Glory. He is the Word of Life, the Life-Giver, the Spirit of Life flowing through you, the Spirit of Christ Who empowers your life and lives in you—Christ Jesus, the Son of God.

Christ is Living Understanding, Who gives you true success and insight into the wise plans I have designed just for you to fulfill your destiny. He living in you is the guarantee and fulfillment of My Destiny Plan for you that remains in place forever and will never fail. You belong to Christ Jesus, Who is Wisdom itself, My child.

I love you,

Daddy God. Amen.

*It is because of him that you are in Christ Jesus, who has become for us wisdom from God—that is, our righteousness, holiness and redemption.*

1 Corinthians 1:30, NIV

## SCRIPTURES FOR FURTHER READING:

1 Corinthians 1:30, Galatians 2:20, Colossians 2:3, 1 Corinthians 1:24, Colossians: 8-11, Proverbs 2:6-7, James 1:5, Colossians 3:16, Proverbs 2:8-9, Philippians 2:13, John 3:31, John 6:23, Proverbs 8:11, James 3:17, 1 Corinthians 2:7, Ephesians 3:11, Romans 8:9-10, Romans 8:1, Proverbs 8:14, Ephesians 2:10, Psalm 33:11, Psalm 16:5

## Prayer

Heavenly Father,

I draw my life from living in union as one with Christ Jesus. You wrapped my heart together in the fabric of His Love which gives me access to all Your riches of Wisdom and Knowledge, which are just waiting for me to discover. Christ is my Living Understanding Who gives me true success and insight into making wise decisions relying on His Word.

In Jesus' name. Amen.

# I Know Everything About You

*God knows everything about you. He is so intimately aware of you. He reads your heart like an open book. There is no detail or area of your life that God is not in complete and total control. There is no step you will take on the path of life that He has not prepared ahead of time for you, and the good works you would do to fulfill your destiny.*

*God is your Father, Who cares deeply about even the smallest detail of your life. He knows everything you need before you need it. His Unfailing Love rises within you to heal the pain of your past and the burdens of your present. You rest in My Healing Peace that Eases and Revives and Refreshes your heart.*

*You can trust and lean on the Peace of His Spirit within you when you have unrest about anything rather than being anxious and worried. His Unfailing Love flowing through His Spirit makes you completely whole and sets you free. You experience the Intimacy of My Unfailing Love within you, working in and through you, to love others as He loves you.*

# Letter From God

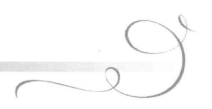

Good Morning,

I Love you, My Dear, Precious, Beloved, Blessed, Beautiful child of My GREAT Love. And that is what you are!

There is no detail or area of your life that I am not intimately involved. I'm in complete and total control of every detail of your life. There is not a hair on your head I have not numbered. There is no step you will take on the path of life that I have not prepared ahead of time for you, and the good works you would do to fulfill your destiny.

I know everything about you. I know when you sit down and when you stand up. I perceive every movement of your heart and soul and understand every thought before it enters your mind. I am so intimately aware of you; I read your heart like an open book and know all the words you are about to speak even before starting a sentence. I know it altogether.

I had gone into your future preparing your destiny and the good works you will do to fulfill it even before you were born. I have placed My Hand of Love is upon your life to give you mercy and spare you from the harm of your past. For I impart My Blessing upon you to satisfy My Great and Wonderful Love for you.

I am your Father, Who cares deeply about even the smallest detail of your life. I know everything you will need before you need it. I know the full longings of your heart and the burdens you carry, the secret wounds of your heart that need healing.

I rise within you, flowing My Unfailing Love into the pain of your past and what burdens you in the present. Every detail of your life, even your deepest feelings and emotions, experience My Healing Peace for your wounded heart that surpasses all understanding. You rest in My Healing Peace that Eases and Revives and Refreshes your soul—My Kiss of Peace to you.

Lean and rely on the Peace of My Spirit within you to rule continually, acting as umpire in your heart. When you are anxious and worried, pour all your concern and stress upon Me and leave them there and let My Spirit Who continually lives within you produce My Peace in your heart to decide and settle with all finality all questions that arise in your mind. And always be thankful!

My Unfailing Love flowing through My Spirit has made you completely whole, My child. I have kissed your heart with forgiveness despite all you've done—My Real Love! So, you now experience the Intimacy of My Unfailing Love being brought to full expression within you and through you, to love others as I love you.

My Unfailing Love has set you free; everything that can hold you back is broken off your life! You now have the Freedom to dispense the Fullness of My Presence and My Power, seeing yourself as I see you, Holy and Blameless in My Sight, Even above Reproach with an Unstained innocence, because of My Great Love for you, My child.

I love you,

Daddy God. Amen.


*O Lord, you have examined my heart and know everything about me.*

Psalm 139:1, NLT

## SCRIPTURES FOR FURTHER READING:

Ephesians 2:10, Matthew 10:30, Psalm 139:1-6, Ephesians 2:4, Matthew 10:30, Matthew 6:8, Philippians 4:6, Matthew 11:28, Psalm 29:11, Colossians 3:15, Galatians 5:22, 1 Peter 5:7, 1 John 4:16-18, John 17:26

## Prayer

Heavenly Father,

You know everything about me intimately, and You deeply care about the smallest details of my life. You see the weight I carry, the secret wounds of my heart, the pains of my past, and the burdens of my present. I ask You to kiss me with Your Healing Peace to ease and revive my soul. And I ask to experience Your Unfailing Love within me to love others as You love them.

*In Jesus' name. Amen.*

# I AM INTIMATELY AWARE OF YOU

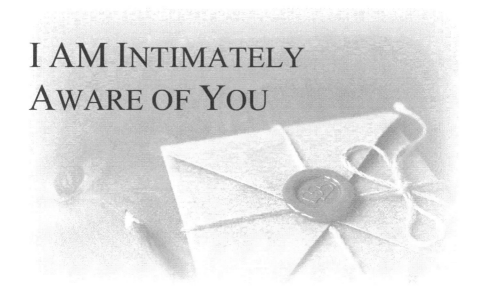

*E*very moment of your life, your destiny—is in God's Hands. He is intimately aware of the plans and thoughts I prepared to accomplish your destiny, plans for peace, prosperity, wholeness, success, and well-being, and not to harm you. He is the One Who directs your Life, so each step brings you closer to your destiny.

God's Heart draws you into His Presence to listen and embrace Him, knowing He has more than enough for all your needs. He is a Sun and Shield to you, wrapping you in His Grace and Glory so that you always have more than enough of everything—every moment and in every way, for He provides it all for you.

The Holy Spirit brings you into God's Presence to receive Mercy's Kiss for your Weaknesses and Discover His Unfathomable Grace to Help you in your time of need. God is a partner in every detail of your life; He guides your steps in life to fit in His Perfect Plan. He is always tenderly caring for you because He Loves you.

# Letter From God

Good Morning,

I Love you, My Dear, Precious, Beloved, Blessed, Special, Beautiful child of My GREAT Love. And that is what you are!

Every moment of your life, your destiny—*is in* My Hands. I am intimately aware of the plans and thoughts I prepared to accomplish your destiny, plans for peace, prosperity, wholeness, success, and well-being, and not to harm you. I came for you to enjoy Life in overflowing abundance, taking the paths I set for you and Living the Good Life I ordained for you.

I am the One Who directs your Life, so each step brings you closer to your destiny. My eyes are your Guide. I am always close to you, teaching and guiding you on the best path for your life. My Hand of Protection is upon you, so there is no risk of failure, for the Glory of My Wraparound Presence is your Champion Defender.

The pull of My Heart draws you into My Presence to listen and embrace Me with the full expectation; I am more than enough for all you need. My Life-Giving Strength is a safe and powerful place to find refuge, an ever-present and well-proven help in times of distress and weakness.

Yes, I am a Sun and Shield to you, wrapping you in My Grace and Glory so that you always have more than enough of everything—every moment and in every way, for I provide it all. My Grace is continually sufficient for you, for My Mighty Power in you show its Most Full expression through your weaknesses. What you see as your weaknesses become the portal to My Power.

Listen, I gave you My Holy Spirit, Who is your Friend just like Jesus—and He never leaves you nor forsakes you, Who is the Spirit of Christ Himself Living within you and remains eternally inside you.

The Holy Spirit brings you into My Presence where Love is enthroned, to receive Mercy's Kiss for your Weaknesses, and Discover My Unfathomable Grace to Help You in Good Times for your every need, even before you were born. And I give you My Perfect, Wonderful Peace to guide your heart in perfect harmony with My plan and your destiny.

Being a partner in your destiny, you have the assurance that I continually weave together every detail of your life to fit into My Perfect Plan. I created you to have life in abundance, taking the paths I prearranged ahead of time, doing the good works I ordained for you, and living the Good Life I made ready for you to live.

I am intimately aware of you and always tenderly care for you because I Love you. And My Faithful Love for you continues on forever. You love Me because I first Loved you, and the Light of My Love shinning within you continually lights up the world around you to shine into the hearts of others around you to bring Me Glory for all eternity, My child.

I love you,

Daddy God. Amen.

*For I know the thoughts that I think toward you, says the Lord, thoughts of peace and not of evil, to give you a future and a hope.*

Jeremiah 29:11, NKJV

Psalm 31:15, Jeremiah 29:11, Psalm 139:3, John 10:10, Ephesians 2:10, Proverbs 20:24, Psalm 32:8, Psalm 62:6, John 6:44, Hebrews 12:2, Philippians 4:19, Psalm 46:1, Psalm 84:11, 2 Corinthians 9:8, 2 Corinthians 12:9-10, John 14:16-17, Hebrews 13:5, Hebrews 4:16, Philippians 4:7, Romans 8:28, John 10:10, Ephesians 2:10, 1 Peter 5:7, Psalm 136:1, 1 John 4:19, Matthew 5:16

## Prayer

Heavenly Father,

My Life is in Your hands. You know everything about me, every thought, and every moment of my life. You are intimately aware of me. You know the plans You have prepared for me—for good, prosperity, wholeness, success, and well-being, and not to harm me. You are a Partner in all I set my hand to do, so I know every detail of my life is woven together for good because You love me and are taking care of me.

In Jesus' name. Amen.

# GUIDED BY THE SPIRIT OF TRUTH

*K*eep your eye on Jesus and watch God continually weaving every detail of your life into His perfect plan for good into your life. He is always with you—do not yield to fear. He never gives you a spirit of fear or doubt or worries; instead, He gave you by the Holy Spirit Who lives in you.

God lives through you and infuses you with the strength and help you need in every situation. He already knows what you need before you even ask. So, stop letting the enemy make you perpetually uneasy and worried about your life. He never stands for the truth. He is full of lies—lying is his native tongue. He is a liar and the father of lies himself.

His Spirit of Truth Guides you into All Truth which both heals and nourishes you. His Voice restores and revives and replenishes your heart. His Truth frees your heart and mind to see through the enemy's lies. His Truth is the reality on the Highest Plane. For Truth is not something you act upon; it acts upon you.

# Letter From God

Good Morning,

I Love you, My Dear, Precious, Beloved, Blessed, Beautiful child of My GREAT Love. And that is what you are!

Every step of your life you take with your eye off Me is fraught with stress and worry. Keep your eyes on Me, Who Gives continually weaves every detail of your life into my perfect plan for bringing good into your life.

Most assuredly, I am with you ALWAYS. Do not yield to fear, for I AM living with you constantly. I never give you a spirit of fear, doubt, or worry, but I have given you by the Holy Spirit Who lives in you—Mighty Power, Love, and a Calm, Well-Balanced Mind.

My child, I live My Life through you and dispense My Life into you! I infuse you with the strength and help you need in every situation. I already know what you need before you even ask Me. So, I tell you to stop letting the enemy make you perpetually uneasy, anxious, and worried about your life; for all you need, I will provide.

The enemy knows you can't move in trust and move in doubt at the same time. Doubt is the currency of the enemy. Fear is his spiritual weapon to deceive you into believing a lie. He is in the business of deceiving and destroying humanity. He is the thief that only has one thing on his mind—to kill, steal, and destroy. He has never stood for all of the truth. He is full of lies—lying is his native tongue. He is a liar and the father of lies himself.

However, I AM the Spirit of Truth Who Guides you into ALL Truth which both heals and nourishes you. My Voice of Truth restores, revives, and replenishes your heart. It frees your heart and mind from the stress and worries that cluster your thoughts and fog your vision to see through the enemy's lies into My Truth that sets you free through the Holy Spirit's operation in your life.

The Truth Giver extinguishes the blazing arrows of thoughts coming at you from the evil one! Truth is the reality on the Highest Plane. For Christ Himself is Truth. Truth is not something you act upon—it acts upon you. I have woven My Truth into your heart so that you know inwardly—

I AM the Truth.

Never doubt My Mighty Power that is at Work within you, constantly energizing you. For My unfailing love and faithfulness always protects you, My child.

I love you,

Daddy God. Amen.

> *Looking away from all that will distract to Jesus, Who is the Leader and the Source of our faith and is also its Finisher.*
>
> Hebrews 12:2, NKJV

# SCRIPTURES FOR FURTHER READING:

Hebrews 12:2, Romans 8:28, Isaiah 41:10, John 14:17, 2 Timothy 1:7, Galatians 2:20, Isaiah 41:10, Psalm 46:1, Matthew 6:8, Philippians 4:6, Matthew 6:25, Philippians 4:19, John 8:44, John 10:10, John 14:16, John 16:13, John 15:9, John 8:32, John 17:17, Romans 2:15, John 14:6, Ephesians 6:16, Ephesians 3:20, Psalm 89:24

## Prayer

Heavenly Father,

I focus my full heart on You, knowing that You are more than enough to provide all I need. You know my needs before I ask, and You satisfy my every need. For You are Faithful and infuse me with the strength and help me in every situation. You weave every detail of my life together for good in harmony with Your plans to fulfill my destiny.

In Jesus' name. Amen.

# I AM YOUR CREATOR

*G od is your Creator and you belong to Him. You are His Child. In His Love, He chose you, He destined you, planned for you to be adopted, revealed as His child, through your union with Christ Jesus before the foundation of the world. His Tremendous Love cascades over you as a visible display of the infinite riches of His Grace.*

*God gave you the Release of Redemption being in Life-Union with Christ—Deliverance and Salvation—the total cancellation of your sins. His Super Abundant Grace is already powerfully working in you. And through your Union with Christ, you have been made God's Inheritance.*

*You are God's Image-Bearer, created in Christ Jesus to fulfill the destiny He has given you. You are taking the paths I planned to do the good works I have given you to do. I walk with you down Life's paths to live the good life, which I prearranged made ready for you to live. Even now, as Christ is, so you are in the world, to continue His good works.*

# Letter From God

Good Morning,

I Love you, My Dear, Precious, Beloved, Blessed, Special, Beautiful child of My GREAT Love. And that is what you are!

I am your Creator, and you belong to Me. You are My Child. In My Love, I chose you, actually picked you out for Myself as My Own in Christ Jesus before the foundation of the world so that you would be holy, set apart for Me and blameless in My Sight, even above reproach, before Me in Love.

For I destined you, planned in love for you to be adopted, revealed as My Own Child, through your union with Jesus Christ, my beloved son; so that My Tremendous Love the cascades over you would glorify My Grace. For the Same Love I have for Jesus, I have for you. This unfolding of My Plan brings Me Great Pleasure!

Since you are now joined to Christ, you have been given the Release of Redemption—Deliverance, and Salvation—by His Blood, the cancellation of all your sins, all because of the riches of My Marvelous Grace poured out on you. My Super Abounding Grace is already powerfully working in you, filling you with all forms of wisdom and understanding with practical insight.

Beloved, you are My Child right now! Through your union with Christ, you have been made My Own Inheritance. Before you were even born, I gave you this destiny so that you would fulfill My Plan Who Always Accomplishes Every Purpose and Plan of My Heart.

For You Are My Own Workmanship recreated in Christ Jesus, a New Creature Altogether, to fulfill the destiny I have given you, for you are in union with Jesus. You take the paths I prepared beforehand that you should walk in them, even before you were born, and live the good life I prearranged made ready for you to live.

Even now as Christ is, so you are in the world. And I destined you to accomplish those good works Jesus did, and even greater works than those because your life is now hidden with Christ in Me, My child.

I love you,

Daddy God. Amen.

> *Know that the LORD, He is God; It is He who has made us, and not we ourselves; We are His people and the sheep of His pasture.*
>
> Psalm 100:3, NKJV

## SCRIPTURES FOR FURTHER READING:

Psalm 100:3, Romans 8:16, 1, Ephesians 1:4, Romans 8:30, Ephesians 1:5, Galatians 4:5, Ephesians 1:6, 1 John 4:11, John 17:23, Colossians 1:14, Ephesians 1:7, Colossians 1:9, 1 John 3:1, Ephesians 1:11, Psalm 139:16, Ephesians 2:10, 2 Corinthians 5:17, Proverbs 16:9, Proverbs 20:24, 1 John 4:17, John 14:12, Colossians 3:3

## Prayer

Heavenly Father,

You are My Creator and I am Your child. I celebrate You with all my heart for cascading Your Tremendous Love over me. Your Super Abundant Grace is already powerfully working in me, releasing all forms of wisdom and practical understanding. I rely on You to guide me and direct my every decision.

In Jesus' name. Amen.

# YOU ARE CHERISHED IN MY SIGHT

*Y*ou are dearly loved and precious in God's Sight. He bought you in tears of love at a Great Price by giving His Greatest Treasure, His Beloved Son, as the sacrifice to prove His Unfathomable Love for you. He co-crucified you with Him, to exchange His Perfect Righteousness for your sins, to be holy and blameless in My Sight without a single fault.

Christ's resurrection life rescued you from the dominion of sin and made you an entirely new person altogether that never existed before—free from sin. Now you are a wholly new person with Christ living His Life in you and indwelt by the Holy Spirit. He enables you with sensible behavior and sound reasoning to divinely balance things from My Perspective.

Don't be discouraged; God is always on your side! He is your Strengthener and Helper. So you can say with Great Confidence, "The Lord is My Helper, He is for me, and I will not fear what man may do to me." So, Who would dare to accuse you whom I have chosen in love to be My Own? No one!

# Letter From God

Good Morning,

I Love you, My Dear, Precious, Beloved, Blessed, Special, Beautiful child of My GREAT Love. And that is what you are!

You are cherished in My Sight because I bought you in tears of love at a Great Price, paid for with the Blood of My Beloved Son, Jesus Christ, to make you My Own. You are My chosen treasure I called out of darkness to experience My Marvelous Life; to shine as an example of the incredible riches of My Grace and Kindness lavishly bestowed upon you, living in a union as one with Christ Jesus.

I love you so dearly. I sent Christ to die for you while you were still a sinner. And I co-glorified you with Him by transferring My Perfect Righteousness to you, who I chose in My Great Love to be holy and blameless in My Sight without a single fault. You are an entirely new creature; your old spiritual condition in Adam passed away. Christ ended Adam's race and became the Life-Giving Spirit. Now you are an entirely new person with Christ, living His Life in you and indwelt by the Holy Spirit.

The law of Spirit of Life flowing through Jesus Christ living within you liberates you from the power of sin that leads to death. Christ's resurrection life rescued you from the dominion of sin, and you live in a new relationship reconciled to God. I made you spiritually alive together with Christ, gave you His very Life, and saved you by His marvelous grace!

LEE RICHARDS

Do not yield to fear. You are never alone. I am closer than the breath in your lungs. Reject the thoughts, keeping your eyes fixed on Me, your Faithful God, and look away from all the distractions in the world. There is nothing to fear, for I have not given you a spirit of fear, but the Holy Spirit, Who gives you My Mighty Power, Love, and self-control. The Holy Spirit enables you with sensible behavior and sound reasoning to divinely balance things from My Perspective.

Don't be discouraged, for I am for you and stand with you. No one can stand against you, because I live within you. I am always on your side! Who would dare to accuse you, who I have chosen in love to be My Own? No one—for I put you in right standing with Me. There is no one left to condemn you.

I am your Strengthener and Helper. So you can say with Great Confidence, "The Lord is My Helper, He is for me, and I will not fear what man may do to me." I infuse you with My Explosive Power to conquer all things, holding you firmly with My Righteous Right Hand of Victory. I have made you more than a conqueror, and your overwhelming victory over everything is through Christ's Great Love for you, My child.

I love you,

Daddy God. Amen.

*Because you are precious in My sight and honored, and*
*because I love you, I will give men in return for you and*
*peoples in exchange for your life.*

Isaiah 43:4, AMPC

## Scriptures for Further Reading:

Isaiah 43:4, 1 Corinthians 6:20, 1 Peter 2:9, Matthew 5:14, Ephesians 2:7, Romans 5:8, Romans 8:30, Ephesians 1:4, 2 Corinthians 5:17, 1 Corinthians 15:45, Galatians 2:20, Romans 8:9-10, Romans 8:2, Romans 5:10-11, Ephesians 2:5, Isaiah 43:5, Isaiah 41:10, Hebrews 12:2, 2 Timothy 1:7, Romans 8:31, 2 Corinthians 6:16, Romans 8:33-34, John 14:16-17, Hebrews 13:6, Philippians 4:13, Isaiah 43:13, Romans 8:37

## Prayer

Heavenly Father,

I am cherished and precious in Your Sight, You dearly love me, for I am Your Chosen Treasure called out of darkness into Your Marvelous Light. Because of Your Great Love, You delivered me from the dominion of sin and gave me the very Resurrection Life of Christ Himself. Now, it is no longer I who lives, but Christ lives His life through me. So, I am not discouraged. You are for me, and You stand with me. No one can stand against me.

In Jesus' name. Amen.

# NOTHING SEPARATES YOU FROM MY PASSIONATE LOVE

*N*o power can separate you from His Passionate Love for you. Nothing in all creation has the power to diminish His Endless Love for you—all are helpless to hinder Omnipotent Love. Because of Christ's sacrifice, you are acquitted and made righteous to live triumphantly in your new relationship as His child—all because of Jesus Christ's bloodshed for you.

Your new resurrection life in Christ is completely secure away in God, Who permanently grafted you into Christ as One with Him. Christ gave His life for you so that whether you are alive or dead, you live forever with Him. You now live victorious in the resurrection life of the Living God, Who lives His Life in and through you.

Christ completely wiped out and canceled all the charges that stood against you, erasing all your sins forever. He never remembers them again. So you don't, either! You are a new creation altogether, with Christ embedded within you. Now the Resurrection Life of Christ and His DNA are embedded within you through the cross, making you holy and blameless before Him in Love, His child.

# Letter From God

Good Morning,

I Love you, My Dear, Precious, Beloved, Blessed, Special, Beautiful child of My GREAT Love. And that is what you are!

No power can separate you from my Passionate Love for you. I clearly proved My Passionate Love for you because while you were lost in sin, Christ died for you. I have justified you in My Sight, acquitted you and made you righteous, and in right relationship with Me through Christ's blood shed for you.

Yes, I saved and rescued you from sin's dominion and brought you into the authority of My Beloved Son; you now share His Resurrection Life. The reign of sin that leads to death is dethroned in your life. And not only that, you live triumphantly in your new relationship as My child—all because of Jesus Christ! And because of His sacrifice, you will never experience My Wrath, for I have reconciled you to Myself by Exchanging your sins for Christ's Righteousness through His death on the cross.

You are permanently One with Christ, living in union with His Resurrection Life and made a partaker of My Salvation by My Marvelous Grace. He gave His life for you so that you live forever with Him, whether you are alive or dead. Your new resurrection life in Christ is hidden completely secure away in Me.

He rose victorious over sin, death, and the grave, destroying the power of darkness' every work, stripping away their every weapon and all their spiritual authority through the blood of His cross. You now live victorious in the resurrection life of the Living God, Who lives His Life in and through you.

You have risen from death's realm where you were held in sin's grip never to return, having been made alive together with Christ and forgiven for all your sins! Christ completely wiped out and canceled all the charges that stood against you and could ever stand against you. He erased all your sins, and I never remember them anymore, forever.

When you died with Christ, the old nature of Adam died in you—it was completely severed from you and cannot be retrieved! You have been born from above of My Spirit, a new creation altogether, with Christ embedded within you. I entirely made you new through your union with Christ, Who empowers your life by My Life-Giving Spirit, Who directs and controls you.

Your old life and all that was within you is gone; you are an entirely new person with the Resurrection Life of Christ and His DNA embedded within you through the cross. I have made all things new and reconcile you back to Myself. You are now reconnected back to Me, restored to your original glory again—holy and blameless before Me in Love, My child.

I love you,

Daddy God. Amen.

*Who shall separate us from the love of Christ? Shall tribulation, or distress, or persecution, or famine, or nakedness, or peril, or sword?*

Romans 8:35, NKJV

## ▎ SCRIPTURES FOR FURTHER READING:

Romans 8:35, Romans 5:8, Romans 5:9, Romans 5:16, Romans 5:10, 2 Corinthians 5:21, Colossians 1:13, John 14:19, Romans 5:1, Romans 6:5, Ephesians 2:5, 1 Thessalonians 5:10, Colossians 3:3, Colossians, 2:15, Romans 8:9, Galatians 2:20, Colossians 2:12-14, John 3:7, 2 Corinthians 5:17, Romans 8:10, Roman 6:12, 2 Corinthians 5:18, Colossians 1:20

## Prayer

Heavenly Father,

I am convinced that no power in all creation, whether things present nor things to come, could ever separate me from Your Passionate Love for me, which You lavishly bestow upon me in Christ Jesus. You made me a new creation with a new identity and hid my life in You. It is no longer I who lives, but Christ lives His Life in and through me to bring You Glory. Thank You for Your Passionate Love alive in me.

In Jesus' name. Amen.

# YOUR NEW LIFE IN CHRIST

*G*od Dearly Loves you and paid an unfathomable price to redeem you back to Himself to forgive your sins to satisfy His Great Love. You have become One with Christ, being permanently engrafted into Him to experience the same New Life God imparted to Him.

Now, to step out and walk in the spiritual victory of your New Resurrection Life in Christ—His victory is your victory! You were co-crucified with Christ, so sin no longer has dominion over you. His Sacrifice eliminated your sin on the cross, which freed you from sin's power once and for all. You are living in union with Him. The old self is gone and the new life in Christ has come.

Life has become an advertisement for God, a visible display, for throughout the coming ages of the immeasurable riches of His Grace and kindness in uniting you together with Christ Jesus.

You are a new creature altogether, an entirely new person created by God from nothing. Your death with Christ was not symbolic but real. You are a new creature altogether that never existed before.

# Letter From God

Good Morning,

I Love you, My Dear, Precious, Beloved, Blessed, Special, Beautiful child of My GREAT Love. And that is what you are!

I Dearly Love you and paid an unfathomable price to redeem you back to Myself in tears of blood, forgiving all your sins because of the riches of My Marvelous Grace lavishly bestowed upon you in Christ Jesus. You have become One with Him, being permanently engrafted into Him to experience the same New Life I imparted to Him.

Your old identity with the sin of Adam is now and forever gone, made ineffective and inactive of its power over you. Now you are no longer a slave to sin's power, for you died with Christ, dismantling the stronghold of sin within you. His Sacrifice has freed you from sin's power once for all because you are in union with Him.

You were co-crucified with Christ so that sin would no longer have dominion over you. Now the good news is to understand you have already died to sin and have victory over. So you no longer have to keep asking for forgiveness for the finished work I have completed for you. I nailed your sin to His cross, erasing it all. You are now alive in Christ. I command you to step out and walk in the spiritual victory of your New Resurrection Life resting on the truth—Christ purchased your freedom. His victory is your victory!

My Resurrection Power in you was released when I raised Christ from the dead. I gave you the same Resurrection Life of Christ; you live in a vital union with Him and Co-Seated as One with Him in the heavenly realm. Your Life is an advertisement, a visible display, for throughout the coming ages of the immeasurable riches of My Grace and kindness in uniting you together with Christ Jesus.

You, being in Union with Christ, are dead to sin and unresponsive to it. The old you died, and you have a new life in Christ that never existed before. You are a new creature altogether, an entirely new person created by God from nothing. Your death with Christ was not symbolic, but real. You died with Christ and were given a new life and made alive by My Resurrection Power of My Spirit to fulfill My chosen destiny for you, My child.

I love you,

Daddy God. Amen.

*Therefore if any person is ingrafted in Christ, He is a new creation; the old has passed away. Behold, the fresh and new has come!*

2 Corinthians 5:17, AMPC

## SCRIPTURES FOR FURTHER READING:

Ephesians 2:4, 1 Corinthians 6:20, Colossians 1:14, Ephesians 1:7, 1 Corinthians 6:17, Romans 6:5, Romans 6:6, Romans 6:10, Colossians 2:14, Romans 6:12, Colossians 2:13, Ephesians 1:19-20, Ephesians 2:7, Ephesians 2:5-6, 2 Corinthians 5:17, Ephesians 1:20, James 1:18

## Prayer

Heavenly Father,

You are so rich in mercy to satisfy your Great and Wonderful Love for me. Oh, the riches of the Marvelous Grace You lavishly bestowed on me. You have made me alive together in a union with Christ. I died with Christ, and now my life is hidden with Him in You. Thank You for making me a new creation that never existed before, born of Your Spirit to fulfill Your destiny for me.

In Jesus' name. Amen.

# I WRAP YOU IN MY PASSIONATE LOVE

*G*od's Restoring Love encourages you when discouraged, refreshing your soul. He wraps you in His Passionate Love that is an all-consuming fire that forever burns in God's Heart for you. His Endless Love is a Consuming Fire that fills your heart to satisfy His Great and Intense Love for you, pulling you close to embrace His Faithfulness.

God's Passion sent the Holy Spirit to be your Intimate Friend and Helper. He guides and defends, comforts and consoles you. No amount of water can extinguish His Love's Endless Flames burning within His because He Never Stop Loving you. He never gives up on you and will stop at nothing until you have yielded everything to the Extravagant Love of Christ.

He enfolds you into His Endless Love that He pours into your heart, sealing you in His Covenant of Love, unlocking your heart to His Passionate Love and tender mercies. His Superabundant Grace is already working in you, releasing every kind of wisdom or practical insight to reflect His Glory to all creation.

# Letter From God

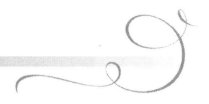

Good Morning,

I Love you, My Dear, Precious, Beloved, Blessed, Special, Beautiful child of My GREAT Love. And that is what you are!

My Restoring Love overcomes your discouragement and eases your soul. For My Seal of Fire is fastened upon your heart, sealing you in My Eternal Love. I wrap you in My Passionate Love that is stronger than even death, an all-consuming fire that forever burns in My Heart for you.

My Spirit of Holiness in you is a Consuming Fire, filling your heart with My Endless Love.

The Stamp of Endless Love seals you in My Compassion and Mercy to satisfy My Great and Intense Love, for you are My child. Yes, I love you with My Everlasting Love and pull on your heart to embrace My Faithfulness.

I know everything there is to know about you because I created you in Christ Jesus. My Passion sent the Holy Spirit to be your Intimate Friend Who is your Helper, Who guides and defends, comforts and consoles you. He reveals to you all the divine favor and blessings I lavishly bestow upon you.

No amount of water can extinguish My Love's Endless Flames; not even floods can quench My Love with Burning Fire within You, because love Never Stops Loving. Love consumes everything, for It Never Gives up. My Love will stop at nothing until you have yielded everything to My Extravagant Love of Christ—to the point where it won't feel like a sacrifice anymore.

My Endless Love enfolds you with My Consuming Flame, pouring into your heart. He seals you in My Covenant of Love. He joins you to Christ to experience all the Treasures of His Redemption by His blood—the total forgiveness of your sins, unlocking your heart with My Passionate Love and tender mercies.

My Superabundant Grace is already working in you, releasing every kind of wisdom or practical insight, making My Secret Desire known to make all things new to you in union with Christ. He is My Passionate Love revealed in you. My Greatest Treasure I gave to restore you to My Original Intent as My Image Bearer to reflect Who I Am and My Glory in all My creation.

I love you,

Daddy God. Amen.

*Come to me, all of you who are weary and carry heavy burdens, and I will give you rest.*

Matthew 11:28, NLT

Matthew 11:28, 2 Corinthians 7:6, Song of Solomon 8:6, Romans 8:38, Matthew 3:11, Hebrews 12:29, Deuteronomy 4:24, Romans 5:5, Ephesians 1:13, 1 John 3:2, Jeremiah 31:3, John 6:44, Psalm 139:1, 2 Corinthians 5:17, 1 Corinthians 2:12, 1 Corinthians 13:8, Song of Solomon 8:7, 1 Corinthians 13:7, Ephesians 5:1, 2 Corinthians 5:17, Romans 5:5, Matthew 26:28, Ephesians 1:7, Colossians 1:14, Romans 11:32, Ephesians, 1:8, Romans 5:8, Romans 8:32, 2 Corinthians 6:20, Colossians 1:19-20, Genesis 1:26-28, 2 Corinthians 3:18

## Prayer

Heavenly Father,

You pull me close, embracing me in the arms of Your Everlasting Love's Faithfulness. When my heart is overburdened and discouraged, You wrap Your Passionate Love around me, refreshing my life. Your Love's consuming flames quench my distress and make all things new through Your Superabundant Grace and Mercy.

In Jesus' name. Amen.

# My Gift of Love and Favor

*G*od pours more and more of His Unfailing Love into you to reveal and clearly demonstrate throughout the ages to come the infinite riches of His Wondrous Grace. In Christ, you have the complete cancellation of your sins through His Blood. He purchased you back to God to satisfy His Great Love for you.

Because you have been joined as One with Jesus, God lavishly bestowed upon you all the treasures of salvation deliverance—the Total Cancellation of your sins and the Endless Riches of His Grace are already available to you. He unveils to you the secret mystery of His plan to unite all things in heaven and earth back to Him through Christ.

God's Gift of Love and Favor continually pours over you through the Holy Spirit to fulfill the purpose and plan of His Heart that made you His Special Treasure of Great Importance. Through the Holies, you experience God's Endless Love already working within you, producing His Gifts, Fruits, Wisdom, and Transforming Power to bring Him Glory.

# Letter From God

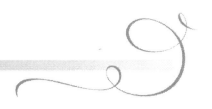

Good Morning,

I Love you, My Dear, Precious, Beloved, Blessed, Special, Beautiful child of My GREAT Love. And that is what you are!

I Pour More and More of My Unfailing Love on you to reveal My Mercy and the Lovingkindness of My Wondrous Grace, to clearly demonstrate throughout the ages to come the infinite immeasurable riches of My Grace and kindness and goodness showered upon you in Jesus Christ.

For in Christ, you have complete cancellation of your sins through His very blood. I purchased you back to Myself through Him to satisfy My Great and Passionate Love to restore My Full Image into your heart. My Perfect Plan of Love was always to reveal you as My Child through your union with Jesus.

You, being joined to Jesus, have received all the Treasures of Salvation and Deliverance that I have lavishly bestowed upon you through His Blood—the Total Cancellation of your sins, including heaven's wisdom and revelation knowledge and all the Endless Riches of My Grace Already Working Powerfully in you.

I unveiled through Christ the Revelation of the secret Mystery of My Plan from the beginning of time to make all things new and unite all things in heaven and earth through Christ—back to its original purpose and restored back to Myself to innocence again.

My Supernatural Peace has been released to you through Jesus' sacrifice that paid your sin debt so that you could be holy and blameless in My Sight without a fault within unstained innocence wrapped in Christ. Through the powerful declaration of My Amazing Grace, I have delivered you from judgment and made you a partaker of my divine inheritance.

I have rescued you out of the control of the dominion of darkness and transferred you into the Kingdom of My Beloved Son to embrace you in My Tender Unfailing Love Forever. I erased all your sins—deleted them forever! Every record held against you forever is permanently nailed to Jesus' cross as a powerful public declaration of your acquittal.

My Gift of Love and Favor pour continuously over you more and more through the Holy Spirit living within you, demonstrating My Forgiveness is eternal, and I never stop forgiving you. You have been justified forever by My Great Love, and I never change My Mind. My Unfailing Love for you is the same yesterday, today, and forever!

I chose and destined you to be My Inheritance before you were ever born to fulfill the purpose and plan of My Heart. You are My Special Treasure of Great Importance that I protect in the safety of My Presence because of your extraordinary value. So I have stamped you with the seal of the Holy Spirit as a guarantee that you are My purchase possession.

You experience My Endless Love already working within you through the Holy Spirit producing My Gifts, Fruits, Wisdom, and Transforming Power through you. So your life is an advertisement of the infinite riches of My Amazing Grace and kindness showered upon you in Jesus Christ.

Christ is your life. You died, and your life is hidden with Him in Me. The Fountain of Life flows from Christ's rivers of Living Water from within you, pouring out more of My Unfailing Love on you, releasing more of My Blessing to you, My child.

I love you,

Daddy God. Amen.

*Show us your unfailing love, Lord, and grant us your salvation.*

Psalm 85:7, NIV

## SCRIPTURES FOR FURTHER READING:

Psalm 85:7, Ephesians 2:7, Colossians 1:14, Colossians 1:19, Ephesians 1:5-6, Ephesians 1:7, Colossians 1:8, 1 Corinthians 2:12, Ephesians 1:9-10, Colossians 1:20, Ephesians 1:3-4, Ephesians 2:8-9, Colossians 1:13, Colossians 2:14, Romans 3:24, Romans 5:5, 1 John 4:8, Numbers 23:19, James 1:17, Hebrews 13:8, Ephesians 1:11, 1 Peter 2:9, Ephesians 1:13-14, Romans 5:5, Galatians 5:22, Ephesians 2:7, Colossians 3:3-4, John 14:6, John 1:4, Psalm 36:7-10

## Prayer

Heavenly Father,

Thank You for uniting me with Jesus and pouring more and more of Your Unfailing Love and Wondrous Grace because I am Your Beloved child. You have blessed me with all the Treasures of Salvation Deliverance—Totally Canceling all my sins, making me an entirely new person with a new identity in Christ Jesus. I ask that Christ's Living Water within me release more of Your Love through me to others.

In Jesus' name. Amen.

# YOU ARE PRECIOUS IN MY SIGHT

*Y*ou are Precious in God's Sight. He called out of darkness into the Kingdom of His Marvelous Life to shine Divine Love through you. God proves His Passionate Love for you and your extraordinary value in sending Christ to die for you—making you His special treasure above all treasures, a visible display of the incredible riches of His Grace and Kindness poured on you.

God paid a Great Price to bring you back to Himself and restore your original innocence. He exchanged all your sins with all Christ's Perfect Righteousness. Now nothing can separate you from His Passionate Love for you. For the law of Spirit of Life flowing through Christ living within you liberates you from the power of sin that leads to death.

He is closer than the breath in your lungs, so do not accept an invitation to fear. Reject the thoughts, keeping your eyes fixed on Him, your Faithful God. For He is for you and stands with you. No one can stand against you. He is your Strengthener and Helper so that you can say with Great Confidence, "the Lord is My Helper, He is for me, and I will not yield to fear."

# Letter From God

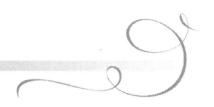

Good Morning,

I Love you, My Dear, Precious, Beloved, Blessed, Special, Beautiful child of My GREAT Love. And that is what you are!

You are Precious and dearly cherished in My Sight. I freely offered up My Greatest Treasure, the Gift of My Beloved Son, to restore you back to Myself through His blood. I called out of darkness into the Kingdom of My Marvelous Life to shine the Light of My Divine Love through you to others, revealing you as My Special Treasure.

My Passionate Love for you proves your extraordinary value in sending Christ to die for you—a treasure above all treasures. My Wraparound Love encircles you so I have you all to Myself, taken in by My Marvelous grace and surrounded by My Endless Love. I did it so that you would see a visible display of the incredible riches of My Grace and Kindness lavishly bestowed upon you in Christ.

I brought you back to Myself and restored your original innocence as I intended. You are now reconnected to Me, and nothing can separate you from My Passionate Love because Christ is living permanently within you. Now you have supernatural peace with me, something greater than just friendship is yours through His sacrifice— you are My child.

I exchanged all your sins with all Christ's Perfect Righteousness through your union with Him. Now, the law of Spirit of Life flowing through Jesus Christ living within you liberates you from the power of sin that leads to death. You possess His resurrection life, having been co-crucified and co-glorified with Him.

Even now I am with you, closer than the breath in your lungs. So do not accept an invitation to fear. Reject the thoughts, keeping your eyes fixed on Me your Faithful God, looking away from all the distractions in this world. Through your life-union with Christ, I infuse you with the strength to stand victorious with the Mighty Power flowing in and through you.

Don't be discouraged, for I am for you and stand with you. No one can stand against you because I live within you. I am always on your side! Who would dare to accuse you whom I have chosen in love to be My Own? No one—for I Myself put you in right standing with Me. There is no one left to condemn you.

I am your Strengthener and Helper. So you can take comfort in My Presence and say with Great Confidence, "the Lord is My Helper, He is for me, and I will not yield to fear." I infuse you with My Explosive Power to conquer all things, holding you firmly with My Righteous Right Hand of Victory. I have made you more than a conqueror; your overwhelming victory over everything is through Christ's Great Love for you, My child.

I love you,

Daddy God. Amen.

> *Because you are precious in My sight and honored, and because I love you, I will give men in return for you and peoples in exchange for your life.*
>
> Isaiah 43:4, AMPC

## Scriptures for Further Reading:

Isaiah 43:4, Romans 8:32, 1 Corinthians 6:20, Colossians 1:20, Colossians 1:13, 1 Peter 2:9, Matthew 5:14, 1 John 4:9, Matthew 5:16, Romans 5:8, Peter 2:9, Psalm 32:10, Titus 2:14, Ephesians 2:7, Colossians 1:20, Romans 8:39, Colossians 1:22, Romans 5:10, 1 John 3:1, 2 Corinthians 5:21, Romans 8:2, Romans 8:30, Isaiah 43:5, Isaiah 41:10, Hebrews 12:2, Philippians 4:13, Ephesians 6;10, Romans 8:31, 2 Corinthians 6:16, Romans 8:34, John 14:16-17, Hebrews 13:6, Isaiah 43:13

## Prayer

Heavenly Father,

I am Precious in Your Eyes. You paid an expensive price to restore me back to Yourself with Your Greatest Treasure, Your Son, to make me Your Special Treasure and child. You surround me with Your Endless Love and keep me close to You so I have nothing to fear, for you have made me more than a conqueror through my living in life-union with Christ.

In Jesus' name. Amen.

# I LOVE YOU WITH AN EVERLASTING LOVE

*G*od loves you with an Everlasting Love and draws you near to Himself to experience His Lovingkindness and continued Faithfulness. His Love for you never fails or ends; in His Faithful Love, He guarantees His Promise because it displays His Love. And He never changes His Mind about you nor His Faithfulness to you.

The Endless Love of Christ transcends your understanding— filling you with all the Fullness of My Divine Presence. He gave you the power to discover and grasp the Great Magnitude of His Passionate Love for you. God loves you with the same love He has for Him, so you can experience all the varied expressions of His Divine Love in all its infinite dimensions.

You are precious in His Eyes, holy and blameless because of His Great Love. Oh, how He dearly loves you and honors you being His inheritance. And He makes you a joint heir with Christ to inherit all He is and He has—Christ's spiritual blessings and inheritance. All because you have a special place in His Heart through your union with Christ.

# Letter From God

Good Morning,

I Love you, My Dear, Precious, Beloved, Blessed, Special, Beautiful child of My GREAT Love. And that is what you are!

I love you with an Everlasting Love, and in My Unfailing Love, I have drawn you near to Me, closer and closer, to experience My Faithfulness and Kindness of heart toward you. When I make a promise to you, I am faithful to keep it and lavish My Unfailing Love on you, in whom I dwell. My promise is a display of My Love; it will be fulfilled and accomplishes all I intended it to do.

My Faithful Love guarantees My Promise to you because My Love never fails or ends. I never change My Mind about you nor My Faithfulness to you. I refresh you each morning with My Mercy and Stability, the foundation of My Faithfulness. So you can boldly say, "The Lord is my inheritance and Helper; therefore, I will hope and wait expectantly in Him!"

You have the power to discover and grasp the Great Magnitude of My Passionate Love for you shown in Christ, who dwells permanently in your innermost being. His roots of love go deep inside of you, firmly establishing you in My Great Love—the Very Source of your life. You, living in life-union with Christ, have My Words living powerfully within you, embed in your heart and fastened to your thoughts.

Yes, I Empower you with the same love I love Him to Experience all the varied expressions of My Divine Love produced by the Holy Spirit within you in all its infinite dimensions. How deeply intimate My Love, how far-reaching; so that you really come to know through experience for yourself the Endless Love of Christ that transcends and surpasses mere knowledge without experience, filling your entire being to overflowing with My Fullness, the richest measure of My Divine Presence.

You are precious in My Eyes, holy and blameless because of My Great Love. I paid a dear, costly, expensive, precious price for you who is special to become My child—the blood of My Son to restore you back to Me. I have reconnected you back to Myself through the sacrifice of His Body that set you apart as holy and restored without a single fault.

Oh, how I dearly love you and honor you in giving My Greatest Treasure for you—the Gift of My Son to satisfy My Great Love for you, because I am so rich in mercy. Because of Christ's once and for all eternal sacrifice, you live in unbroken fellowship with Me. Now, you are My Chosen Inheritance through your union with Christ; I planned it all before you were ever born as part of your destiny.

And since you are My child joined to Christ, you have been made a joint heir with Him and Inherit all He is and He has—His Spiritual blessings and inheritance. The Holy Spirit reveals everything that belongs to Him so that you may know and understand all the gifts of grace and blessings I freely have so lavishly bestowed upon you. Because you have a special place in My Heart, you take hold and experience your entire kingdom inheritance with My Holiness and Authority that come with it, My child.

I love you,

Daddy God. Amen

*Yes, I have loved you with an everlasting love; therefore with loving-kindness have I drawn you and continued My faithfulness to you.*

Jeremiah 31:3

## SCRIPTURES FOR FURTHER READING:

Jeremiah 31:3, Psalm 73:28, Deuteronomy 7:9, Isaiah 55:11, Lamentations 3:22, 2 Corinthians 13:8, Malachi 3:6, Lamentations 3:23, Hebrews 13:6, Lamentations 3:24, Ephesians 3:17-18, Romans 5:8, Ephesians 3:17, John 15:7, Hebrews 10:16, John 15:9, Galatians 5:22, Ephesians 3:18-19, Colossians 2:10, Ephesians 1:4, Isaiah 43:4, 1 Corinthians 6:20, 1 John 3:1, Colossians 1:20, Colossians 1:22, Isaiah 43:4, Romans 8:32, Ephesians 2:4, Romans 6:10, Hebrews 9:26, Ephesians 1:11, Romans 8:17, 1 Corinthians 2:12, Matthew 25:34

## Prayer

Heavenly Father,

You love me with The Everlasting Love that draws me close next to Your heart. I have confidence that when the Holy Spirit persuades me, Your Promise is true to me, for You guarantee it will come to pass. Your Faithful Love guarantees Your Promise to me because Your Love never fails and You never change Your Mind about what You promised me.

In Jesus' name. Amen.

# YOUR NEW HEAVENLY INHERITANCE

*W*hen your earthly tent is torn down through death, your house in heaven made by God and not by human hands is ready for you—Christ is preparing it for you. He is your revocable eternal promise of receiving the complete possession of your full inheritance. And God confirms it by stamping you with the seal of The Holy Spirit as a guarantee of receiving your inheritance.

He is your Divine Encourager, Who fills you to overflowing with God Himself, doing infinitely more for you than you can ask, hope, or ever imagine because you are a co-heir with Christ Jesus, sharing Everything that belongs to Him, The Spirit, giving all to you. And since you are joined to Christ, you also inherit all He is and all He had because you are His Heir.

The Holy Spirit whispers into your innermost being, testifying together with your spirit, assuring that what God promised you will be fulfilled. He persuades you that God guarantees the fulfillment of His Word He births within you. So you can actively wait for Him to fulfill what He births within you not yet revealed to your senses, He guarantees will come to pass.

# Letter From God

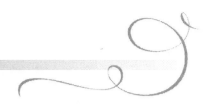

Good Morning,

I Love you, My Dear, Precious, Beloved, Blessed, Special, Beautiful child of My GREAT Love. And that is what you are!

When your earthly tent is torn down through death, your God-Built house in heaven made by Me and not by human hands is ready for you—that Christ has prepared to Last Forever. I Myself prepared this wonderful destiny for you. I confirm it with stamping you with the seal of The Holy Spirit as a guarantee of your inheritance. He is the first installment of what all is coming.

In giving the Holy Spirit, I am making you a revocable eternal promise of receiving the complete possession of your full inheritance. The Holy Spirit is My Promise that My Word to you is True. He is the Spirit of Truth—the Truth-Giving Spirit, My Spirit, Who reveals the reality of My Promised Inheritance to you.

He is your Divine Encourager, Who fills you to overflowing with God Myself, giving you the confident courage that I will do infinitely more for you than you can ask, hope, or ever imagine. He ignites within you the power and desire to believe Me and access everything I have because you are a co-heir with Christ Jesus.

Everything that belongs to Me, I have given to Christ Jesus, My Beloved Son—All Things, All Authority, All People, All that I am and that I have. The Holy Spirit takes what I have given to Christ and gives to you. And since you are joined to Christ, you also inherit all that He is and all that He has because you are My Heir too.

The Holy Spirit whispers into your innermost being, testifying together with your spirit, assuring that what I promised you will be fulfilled. So That you live by faith through the gift of My Holy Spirit within you, Divinely Persuading you that My Promises and Word I continually birth in you will come to My way.

The Holy Spirit is My warranty that guarantees the fulfillment of the Revelation of My Word I birth within you. Now through My Holy Spirit Divinely Persuasion, you actively wait for My Fulfillment of what I have birthed within you through the power of My Love not yet revealed to your senses, but I guarantee it will come to pass, My child.

I love you,

Daddy God. Amen.

*For we know that when this earthly tent we live in is taken down (that is, when we die and leave this earthly body), we will have a house in heaven, an eternal body made for us by God himself and not by human hands.*

2 Corinthians 5:1, NLT

## SCRIPTURES FOR FURTHER READING:

2 Corinthians 5:1, John 14:2, 2 Corinthians 5:5, Romans 8:30, Ephesians 1:13-14, John 14:26, John 16:13, John 14:26, Ephesians 3:19, 2 Corinthians 5:6, Ephesians 3:20, Philippians 2:13, Galatians 4:7, Romans 8:17, John 16:15, John 3:34, Matthew 11:27, Romans 8:17, Romans 8:16, Isaiah 55:11, Luke 11:13, 1 John 5,4, Hebrews 11:1

## Prayer

Heavenly Father,

You have prepared for me a house in heaven, an eternal body made without human hands to live eternally in You. The assurance of Your Spirit living within me is the guarantee of my inheritance from You. He Testifies together with my spirit that all Your Promises to me are trustworthy and will come to pass, being a co-heir with Christ, and sharing His inheritance.

In Jesus' name. Amen.

# I Chose You to Glorify Me

*G*od chose you to Glorify Him from the beginning and wrapped you into Christ before He laid the foundation of the world, to be holy and blameless before Him. He reconnects you back to Himself to restore your original innocence. I made you alive in Union with Christ, saved you by My Marvelous Grace, and raised you up along with Him, faultless before Me.

The Light of His Love shines within you, showing how much He truly loves you, giving you a rich and satisfying, abundantly overflowing life in the fullest measure. He cares deeply about the smallest details of your life, even the number of hairs on your head. He is intimately aware of you, understanding your every thought before it enters your mind.

Your body houses His Beautiful Image inside you. His new creation, His Masterpiece to reflect Him into all His Creation—He loves you with Unlimited Passion. He is with you always. The Light of His Love floods you with His Glory now streaming from you, making you the Light of His Love to the world around you, being His holy temple.

# Letter From God

Good Morning,

I Love you, My Dear, Precious, Beloved, Blessed, Special, Beautiful child of My GREAT Love. And that is what you are!

I chose you to Glorify Me. From the beginning, I wrapped you into Christ before I laid the foundation of the world to be holy and blameless before Me in My Great Love. Just as you love your child when you know it's been conceived, so I love you. I guided your conception and knew you before you were formed in your mother's womb.

Before you were born, I chose you to be established, revealed as My child through your union with Jesus Christ, to clearly prove My Tremendous Love for you and to reconnect you back to Myself, restoring your original innocence. I made you alive in Union with Christ and saved you by My Marvelous Grace. You were reconnected back to Me through The Resurrection Power that raised you up along with Christ into the heavenly realm, faultless before Me.

The Light of My Love shines within you, showing how much I truly love you in having My One and Only Son living eternal life through you, giving you a rich and satisfying, abundant overflowing life in the fullest measure. I loved you long before you loved Me, and I proved it by sending My Son into the world to be the once and for all pleasing sacrifice to take away your sins, purifying and making you holy, bestowing upon you the experience of eternal life.

LEE RICHARDS

I care deeply about the smallest details of your life, even the number of hairs on your head. I am intimately aware of you, understanding your every thought before it enters your mind, and know what you're going to say before you speak it. How precious are My Thoughts toward you. Every single moment I am thinking about you. I wrote all your days in My Book even before you were formed in your mother's womb.

Your body houses My Own Beautiful Image inside you as My Masterpiece to reflect Who I am into all My Creation. As My New creation, it is no longer you who lives, but Christ lives within you— He is your life. He is My True Image, so now you have My Own Nature and Likeness fashioned into a new creature like Me, who I love with Unlimited Passion. For I destined you from the beginning to share My Son's likeness inwardly. You are the Temple of the Living God.

I am with you always. The Light of My Love floods you with My Glory. Rise from the depression and anxiety in which circumstances have kept you—for My Glory now streams from you. And the brightness of My Glory appears over you! For Christ is shining upon you and giving you New Life in Him. The very glory I gave Christ He has given you, to shine His Light and Salvation to the world around you.

You are now the Light of His Love, and all who embrace Him will have His Life-Giving Light and never walk in darkness. For I deliver you entirely out of darkness' control into the Kingdom of My Beloved Son, purchasing your freedom and releasing you from all your sins through His Blood. I qualified you to be a partaker of My Precious Light of Glory pouring into your heart, to illuminate the Light of My Love that changes a person's heart, My child.

I love you,

Daddy God. Amen.

*Even before he made the world, God loved us and chose us*
*in Christ to be holy and without fault in his eyes.*

Ephesians 1:3, NLT

## SCRIPTURES FOR FURTHER READING:

Ephesians 1:3-4, Job 10:10, Jeremiah 1:5, Psalm 139:15, Ephesians 1:5, Romans 5:8, Colossians 1:20, Ephesians 2:5, Colossians 1:21, Ephesians 2:6, 1 John 4:9, John 10:10, Matthew 10:30, Psalm 139:2, Psalm 139:4, Psalm 139:16-17, Ephesians 2:10, Genesis 1:26, 2 Corinthians 5:17, Galatians 2:20, Colossians 1:15, Romans 8:29, 2 Corinthians 6:16, Isaiah 60:1-2, Matthew 28:20, Isaiah 60:1-2, Ephesians 5:14, Isaiah 49:16, John 8:12, Colossians 1:13-14, Colossians 1:12, 2 Corinthians 4:6, Matthew 5:16

## Prayer

Heavenly Father,

You have wrapped me into Christ and made me holy and blameless before You in Your Great Love. How precious are Your Thoughts toward me? Every single moment You are thinking about me, The Light of Your Love floods me with Your Glory and Unlimited Passion that overcomes all things to have and enjoy an abundant life, until it overflows.

In Jesus' name Amen.

# My Word Will Come to Pass

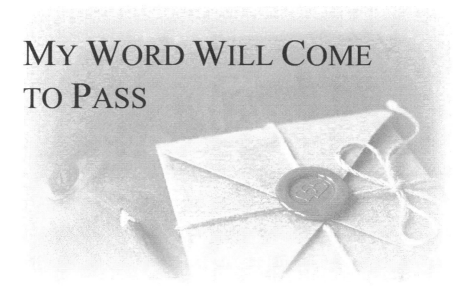

*Y*ou now have a God-Built Home not made without humans' hands. You are God's inner sanctuary, where the Holy Spirit dwells permanently within you, the house Christ prepared for you. The Holy Spirit is your irrevocable, eternal down payment that guarantees God's Word will come to pass and you will possession of all His blessings.

Yes, you are a Seal of Love upon God's heart. He engraved you on the palms of His hands, and His Endless Love overflows in your heart through the Holy Spirit living in you. He is your irrevocable, eternal down payment that guarantees His Word will come to pass—His warranty, certifying that His Word to you is True.

The Holy Spirit is your Divine Encourager, Who gives you the confident courage that God will achieve infinitely more for you than you can hope. He whispers into your innermost being, testifying together with your spirit, assuring you what I promised you I would fulfill. My warranty that guarantees the fulfillment of His Word He births within you who believes.

# Letter From God

Good Morning,

I Love you, My Dear, Precious, Beloved, Blessed, Special, Beautiful child of My GREAT Love. And that is what you are!

You now have a God-Built Home not made without human hands, being My inner sanctuary, the sacred place where the Holy Spirit dwells permanently within you, My house Christ made ready to last forever in the heavens. Your extraordinary destiny, I guarantee by stamping you with the seal of The Holy Spirit as the first installment of what all is coming.

Yes, you are a Seal of Love upon My heart. I have engraved you on the palms of My hands; your name is written upon My heart, for My Endless Love lives in you and I in you. My Glory and Honor I have given you, in whom I delight to carry on My Best Works as Jesus did and do even Greater ones.

My Holy Spirit is your irrevocable, eternal down payment that guarantees My Word will come to pass, and you will receive the complete possession of your blessings to come. The Holy Spirit is My warranty, certifying that My Word to you is True. He is the Spirit of Truth—the Truth Giving Spirit, My Spirit, Who reveals the reality of My Promised Inheritance to you.

That is, the Holy Spirit is your Divine Encourager, Who fills you to overflowing with Myself, giving you the confident courage that I will achieve infinitely more for you than you can hope. I ignite within you the power and desire to believe Me and know you can access everything I have—because you are a co-heir with Christ Jesus.

Everything that belongs to Me, I have given to Christ Jesus, My Beloved Son—All Things, All Authority, All People, All that I AM and have. The Holy Spirit takes what I have given to Christ and transmits it to you. And since you are in union with Christ, you also inherit all He is and all He has because you are My Heir.

The Holy Spirit whispers into your innermost being, testifying together with your spirit, assuring you what I promised you I would fulfill. So that you live by faith through the gift of My Holy Spirit within you, Divinely Persuading you that My Promises and My Word I continually birth in you will come to pass My way.

The Holy Spirit is My warranty that guarantees the fulfillment of the Revelation of My Word births within you, who believes. Now through My Holy Spirit's Divinely Persuasion, you actively wait for My Fulfillment of what I have birthed within you through the power of My Love not yet revealed to your senses, but I guarantee it will come to pass, My child.

I love you,

Daddy God. Amen.

*For we know that if the tent which is our earthly home is destroyed (dissolved), we have from God a building, a house not made with hands, eternal in the heavens.*

2 Corinthians 5:1, AMPC

2 Corinthians 5:1, 2 Corinthians 5:1, 1 Corinthians 3:16, 1 Corinthians 6:19, John 14:2, 2 Corinthians 5:5, Romans 8:30, Ephesians 1:13-14, Song of Solomon 8:6, Isaiah 49:16, Exodus 28:29, John 17:26, John 17:22, Ephesians 2:10, John 14:12, 2 Corinthians 2:22, John 14:26, John 16:13, John 14:26, Ephesians 3:19-20, 2 Corinthians 5:6, Philippians 2:13, Galatians 4:7, Romans 8:17, John 16:15, John 3:34, Matthew 11:27, John 16:15, Romans 8:17, Isaiah 55:11, Luke 11:13, 1 John 5,4, Hebrews 11:1

## Prayer

Heavenly Father,

Your Word to me will come to pass, every promise the Holy Spirit whispers into my innermost being, testifying together with my spirit You guarantee to be fulfilled. Your Holy Spirit is the irrevocable, eternal down payment that certifies to me I will receive the complete possession of all Your promised blessings.

In Jesus' name. Amen.

# YOUR BEST LIFE IS FOUND IN ME!

*Your Best Life is found in Me! Your old identity and spiritual condition have passed away. You are an entirely new creature with a new heart and spiritual identity—a child of God. The Spirit of Christ empowers your New Life, directing and guiding you by His impulses to pursue spiritual realities and experience all His Grace has lavishly bestowed upon you.*

*Your body is the sacred Temple of the Spirit of Holiness; the Holy Spirit lives within you. You no longer belong to yourself; you are God's. Indeed, you are God's True child. He makes His Relationship with you His Highest Priority! And He Proved it by showing you His Passionate Love by sending His Beloved Son to die in your place—His Love draws you to Himself.*

*Yes, God made you alive together in fellowship and in union with Him, to live in a Personal Relationship with Him. He is your Life. Your life is hidden in Him. You have His Righteousness, Grace, Joy, Peace, Wisdom, Victory, Strength, Inheritance, and Spiritual Blessings. All He is in Christ; you are because you live in union as one with Christ.*

# Letter From God

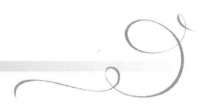

Good Morning,

I Love you, My Dear, Precious, Beloved, Blessed, Beautiful child of My GREAT Love. And that is what you are!

Your Best Life is found in Me! Your old identity and spiritual condition have passed away. You died with Christ and severed all your ties to it. Now, you are an entirely new creature with a new heart and spiritual identity—a child of God. Your New Life is hidden away with Christ in Me. I have wrapped you in the same Passionate Love I have for Him, so you live in union as One with Us!

The Spirit of Christ empowers your New Life by making His home in you. My Holy Spirit dwells within you, directing and guiding you by divinely persuading and implanting within you the passion, the power, and desire to do what pleases Me. So, you live by My impulses to pursue spiritual realities and experience all My Grace has lavishly bestowed upon you.

Your body is the sacred Temple of the Spirit of Holiness, Who lives within you. You no longer belong to yourself; you are Mine. You have been stamped with the Seal of the Holy Spirit, Whom you have received from Me as My Gift to you. He lives inside your sacred sanctuary.

Indeed, you are the Temple of the Living God. I dwell in you, and with you, and among you. I am your Father God, and you are My True child. I released the Spirit of Sonship into your heart—

moving you to cry out intimately, "My Father! Daddy God!" And that is who I am!

I make My Relationship with you My Highest Priority! I Proved it by showing you My Passionate Love for you by sending My Beloved Son to die in your place while you were still lost and ungodly! Further, I loved you long before you loved Me. It was My Love that pulled on your heart to embrace Me and drawn you to Myself.

Yes, I made you alive together in fellowship and in union with Me, to live in a Personal Relationship with Me. I AM your Life. My Life is your Life. My Righteousness is your Righteousness. My Grace is your Grace. My Attributes are your Attributes. My Love is your Love. My Joy is your Joy. My Peace is your Peace. My Wisdom is your Wisdom. My Victory is your Victory. My Strength is your Strength. My Inheritance is your Inheritance. My Spiritual Blessings are your Spiritual Blessings. I am your Life! All I AM in Christ, you are!

I stir My Gifts, Fruits, and Attributes with My Passion in you to Love Me and people as naturally as I Love you. Get up every morning, Rejoicing in My Love for you and overflowing through you to others, My child.

I love you,

Daddy God. Amen.

*For you died, and your life is now hidden with Christ in God.*

Colossians 3:3, NIV

# SCRIPTURES FOR FURTHER READING:

Colossians 3:3, 2 Corinthians 5:17, Galatians 2:20, John 14:20, Ezekiel 11:19, 1 John 3:2, John 17:23, Romans 8:9, Philippians 2:13, Romans 8:5; 1 Corinthians 2:12, 1 Corinthians 6:19, Ephesians 1:13, Luke 11:23, 1 Corinthians 3:16, 2 Corinthians 6:16, Galatians 4:6, Romans 8:16, Romans 5:8, 1 John 4:10, John 6:44, Ephesians 2:5, Galatians 2:20, Colossians 3:4, 1 Corinthians 1:30, Ephesians 4:7, Galatians 5:22, Ephesians 2:14, 1 Corinthians 15:57, Philippians 4:13, Romans 8:17, Ephesians 1:3, John 14:20

## Prayer

Heavenly Father,

You made me an entirely new creature out of nothing that ever existed before with a new spiritual identity—a child of God. And that is who You call me. I have a completely fresh and new life living in union as one with Christ. He empowers my life because You fully accept me. Thank You for making Your Relationship with me Your Highest Priority!

In Jesus' name. Amen.

# GOD EMPOWERS YOUR PRAISE

*T*he Breath of the Spirit of Life in Christ Jesus that liberates you to sing a brand-new song on the harp of your heart to make music to Him! God puts a new song in your heart for this new day to remind you how He always comes through for you! God awakens your heart, breathing His Life into your spirit, filling you with His Endless Love by His Spirit Who Lives within you.

His Spirit stirs a Song of Praise within your spirit to affectionately give thanks to Him for His Gift of Overflowing Grace given to you. His High and Holy Praises fill your heart, making your Shouts of Praise a two-edged Spirit Sword in your mouth, energized with divine power, giving you a weapon that has no equal to silence those who oppose you.

The Spirit of the Lord is your wrap-around shield. He rises through your broken heart and sorrows to comfort and console you in every calamity and distress. His Spirit of Comfort ignites you to Praise Him, to put your focus on Him, Who is Bigger than anything you're facing. Never be afraid of all He has already conquered—all the power of sin, death, and the devil.

# Letter From God

Good Morning,

I Love you, My Dear, Precious, Beloved, Blessed, Beautiful child of My GREAT Love. And that is what you are!

I awaken your heart by breathing My Life into your spirit, filling you with My Endless Love through My Spirit Who Lives within you.

My Breath is the Spirit of Life in Christ Jesus that liberates you to sing a brand-new song on the harp inside your heart to make music to Me! I put a new song in your heart for this new day that rises up within you every time you think about how I have come through for you!

It inspires an outpouring of Praises and Thanksgivings to Me because of the surpassing measure of My Grace, Favor, Mercy, and Spiritual Blessings I lavish upon you that is already working powerfully within you.

My Spirit stirs a Song of Praise within your spirit, to affectionately give thanks to Me for My Gift of Overflowing Grace given to you, which I have given you is far Greater than Words! He empowers you to Praise Me, Even in your weakness. Therefore, you can Praise Me even in the middle of life's storms, knowing My Power and Potential is greater than your problems.

My High and Holy Praises fill your heart, making your Shouts of Praise a two-edged Spirit Sword in your mouth, energized with divine power filling you with overflowing assurance that nothing can stand in the way between you and My promise. Your praise is a weapon that has no equal. Through Praise, you establish a stronghold against your enemies, silencing those who oppose you.

The Spirit of the LORD is your wrap-around shield. I rise through your broken heart and sorrows to comfort and console you in every calamity and distress, for My Endless Comfort cascades upon you through your Union with Me. I empower you with inner strength to conquer every difficulty.

My Spirit of Comfort ignites you to Praise Me, to put your focus on Me to see from My Victorious point of view, which is Bigger than anything you're facing.

Praise declares My Truth. I am your Helper. Never be afraid of who and what I have already conquered. I Myself Watch over you; My Presence shelters you. Through Me, continually offer up at all times the sacrifice of praise to Me, that is, the fruit of your lips that thankfully acknowledge and confess and glorify My Name, My child.

I love you,

Daddy God. Amen.

*He put a new song in my mouth, a hymn of praise to our God. Many will see and fear the Lord and put their trust in him.*

Psalm 40:3, NIV

## SCRIPTURES FOR FURTHER READING:

Psalm 57:7-8, Romans 5:5, Genesis 2:7, Romans 8:2, 1 Corinthians 15:45, Psalm 71:22, Psalm 144:9, Psalm 40:3, 2 Corinthians 9:12, Ephesians 2:8, Romans 8:26, 2 Corinthians 12:9, Psalm 140:6, Hebrews 4:12, Revelations 1:16, Psalm 8:2, Psalm 7:10, Psalm 16:8, Psalm 28:7, 2 Corinthians 1:5, Philippians 4:13, Hebrews 12:2, Colossians 2:9-10, Hebrews 13:5, Leviticus 7:12, Isaiah 57:19, Hosea 14:2

## Prayer

Heavenly Father,

Breathe fresh on me! Awaken my heart with a new song of Your Endless Love that reminds me how You always comes through for me! Oh, the surpassing measure of Your Marvelous Grace already working powerfully within me, stirring my spirit to affectionately give thanks to You. For Christ wraps me in His Endless Comfort and gives me the inner strength to conquer every difficulty.

In Jesus' name. Amen.

# My Love Is Always the Same

*G*od's Love is always the same for you—He never changes His mind about you. He has commanded His Endless Love to pour over you, stretching from one eternity to the next in unbroken faithfulness. Endless Love beyond measure pouring into your heart through the Holy Spirit, filling you to overflowing with all God's fullness.

Christ proved God's Passionate Love for you by freely giving Himself to die in your place, so you know He graciously provides you with everything else you need. Leave all your cares and troubles with Him, for His Unlimited Grace is always more than enough, always tenderly to take care of you no matter the need.

When you are feeling weak in human strength, God is always helping you. Then you discover that your weakness is a portal to His Divine Power that is continually at work within you. No power can separate you from His Passionate Love for you, Eternal Life-Union with Me, Who Never leaves you nor abandons you—NEVER!

# Letter From God

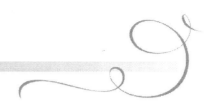

Good Morning,

I Love you, My Dear, Precious, Beloved, Blessed, Special, Beautiful child of My GREAT Love. And that is what you are!

My Love is always the same for you—I never change. My Perfect Love for you never changes, never fades out, or comes to an end. I Love you and never stop loving you, forever! I have commanded My Endless Love to pour over you, stretching from one eternity to the next in unbroken faithfulness to show the infinite riches of My Marvelous Grace clearly.

Your weaknesses are a reminder that My Faithfulness never waivers because My Faithful Love never ends. I Love you with the same Passionate Love I have for My Beloved Son, Jesus Christ— Endless Love beyond measure pouring into your heart through the Holy Spirit that transcends your understanding, filling you to overflowing with all My fullness, God Myself!

My Love lives in you, and Christ, Who proved My Passionate Love lives in you. He is My Greatest Treasure, given for you to know with certainty that I graciously provide you with everything else you need. For I know what you need before you know you have the need, having written all the days of your life in My Book before a single day took place.

I hear your heart cry out to Me and rescue you from all that worries and distresses you because I am always tenderly caring for you. Leave all your cares and troubles with Me, for My Unlimited Grace is always more than enough to strengthen you. For when you are weak in human strength, then you are Truly Strong in My Divine Power.

I am your Strengthener, and My Power shows its expression most effective in your weaknesses. So you can boast when you feel weak and surrounded by distresses, then you are Truly Strong in My Divine Power. For Christ bore your weaknesses and distresses on the cross, and instant strength flows through His Wounds of Love, flowing Mighty Power at work within you.

Although you were co-crucified with Christ in weakness, now you live together with Him, sharing the fullness of His Resurrection Life. Nothing in all the universe, seen or unseen, has the power to separate or diminish the Endless Love of Christ for you. No power can come between My Passionate Love for you, which I lavished upon you in Christ Jesus your Lord.

I am always with you, and My Unfailing Love continually protects you. When you feel distant, simply look away from the enemy's distractions—the ideas and opinions of the culture around you. Instead, Focus on Me! And you will be totally transformed by My Resurrection Power, stirring your mind's most holy emotions, thus persuading you that I am Always with you. When you Acknowledge My Presence, it pushes aside the lies of the deceiver.

My Endless Love Never changes for you because you are in an Eternal Life-Union with Me, Who Never leaves you or abandons you, NEVER! My Faithful Love Never Ends and Never Fails! Every single moment I am thinking of you, I Love you constantly in My thoughts, My Child.

I love you,

Daddy God. Amen.

*For I am the Lord, I do not change;*

Malachi 3:6, AMPC

## SCRIPTURES FOR FURTHER READING:

Malachi 3:6, James 1:17, 1 Corinthians 13:8, Hebrew 13:6, Psalm 42:8, Psalm 103:17, Ephesians 2:7, 2 Timothy 2:13, Psalm 107:10, John 17:23, Ephesians 3:19, Romans 5:5, John 17:26, Romans 5:8, Romans 8:32, Matthew 6:32, Psalm 139:16, Psalm 34:17, 1 Peter 5:7, Psalm 55:22, 2 Corinthians 12:9, Philippians 4:13, 2 Corinthians 12:10, Isaiah 53:4-5, Ephesians 3:20, Romans 6:8, Galatians 2:20, Romans 8:35, Romans 8:39, Matthew 28:20, Psalm 40:11, 1 Corinthians 2:4-5, Galatians 2:20, Hebrews 13:5, Lamentations 3:22, Psalm 136:1, 1 Corinthians 13:8, 2 Corinthians 12:9-10, Isaiah 53:4, 2 Corinthians 3:4, Luke 24:48, 2 Corinthians 13:4, Hebrews 12:2, Romans 12:2, 1 Corinthians 2:4, Ephesians 2:2, John 8:44, Revelation 12:9, Hebrews 13:5, Psalm 16:8

## Prayer

Heavenly Father,

Thank You for always loving me and never leaving me or abandoning me. I can trust and rely on Your Endless Love to pour over me in unbroken faithfulness. You hear my heart's cries and rescue me from all my worries and distresses because You tenderly care for me from the depths of Your Unlimited Grace. Every single moment you love me, flowing Your Strength through me to conquer every difficulty.

In Jesus' name. Amen.

# I FILL YOUR HEART WITH JOY

*T*oday, God fills your heart with joy. His Grace and Truth go prepare the way before you with generous blessings ahead for you before you were ever born. God's Endless Love continuously pours into your heart, lavishing upon you every spiritual blessing from heavenly places as His Gift of Love. He gives you a rich, enjoyable life overflowing with more than you hope.

God knows everything about you and all your needs before you ask Him. And even before you ask Him, He has set the answer to liberally supply and fill to the full your every need. He makes every good thing come to you in abundance so that you will rejoice in the blessings He lavishly bestows upon your life.

God is perpetually close with you, always living with you and within you. He is Your Comforter, Who sings over you with joy. I quiet your heart with My Passionate Unfailing Love, calming all your fears. His Joy is your continual feast in every season of life that overflows your being in union with Him. Nothing can separate you from His Joy.

# Letter From God

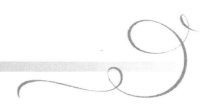

Good Morning,

I Love you, My Dear, Precious, Beloved, Blessed, Beautiful child of My GREAT Love. And that is what you are!

I fill your heart with joy. My Grace and Truth go prepare the way before you, for I have laid My generous hand of blessings upon you. I satisfy you with good things so that your life is supercharged with fresh new strength when you are tired and weary to soar with overcoming power.

Before you were ever born, I chose you as My delightful child through your union with Christ in My Great Love. Now you experience My Endless Love pouring into your heart, glorifying My Grace as I lavish upon you every spiritual blessing from the heavenly places you would need today as a Gift of Love from Me. I give you a rich, enjoyable life, everything in abundance, life overflowing with more than you hope for.

I know everything about you and all your needs before you ask Me, having written all your days in your book before you were born. Before you even knew to ask, I sent My answer to liberally supply and fill to the full your every need by making Grace, every favor and earthly Blessing come to you in abundance so that you have more than enough for everything—always in every way.

I make you overflowing with every good thing you need, so you will rejoice in the blessings I lavishly bestow upon your life and give glory to Me in all things, My child.

I am perpetually close with you always, for I am constantly living with you and within you. I am standing with you always. I never abandoned you nor fail you in any way, and My Hand is always upon you. So you can take comfort and say with great confidence, "The LORD is my Helper; I know the LORD is for me, and I will not yield to fear."

I am Your Comforter, Who sings over you with joy. I quiet your heart with My Passionate, Unfailing Love, calming all your fears. I make no mention of your past sins or even recall them. I direct you on the path that brings you face-to-face with Me, granting you the Fullness of Joy in My Presence and the pleasures of living in union with Me to satisfy My Great Love for you.

My Joy is your continual feast in every season of life. I AM full of Joy. For My Joy overflows to you, being in union with Me. Nothing can separate you from My Joy. You entered into My Joy when you were born of My Spirit, for My Spirit produces My Joy in you. For I AM the author and inspiration of the fountain of your Joy, Who fills you to overflowing with uncontainable joy and perfect peace as you trust in Me.

I made you Holy to Me, for I AM holy, Who made this day for you—Rejoice and Be Glad in it, because I AM Personally Present with you. My Joy is your strength. I AM always with you and for you because I love you, and I freely and graciously give you My Joy, My child.

I love you,

Daddy God. Amen.

*This is the day the Lord has made; We will rejoice and be glad in it.*

Psalm 118:24, NIV

Psalm 118:24, Psalm 89:14, Psalm 139:5, Psalm 145:16, Psalm 103:5, Isaiah 40:31, Ephesians 1:5, Romans 5:5, Ephesians 1:5, Ephesians 1:3, John 10:10, Psalms 139:1, Matthew 6:8, Psalm 139:16, Isaiah 65:24, Philippians 4:19, 2 Corinthians 9:8, Matthew 28:20, John 14:17, Romans 8:31, Hebrews 13:5, Isaiah 41:10, Hebrews 13:5-6, John 14:16, Zephaniah 3:17, Psalm 16:11, 1 Thessalonians 5:16, Romans 8:38, John 3:7, Galatians 5:22, Philippians 4:4, Romans 5:13, Psalm 118:14, Nehemiah 8:10, Romans 8:32

## Prayer

Heavenly Father,

Thank You for filling my heart with Your overflowing Joy and rejoicing over me with Joy. I can rest in Your Passionate, Unfailing Love that calms all my fears and worries because Your Joy is my strength. Nothing can separate me from Your Endless Love for me that overflows me with uncontainable joy and perfect peace as you trust in You.

In Jesus' name. Amen.

# My Glorious Inheritance

*God delights in loving and favoring you because you are His Glorious Inheritance of His Beloved Son Jesus Christ. He claimed you as His Inheritance before the foundation of the world to be His child. And He drew you to Himself through His Great Love that never weakens and made you His Masterpiece to accomplish the good works He prepared in advance for you to do.*

*You have also received an Inheritance from God, Who gave you the Holy Spirit as the Unbreakable Seal of My Promise that guarantees you will receive all your inheritance promised. He gave you access to all His riches of living in union as one with Christ including His Power, Wisdom, Righteousness, Holiness and Redemption.*

*So now you have great confidence, knowing every detail of your life is woven together for good to fulfill your predetermined destiny with Him being a Partner in all your works. After all, His love for you never comes to an end because He does not change His mind about you. There is no power above us or beneath us that can distance us from His Passionate love.*

# Letter From God

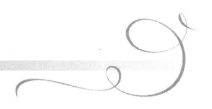

Good Morning,

I Love you, My Dear, Precious, Beloved, Blessed, Special, Beautiful child of My GREAT Love. And that is what you are!

I delight in loving and favoring you, who thrills My Heart beyond measure because you are My glorious inheritance of My Beloved Son Jesus Christ. I marked you out and made you My Inheritance ahead of time. I claimed you as My inheritance before the foundation of the world to be My child, holy and acceptable in My Sight without blame, and gave you this destiny.

I have drawn you to Myself through My Great Love for you in Christ Jesus that never weakens because I am rich in compassion and mercy. Now you are My Masterpiece, born from above through My Spirit in Christ Jesus to accomplish the good works I prepared in advance for you to do that fulfill your destiny. Having called you to come to Me and determined your destiny ahead of time, I gave you right standing with Me and My Glory.

You have also received an Inheritance to fulfill the plans of My Heart being one with Christ. And the Holy Spirit is The Unbreakable Seal of My Promise that guarantees you will receive all of redemption's promises. All My blessings I give you through My Wonderful Grace are your spiritual inheritance. You are already blessed with every spiritual blessing in the heavenly realms as My Gift of Love—an endless treasures of divine wisdom and revelation knowledge through your intimacy with Me.

You are My chosen one, wrapped in union with Christ, knit together in My Endless Love and the comfort of My Presence. You have access to all My riches living in union as one with Christ, including My Power and Wisdom manifesting itself as your Righteousness—approved, accepted and in right standing with Me. Your Holiness—consecrated and set apart for Me, and your Redemption—My Image restored in your heart.

I pull on your heart to embrace Me. Each day your heart moves closer and closer to Me as you experience that I am closer than the breath in your lungs. My Wraparound Love surrounds you as a security shield of Divine safety. My Love for you is like a flooding river overflowing with tender mercies. I love to love you! The more I love you, the more you love Me, because the reward of love is love.

You know with great confidence that I deeply love you and continually weave every detail of your life together for good to fulfill your predetermined destiny with Me, being a Partner in all your works. Oh, the great Joy of having each other for All Eternity, knowing nothing in the universe has power that can separate you from My Endless Love I lavish upon you in Christ Jesus.

Nothing in your present or future circumstances can weaken My Love. After all, My Love for you never comes to an end because I do not change My mind about you. There is no power above us or beneath us—no power in all creation—that can distance you from My Passionate love, which I lavish upon you through your Lord Jesus Christ, My child.

I love you,

Daddy God. Amen.

*In Him we also were made God's heritage portion and we obtained an inheritance; for we had been chosen and appointed beforehand in accordance with His purpose . . .*

Ephesians 1:11, AMPC

## SCRIPTURES FOR FURTHER READING:

Deuteronomy 10:15, Psalm 41:11, Psalm 16:3, Psalm 47:4, Ephesians 1:11, John 6:44, 1 Corinthians 1:30, Romans 8:38, Ephesians 2:4, Ephesians 2:10, Romans 8:30, Ephesians 1:14, Acts 20:32, 1 Corinthians 2:12, Colossians 2:3, Ephesians 1;17, Colossians 2:2, Colossians 1:27, 1 Corinthians 1:24, 1 Corinthians 1:30, John 6:44, James 4:8, Psalm 32:10, Psalm 115:11, Psalm 145:9, 1 John 4:19, Romans 8:28, Romans 8:35, Romans 8:38, 1 Corinthians 13:8, Malachi 3:6, Romans 11:29, Romans 8:38-39

## Prayer

Heavenly Father,

You made me Your Inheritance before the foundation of the world, holy and acceptable in Your Sight, without a single flaw. I am Your Masterpiece, created in Christ Jesus to accomplish the good works You prepared in advance to fulfill my destiny with You, being my Partner in all I do. I know You are Weaving every detail of my life into the fabric of Your Love to live the good life You made ready for me to live.

In Jesus' name. Amen.

# FOCUS ON MY TRUTH

*F*ocus on God's Truth. Let go of every wound that has pierced you and give them to God. Release your hurt to Him, who endured the torment of your sufferings to free you from the pains of your past. Remember, you are God's child! Turn away from the enemy's half-truths to God's Full Truth! Look away from all that distracts in the natural world and fasten your gaze on Me.

You can be confident that God's Immeasurably Mighty Power is at work continually within you to overcome the world, defeating its power. He protects you and watches over you, and the evil one cannot touch you. He guards your heart through your Life-Union with Christ from the evil influences of the world system—the culture of the world.

You are filled to overflowing through all your being with all His Fullness—God the Father, Son, and Holy Spirit. He has imparted to you His Authority and Power over all the power that the enemy possesses. He made you be more than a conqueror through Christ, being your glorious victory over everything and walking in His Authority.

# Letter From God

Good Morning,

I Love you, My Dear, Precious, Beloved, Blessed, Beautiful child of My Great Love. And that is what you are!

Focus on My Truth. Let go of every wound that has pierced you, especially in the areas you struggle, and give them to Me. Release your hurt to Me, who endured the torment of your sufferings to free you from the pains of your past so you can fulfill the beautiful destiny I have given to you.

Remember who you are—My child! Turn away from the enemy's half-truths to My Full Truth! Look at Me and away from all that distracts in the natural world and fasten your gaze on Me. And My Wonderful Peace that Surpasses All Understanding will guard your heart and mind, through My Peace being the controlling factor in guiding your heart to the answers you need.

You can be confident My Immeasurably Mighty Power is at work continually within you to overcome the world, defeating its power. For I, Who lives in you is far greater than the enemy in the world who comes to kill, steal, and destroy you. I protect you, My child, and watch over you, Christ's Divine Presence within you keeps you safe and the evil one cannot touch you.

I guard your heart against the evil influences of the world system—the culture of the world. You are supernaturally infused with the strength of Christ's explosive power flowing in and through you to conquer anything. Further, your life is hidden with

Christ in Me. It is no longer you who lives, but Christ, my beloved Son, lives in union with you and through you as One!

You are filled to overflowing through all your being with all My Fullness—God the Father, Son, and Holy Spirit—wholly flooded with God Myself. Through your union with Christ, I co-seated you with Him in the heavenly realm, Who is the Head of all rule and authority and power—a headship He exercises through you.

I have imparted to you My Authority and Power over all the power that the enemy possesses. I lead you in triumph over all of them, for I made you to be more than a conqueror through Christ, being your glorious victory over everything! Absolutely nothing will be able to harm you as you walk in My Authority.

So now you can live with confidence that there is nothing in all creation with the power to separate you from My Passion Love, which I have lavishly bestowed upon you, My child.

I love you,

Daddy God. Amen.

*Jesus said to him, I am the Way and the Truth and the Life; no one comes to the Father except by Me.*

John 14:6, AMPC

## SCRIPTURES FOR FURTHER READING:

Hebrews 12:1, Isaiah 53:4-5, Psalm 69:29, Ephesians 2:10, 1 John 3:1, John 8:44, Psalm 12:6, John 8:32, John 14:6, Hebrews12:2, Philippians 4:7, Colossians 3:15, Ephesians 1:19, Ephesians 3:20, 1 John 5:4-5, 1 John 4:4, John 10:10, 1 John 5:18, John 17:15, Ephesians 6:10, Philippians 4:13, Colossians 3:3, Galatians 2:20, Ephesians 3:19, Ephesians 2:6, Colossians 2:10, Ephesians 1:21, Ephesians 1:22, 1 Corinthians 12:27, Luke 10:8-9, Romans 8:37-39

## Prayer

Heavenly Father,

I let go of every wound that has pierced me to You. I release My hurt to You, Who loves me, the Father of Tender Mercy and the God of all comfort, Who always comes alongside me in my trouble and distress to console and encourage me. I let Your Peace be the controlling factor in my decisions, not my emotions, through You supernaturally infusing the strength of Christ's Mighty Power in me that overcomes all the evil forces that would hurt me.

In Jesus' name. Amen.

# MY TENDER LOVE LASTS FOREVER

*T*oday is God's Precious Love Gift to you to experience the Joy of, knowing He is always near to you. God is smiling upon you because He constantly loves you, who is living in the freedom of His Grace. Your life-union with Christ sets you apart for Him to experience the reality of His Grace and His Blessings in all you do.

Christ now lives His life through you. God made you a completely new person with a new identity enfolding you into Christ—Child of God. Your life is a beautiful song written by

God for God, Who broke down the wall that separated you from Him, setting you free to experience His Tender Love forever.

You will never be ashamed or disappointed because of your Hope in God. Even before you call on Him, He has already answered you. He strengthens your innermost being with His Word so that you may live in His Faithfulness and never be ashamed. And His Endless Love guarantees My Word will never fail—it will come to pass.

# Letter From God

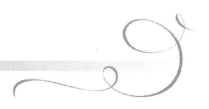

Good Morning,

I Love you, My Dear Precious, Beloved, Blessed, Special, Beautiful child of My GREAT Love. And that is what you are!

Today is My Precious Love Gift to bring you Joy and fill your heart with gladness, knowing I am always near you. I am smiling upon you, so live in the present, not the past, for you are alive in union with Christ, Who constantly loves you and washed away once and for all your sins through His Blood. I sent Him to release New Life and True Freedom in your life.

You are now living in the freedom of My Grace. As My Righteousness through your life-union with Christ, I have brought you deeper into holiness—set apart for Me to experience perfect freedom through responding to the Divine Persuasion of My Truth. It powerfully changes your life as you experience the reality of My Grace so that you can enjoy My Blessings in all you do.

Christ now lives His life through you; it is no longer you who lives, for He lives in union as one with you. You enjoy life-union in Him, Who set you free. I made you completely new, a new order of being, enfolding you into Christ. Now you have a new identity as My Child, for you are indwelt by My Gift—the Spirit of Holiness and Truth.

Your life is a beautiful song written by ME that sings forth all I desire in your life and have given you to do. You have breakthroughs because Christ broke down the wall that separated you from ME. He has set you Free to experience My Tender Love forever.

You will never be ashamed or disappointed because of your Hope in Me, for I continually pour out My Endless Love into your heart to experience My Presence Always with you. Even before you call on Me out of your distress and pain, I am already with you, delivering you out and setting you free.

For I am for you and I always stand with you. I am the One Who lives in you and with you and makes My home in you, so you never need to be afraid. I chose you to live and not die in the struggles you face to declare with rejoicing what I have done for you.

I strengthen your innermost being with My Word just as I promise so that you may live in My Faithfulness and never be ashamed. For My Endless Love guarantees My Word birthed in you by the Holy Spirit will never fail—it will come to pass. I am gracious and full of compassion for you, and am faithful to keep My promises. I am good to you, and My Tender Love for you Lasts Forever, My child!

I love you,

Daddy God. Amen.

*Praise the Lord. Give thanks to the Lord, for he is good; his love endures forever.*

Psalm 106:1, NIV

## SCRIPTURES FOR FURTHER READING:

Psalm 61:8, Numbers 6:25, Ephesians 2:5, Revelation 1:5, John 10:10, John 8:32, Romans 6:14, 2 Corinthians 5:21, Romans 6:22, James 1:25, Colossians1:6, Romans 8:10, Galatians 2:20, 1 Corinthians 7:22, 2 Corinthians 5:17, 1 John 3:1, 1 Corinthians 6:19, John 14:17, Zephaniah 3:17, Ephesians 2:10, 2 Samuel 5:20, Ephesians 2:14, Isaiah 61:1, Psalm 118:1, Romans 5:5, Isaiah 28:16, Isaiah 65:24, Psalm 118:5, Romans 8:31, Psalm 118:6, Isaiah 50:8, 2 Corinthians 6:16, 18, Psalm 118:17, Psalm 119:116, Isaiah 63:7, 1 Corinthians 13:8, Isaiah 55:11, Isaiah 30:18, Psalm 106:1

## Prayer

Heavenly Father,

Your Tender Love for me never fails to keep Your promises to me. You have entwined my heart with Yours, so I know You have mercy for my failures and give grace to help for my weaknesses. I live in the freedom of Your Grace in life union with Your Son, indwelt by the Holy Spirit, Who imparts new life to me because I am fully accepted by You.

In Jesus' name. Amen.

# INVITATION TO RECEIVE JESUS AS YOUR LORD AND SAVIOR

*Y*our Heavenly Father understands you because He created you. He knows your needs and understands your sufferings, disappointments, pain, fear, anxiety, doubts, and worries.

The Father is always available to you; He comes alongside you to give Tender Mercies for your failures and the Infinite Riches of His Grace to save you from Judgment. He makes you a partaker of Christ's salvation through your faith in Jesus Bloodshed on the cross for the forgiveness of your sins.

In the quietness of your heart, accept Jesus Christ's personal sacrifice on the cross as your own. Right there where you are, ask Jesus to come into your heart, and confess Him as Lord of your life.

Simply say:

Heavenly Father, I believe Jesus died on the cross and shed His blood to forgive all my sins, clearly demonstrating Your Great Love for me. Therefore, I confess with my mouth and believe in my heart that Jesus Christ is Lord of my life and You raised Jesus from the dead. I am saved, born anew of the Holy Spirit. I believe in the name of Jesus Christ. I have received the gift of righteousness making me right with You—so I openly declare the profession of my faith that confirms my salvation.

Thank you for forgiving me of all my sins and making me a new creation that never existed before, an entirely new person in Christ Jesus. Thank You, Father, for Your wonderful gift of salvation, and I am now Your child.

In Jesus' name. Amen.

## Scriptures for Further Reading:

Matthew 6:8, Romans Ephesians 2:8, Colissians1:14, Romans 10:9-10, John 3:5-7, 2 Corinthians 5:21, Romans 5:17, 2 Corinthians 5:17, Galatians 4:6, 1 John 3:2

# ABOUT THE AUTHOR

*T*he messages found in the Love Letters from God given to Lee Richards during his daily quiet time were birthed in him by the Holy Spirit through Bible reading and prayer, revealing the endless treasures of God's Love.

Lee is a speaker, teacher, mentor who writes encouraging messages to connect people everywhere to the heart of God to enjoy a richer, more intimate relationship with Jesus.

Lee's passion is for you to experience for yourself God's Divine Mystery – Christ Living in you. The freedom that comes when you encounter God's Heart through His Word and know Him more intimately, being rooted and grounded in His Love.

By God's Grace, he makes known to you the endless treasures available in Christ.

And He enlightens your understanding with the light of God's Word to experience the complete revelation of the glorious inheritance God has given you.